LADY GREGORY
SELECTED PLAYS

Chosen and Introduced
by
Elizabeth Coxhead

Foreword by Sean O'Casey

COLIN SMYTHE
Gerrards Cross   1975

All applications for licences to
give performances of Lady Gregory's Plays
should be addressed to
Samuel French Limited of
26 Southampton Street
Strand . London WC2

First edition published in 1962

This selection copyright © 1962 by The Lady Gregory
Estate

Second English edition published in 1975 by
COLIN SMYTHE LIMITED
Gerrards Cross, Buckinghamshire

ISBN: 0-900675-73-X

Printed in Great Britain by
REDWOOD BURN LIMITED
Trowbridge & Esher

QUEEN MARGARET COLLEGE

100 065 352

30356

LADY GREGORY: SELECTED PLAYS

QUEEN MARGARET COLLEGE LIBRARY

BY THE SAME AUTHOR

The Coole Edition
General Editors: T. R. Henn, C.B.E., Litt.D.
and Colin Smythe

Visions & Beliefs in the West of Ireland
Cuchulain of Muirthemne
Gods and Fighting Men
Our Irish Theatre
The Collected Plays:
  The Comedies
  The Tragedies and Tragic Comedies
  Wonder and Supernatural plays
  Translations, Adaptations & Collaborations
The Kiltartan Books
Sir Hugh Lane: His Life and Legacy
Poets and Dreamers
Seventy Years
The Journals (in two Volumes)
The Lectures
Shorter Writings (in two Volumes)
The Autobiography of Sir William Gregory (editor)
Mr. Gregory's Letter-Box 1813-1830 (editor)
Catalogue of Coole Library, Bibliography and General Index

CONTENTS

FOREWORD

A SPRIG OF ROSEMARY AMONG THE LAUREL

BY SEAN O'CASEY

IT is odd to let the imagination dwell on the group of hog-politicals talking together for a few minutes, and then deciding with an ignorant Irish hey ho nonny O, that the historic House of Coole should be pulled down and rooted up from the roof down to the cellar, and the stones to be scattered far and wide so that the House dwindled down to a place where no-one came. They tried to tear asunder, leaf by leaf, the wreath that the poet Yeats had placed upon her head, failing to realize that this was far beyond the reach of apathy, ignorance, or spite. This was the house that nourished Yeats, giving him wine, if not from the vineyard, then from a vineyard just as good; wine from abroad and honey from her own bees, honey I and she ate when breakfasting together. The house gave him great woods, a fine river, a wide lake, the majestic whirr of wild swans in flight, and evenings of peace full of the linnet's wings . . .

It was Lady Gregory who opened to the poet the warm welcome, spiritual and practical, of an Irish soul; it was her sympathy and help that gave the poet to Ireland, and Ireland who willy-nilly gave the great poet to the world; she should be remembered forever.

In her book *Cuchulain of Muirthemne*, Lady Gregory says: 'If there was more respect for Irish things among the learned men that live in the college at Dublin, where so many of these old writings are stored, this work would not have been left to a woman of the house, that has to be minding the place, and listening to complaints, and dividing her share of food.'

In my opinion, Lady Gregory, if not a great writer, was a first-class one, and a prolific one, too. She wrote many plays

7

and a number of books, (I wonder, at times, why Ireland's National Government, such as it is, does not issue such books as *Gods and Fighting Men, Saints and Wonders, Poets and Dreamers*, and the one about Cuchulain – presenting the Hero in a far more vivid way than the figure now standing in Dublin's Post Office.) Hampered as she was with the many burdens she carried about with her – her little theatre, her home, orchard, woods, the anxiety she felt for Yeats, and worst of all, the burden of bringing safely back the Lane Pictures to Dublin – considering all these, it is more than a wonder this indomitable woman squeezed out the time to leave behind such a fine amount of first-class literary work. Lady Gregory was the last but one (if we count Yeats as a Christian), and since she left, the present-day Irish Protestants in the Irish Republic have ceased to be indomitable, and aren't even interesting, for they aren't even the ghosts of those who went before them: most of them like the *siogaidthe* mentioned in Art MacCooey's song of *One-Eyed Mary*.

Since she died, there has been no whisper or remembrance given, as far as I know, to Lady Gregory; the Abbey Theatre and the Irish Academy of Letters seem to look upon her as a poor has-been; no-one even has placed a laurel wreath round the brows of the bronze head of the gallant lady in the Dublin Municipal Gallery. Perhaps it is just as well, for she was no kind of spirit to be admired by our intellectual and artistic group shivering at the shake of a clerical finger.

One gallant group, led by Michael Scott, the Architect (in more ways than one), has managed to set up a lasting memento to James Joyce. A Martello Tower where Joyce once lived, bought by Mr Scott, has been made into a museum of many things close to the life and work of the greater writer. That, at least, can be set against the scabby destruction of Coole House. No sign remembering Synge, Stephens; Yeats has his grave, and now a Summer School in his honour is held yearly in Sligo; but still none remembering Lady Gregory or George Moore. Perhaps, some time, an Irish Government will issue stamps remembering them all; and if they don't, never mind – they will be remembered, not so much for what they handled or owned, but for what they did; which things are not writ down in water, but engraved deep on the everlasting tablets of Irish History.

Miss Coxhead has already written a fine *Life* of Augusta Gregory, and this book is another tribute to the great gifts which were within the body, mind, and spirit of the gallant one we recognized and knew as Lady Gregory: I commend it to all Irishmen and Irishwomen (and English and American) wherever they may be. It is a fine sprig of rosemary among the Yeatsian laurel.

Lady Gregory, mother of many books, Daughter of Ireland, daughter of wise words, of good deeds, of great humour, lover of tree and sweet herb, of beast and bird, we hail thee still! We do not wish, nor can we afford, to murmur farewell to thee for a long, long time to come.

INTRODUCTION

AUGUSTA PERSSE, the twelfth child in a family of sixteen, was born at Roxborough House, County Galway, on March 15, 1852. The Persses were typical Anglo-Irish landed gentry, Protestant, and narrowly Conservative in their opinions. Her mother and elder sisters were proselytizers among their Catholic tenants, a fact which is still remembered against them; her brothers, by contrast, were crack shots and daring riders to hounds, with a tendency among the younger to indiscipline and wildness. All were sketchily educated at home by tutors and governesses, and none shared Augusta's feeling for literature and longing for the world of art and culture. There was no library, and when she had read the few books in the house she was reduced to borrowing from the village schoolmaster.

But Roxborough itself was an education. It was a great working estate, where the sheep-shearing alone took a week, and where the children of the house lived on terms of friendship with an army of farm-workers and craftsmen. The most potent influence in Augusta's childhood was old Mary Sheridan, for forty years nurse in the family, an Irish-speaker and a walking library of fairy-tales and folklore. She could remember the landing of the French at Killala in 1798, and had secret sympathies with the Fenian rising. The conflict in the mind of the child Augusta, passing from Mary's 'rebelly' stories to the outraged Orangeism of the drawing-room, was to be echoed long afterwards in the sergeant hero of her most famous one-act play, *The Rising of the Moon*.

She grew up into a small, shy, retiring young woman, occupying herself with social work on the estate, visiting the cottagers, helping them to read and write letters to and from their children in America, and gaining her insight into the peasant mind. She longed to learn the mysterious language spoken all around her, but as she says, 'my asking, timid with the fear of mockery, was unheeded.' Irish was a servants' language, not for girls of her class.

When she was twenty-seven, a brother fell ill, and she accompanied him and their mother to the south of France. There they met their neighbour Sir William Gregory of Coole Park, recently retired from the governorship of Ceylon. He was a charming and distinguished widower, who in his younger days had sat in Parliament, fought his duel, won and lost fortunes on the turf; he was also a man of wide culture, and a trustee of the National Gallery in London. A friendship ripened between him and Augusta, and when they returned to Galway he gave her the run of the fine library at Coole. Next year they were married, and in spite of the discrepancy in their ages – he sixty-three and she twenty-eight – there is every reason to suppose it was a love-match. Their only child, Robert, was born in 1881.

The twelve happy years of marriage were spent in travel, and in mingling with the world of art and letters in London, Coole being used merely for a few weeks of shooting each autumn. And under Sir William's tutelage Augusta made up the deficiencies in her education, becoming a very fair scholar in French, Italian and German. 'Quite a student' is how he describes her in a letter to a friend.

His death in 1892 left her only modestly provided for; the estate and rents of Coole would pass to her son when he came of age. She determined to earn money by her pen, first editing Sir William's memoirs, then a collection of papers left by an earlier Gregory who had been Under-Secretary for Ireland (it was this experience, she says, which turned her into a Nationalist). With her son she at last contrived to learn Irish, and became absorbed in the revival of interest in folklore and the ancient literary traditions.

The leaders of this movement were the poet W. B. Yeats, and Douglas Hyde, founder of the Gaelic League, and she came to know them both through her Catholic landowning neighbour, Edward Martyn, and invited them in her turn to Coole. Under their guidance she collected folklore, driving herself through the lanes in her pony-drawn phaeton, and talking to the cottagers, no longer as a daughter of the Big House, but in their own language and on terms of equality. And presently she translated the ancient sagas of Cuchulain and Finn into what Yeats called 'a musical and caressing English, which never goes very

far from the idiom of the people she knows so well.' These
translations opened the eyes of many non-Irish-speakers to the
splendours of their literary heritage.

She had never been particularly interested in the theatre, but
both Yeats and Martyn had written plays on Irish themes
which they were unable to get produced, and the founding of
the dramatic movement can be dated from a lunch meeting at a
friend's house in 1897. 'I said it was a pity we had no Irish
theatre where such plays could be given. . . . Things seemed to
grow possible as we talked, and before the end of the afternoon
we had made our plan.' The plan was to get guarantees from
their friends and bring over an English company to Dublin to
perform the plays, there being no professional Irish companies
at that time.

For three years in succession this was done; then Yeats discovered a body of Dublin amateurs who had been putting on
plays under the brothers Willie and Frank Fay, and at last the
infant Irish theatre spoke in its native idiom. The style of
acting evolved by the Fays, simple and sincere, made possible
the peasant plays of J. M. Synge and of Lady Gregory herself.
His first play, *Shadow of the Glen*, and hers, *Twenty-Five*, were
given by them at the Molesworth Hall in Dublin in 1903.
Then Miss Horniman, an English friend of Yeats, made her
generous offer to buy and convert as a theatre the old Mechan-
ics' Institute in Abbey Street, and so the Abbey Theatre was
born. The bill on the opening night, December 27, 1904, was
Yeats' poetic play *On Baile's Strand* and what many still
consider Lady Gregory's most amusing one-act comedy,
Spreading the News.

Thenceforward her life was bound up with the Abbey, more
intimately than any other person's. She became, with Yeats and
Synge, one of its original triumvirate of directors. She took the
major part in raising funds to keep it going, and in reading
scripts and discovering and encouraging new playwrights.
She supervised rehearsals, produced herself when necessary,
and mothered the company, bringing up hampers of good food
from Coole to supplement the living standard imposed by
meagre wages. With Yeats she bore the brunt of the fight to get
a hearing for Synge's *Playboy of the Western World*, howled

down by the Dublin audience, and for Shaw's *Showing Up of Blanco Posnet* on which the Viceroy tried to impose a censorship ban; the *Playboy* struggle was repeated in America when she took the Abbey players there in 1911. And she kept open house at Coole for poets and playwrights in need of rest and inspiration. Yeats spent the greater part of every summer there, and the house, the woods and the mysterious swan-dappled lake are immortalized in his poems.

Her principal work as playwright was done in the decade from 1902, when she was between fifty and sixty. She had begun by helping Yeats with dialogue and construction (much of the dialogue of his *Kathleen ni Houlihan* is, as he acknowledges, hers), then found her own vein of sparkling one-act peasant comedy, classical in temper and much influenced by Molière, whose works she regularly translated for the Abbey. Her 'Cloon' is unmistakably Gort, the little market town close to Coole, with its workhouse, its rival Protestant and Catholic churches, and its unusual burying-ground at the 'Seven Churches', a group of ecclesiastical ruins three miles to the west.

Indeed, some of the parallels were so close that the Gort butcher, identifying himself with 'Mr Quirke' of *Hyacinth Halvey*, was heard to mutter that 'her Ladyship should get a good slap in a particular quarter.' What he failed to appreciate was the universal element in her characters; the credulity of the market folk in *Spreading the News* may equally be found in the drawing-room, or the quarrellers of *The Workhouse Ward* in a St James's club. Some have even seen a personification of divided Ireland in this last play.

Lady Gregory is capable of pathos, too, if never quite of tragedy; there is deep feeling in *The Gaol Gate*, *Dervorgilla* and *MacDonough's Wife*. And the 'folk-history' play, based on the 'Alfred and the cakes' sort of history handed down in peasant tradition, is something she might almost claim to have invented.

Generally, she is happiest in the one-act form, her three-acters tending to be diffuse, but at least two of them have merit, and I have included them in this necessarily rather arbitrary selection. *The White Cockade* embodies folk-history's version of how James II fled from Ireland after the Battle of the Boyne;

it is comedy shot through with fine heroic feeling. In the three-
act, three-character *Grania*, she uses a part of the Finn legend
to express her view of the 'loveless Irishman', and of the frus-
trations experienced by women in a society permeated by
peasant attitudes. They are not quite exorcized in Ireland yet.

Lady Gregory's later years were shadowed by the First
World War, which took the lives of her son and of her favourite
nephew, the art-dealer Sir Hugh Lane, and by the Irish
'troubles', in which her Republican sympathies caused her to
be regarded as a traitor by her own class. They were also embit-
tered by a fruitless struggle to recover from England a collection
of French Impressionist paintings which Lane had left to
Dublin, in an unfortunately unwitnessed codicil to his will.
(This injustice has now been righted by a compromise.) But she
continued to write plays – her last, *Dave*, is a remarkable
achievement for a woman of seventy-four – and in the 1920s
she had the happiness of discovering in Sean O'Casey a striking new talent and a new friend. He on his side has paid
tribute, not only to her character but to her gifts. 'In the
theatre, among the poets and playwrights, herself a better playwright than most of them, she acted the part of a charwoman,
but one with a star on her breast.'

Up to 1930 she continued to come regularly to Dublin and
keep a stern eye on standards at the Abbey, where she is
remembered as a dumpy little figure in widow's weeds, 'rather
like Queen Victoria'. But her Journals prove that beneath this
slightly formidable exterior there lay a still-young heart and
mind, ready to sympathize with any new theatrical experiment.

She died in 1932 at the age of eighty, and the house of Coole
was pulled down not long afterwards; the only objects of pil-
grimage remaining today are the woods and lake, and the
'autograph tree' carved with the initials of her famous friends.
The inevitable reaction against her work set in, and has per-
sisted far too long, though she has always been esteemed by
the amateur dramatic movement, and there are signs that the
professional stage is rediscovering her. I hope this selection
will help to prove that even beside the genius of Yeats, Synge
and O'Casey, her distinctive and captivating voice deserves
again to be heard.

LADY GREGORY: SELECTED PLAYS

THE RISING OF THE MOON

PERSONS

Sergeant
Policeman X
Policeman B
A Ragged Man

THE RISING OF THE MOON

Scene: Side of a quay in a seaport town. Some posts and chains. A large barrel. Enter three policemen. Moonlight.

(Sergeant, who is older than the others, crosses the stage to right and looks down steps. The others put down a pastepot and unroll a bundle of placards.)

Policeman B: I think this would be a good place to put up a notice. (*He points to barrel.*)

Policeman X: Better ask him. (*Calls to Sergeant.*) Will this be a good place for a placard ?
(*No answer.*)

Policeman B: Will we put up a notice here on the barrel ?
(*No answer.*)

Sergeant: There's a flight of steps here that leads to the water. This is a place that should be minded well. If he got down here, his friends might have a boat to meet him; they might send it in here from outside.

Policeman B: Would the barrel be a good place to put a notice up ?

Sergeant: It might; you can put it there.
(*They paste the notice up.*)

Sergeant: (*Reading it.*) Dark hair – dark eyes, smooth face, height, five feet five – there's not much to take hold of in that – It's a pity I had no chance of seeing him before he broke out of gaol. They say he's a wonder, that it's he makes all the plans for the whole organization. There isn't another man in Ireland would have broken gaol the way he did. He must have some friends among the gaolers.

Policeman B: A hundred pounds is little enough for the Government to offer for him. You may be sure any man in the force that takes him will get promotion.

Sergeant: I'll mind this place myself. I wouldn't wonder at all if he came this way. He might come slipping along there (*points to side of quay*), and his friends might be waiting for him there (*points down steps*), and once he got away it's little chance we'd have of finding him; it's maybe under a load of kelp he'd be in a fishing boat, and not one to help a married man that wants it to the reward.

Policeman X: And if we get him itself, nothing but abuse on our heads for it from the people, and maybe from our own relations.

Sergeant: Well, we have to do our duty in the force. Haven't we the whole country depending on us to keep law and order? It's those that are down would be up and those that are up would be down, if it wasn't for us. Well, hurry on, you have plenty of other places to placard yet, and come back here then to me. You can take the lantern. Don't be too long now. It's very lonesome here with nothing but the moon.

Policeman B: It's a pity we can't stop with you. The Government should have brought more police into the town, with *him* in gaol, and at assize time too. Well, good luck to your watch.

(*They go out.*)

Sergeant: (*Walks up and down once or twice and looks at placard.*) A hundred pounds and promotion sure. There must be a great deal of spending in a hundred pounds. It's a pity some honest man not to be the better of that.

(*A ragged man appears at left and tries to slip past. Sergeant suddenly turns.*)

Sergeant: Where are you going?

Man: I'm a poor ballad-singer, your honour. I thought to sell some of these (*holds out bundle of ballads*) to the sailors.
(*He goes on.*)

Sergeant: Stop! Didn't I tell you to stop? You can't go on there.

Man: Oh, very well. It's a hard thing to be poor. All the world's against the poor!

Sergeant: Who are you?

Man: You'd be as wise as myself if I told you, but I don't mind. I'm one Jimmy Walsh, a ballad-singer.

Sergeant: Jimmy Walsh? I don't know that name.

Man: Ah, sure they know it well enough in Ennis. Were you ever in Ennis, sergeant?

Sergeant: What brought you here?

Man: Sure, it's to the assizes I came, thinking I might make a few shillings here or there. It's in the one train with the judges I came.

Sergeant: Well, if you came so far, you may as well go farther, for you'll walk out of this.

Man: I will, I will; I'll just go on where I was going.
(*Goes towards steps.*)

Sergeant: Come back from those steps; no one has leave to pass down them tonight.

Man: I'll just sit on the top of the steps till I see will some sailor buy a ballad off me that would give me my supper. They do be late going back to the ship. It's often I saw them in Cork carried down the quay in a hand-cart.

Sergeant: Move on, I tell you. I won't have anyone lingering about the quay tonight.

Man: Well, I'll go. It's the poor have the hard life! Maybe yourself might like one, sergeant. Here's a good sheet now. (*Turns one over.*) 'Content and a pipe' – that's not much. 'The Peeler and the goat' – you wouldn't like that. 'Johnny Hart' – that's a lovely song.

Sergeant: Move on.

Man: Ah, wait till you hear it. (*Sings*) –

There was a rich farmer's daughter lived near the town of Ross;
She courted a Highland soldier, his name was Johnny Hart;
Says the mother to her daughter, 'I'll go distracted mad
If you marry that Highland soldier dressed up in Highland
plaid.'

Sergeant: Stop that noise.
(*Man wraps up his ballads and shuffles towards the steps.*)

Sergeant: Where are you going?

Man: Sure you told me to be going, and I am going.

Sergeant: Don't be a fool. I didn't tell you to go that way; I told you to go back to the town.

Man: Back to the town, is it?

Sergeant: (*Taking him by the shoulder and shoving him before*

him.)   Here, I'll show you the way. Be off with you. What
are you stopping for?

Man: (*Who has been keeping his eye on the notice, points to it.*)
I think I know what you're waiting for, sergeant.

Sergeant: What's that to you?

Man: And I know well the man you're waiting for – I know
him well – I'll be going.
(*He shuffles on.*)

Sergeant: You know him? Come back here. What sort is he?

Man: Come back is it, sergeant? Do you want to have me
killed?

Sergeant: Why do you say that?

Man: Never mind. I'm going. I wouldn't be in your shoes if
the reward was ten times as much.   (*Goes on off stage to left.*)
Not if it was ten times as much.

Sergeant: (*Rushing after him.*)   Come back here, come back.
(*Drags him back.*)   What sort is he? Where did you see
him?

Man: I saw him in my own place, in the County Clare. I tell
you you wouldn't like to be looking at him. You'd be afraid
to be in the one place with him. There isn't a weapon he
doesn't know the use of, and as to strength, his muscles are
as hard as that board   (*slaps barrel*)

Sergeant: Is he as bad as that?

Man: He is then.

Sergeant: Do you tell me so?

Man: There was a poor man in our place, a sergeant from
Ballyvaughan – It was with a lump of stone he did it.

Sergeant: I never heard of that.

Man: And you wouldn't, sergeant. It's not everything that
happens gets into the papers. And there was a policeman in
plain clothes, too . . . It is in Limerick he was. . . . It was
after the time of the attack on the police barrack at Kil-
mallock. . . . Moonlight . . . just like this . . . waterside. . . .
Nothing was known for certain.

Sergeant: Do you say so? It's a terrible county to belong to.

Man: That's so, indeed! You might be standing there, looking out that way, thinking you saw him coming up this side
of the quay   (*points*),   and he might be coming up this other

side (*points*),   and he'd be on you before you knew where you were.

Sergeant: It's a whole troop of police they ought to put here to stop a man like that.

Man: But if you'd like me to stop with you, I could be looking down this side. I could be sitting up here on this barrel.

Sergeant: And you know him well, too?

Man: I'd know him a mile off, sergeant.

Sergeant: But you wouldn't want to share the reward?

Man: Is it a poor man like me, that has to be going the roads and singing in fairs, to have the name on him that he took a reward? But you don't want me. I'll be safer in the town.

Sergeant: Well, you can stop.

Man: (*Getting up on barrel.*) All right, sergeant. I wonder, now, you're not tired out, sergeant, walking up and down the way you are.

Sergeant: If I'm tired I'm used to it.

Man: You might have hard work before you tonight yet. Take it easy while you can. There's plenty of room up here on the barrel, and you see farther when you're higher up.

Sergeant: Maybe so. (*Gets up beside him on barrel, facing right. They sit back to back, looking different ways.*) You made me feel a bit queer with the way you talked.

Man: Give me a match, sergeant (*he gives it, and man lights pipe*);   take a draw yourself? It'll quiet you. Wait now till I give you a light, but you needn't turn round. Don't take your eye off the quay for the life of you.

Sergeant: Never fear, I won't. (*Lights pipe. They both smoke.*) Indeed it's a hard thing to be in the force, out at night and no thanks for it, for all the danger we're in. And it's little we get but abuse from the people, and no choice but to obey our orders, and never asked when a man is sent into danger, if you are a married man with a family.

Man: (*Sings*) –

As through the hills I walked to view the hills and shamrock plain,
I stood awhile where nature smiles to view the rocks and streams,
On a matron fair I fixed my eyes beneath a fertile vale,
As she sang her song it was on the wrong of poor old Granuaile.

Sergeant: Stop that; that's no song to be singing in these times.

Man: Ah, sergeant, I was only singing to keep my heart up. It sinks when I think of him. To think of us two sitting here, and he creeping up the quay, maybe, to get to us.

Sergeant: Are you keeping a good lookout?

Man: I am; and for no reward too. Amn't I the foolish man? But when I saw a man in trouble, I never could help trying to get him out of it. What's that? Did something hit me? (*Rubs his heart.*)

Sergeant: (*Patting him on the shoulder.*) You will get your reward in heaven.

Man: I know that, I know that, sergeant, but life is precious.

Sergeant: Well, you can sing if it gives you more courage.

Man: (*Sings*) –

Her head was bare, her hands and feet with iron bands were bound,
Her pensive strain and plaintive wail mingles with the evening gale,
And the song she sang with mournful air, I am old Granuaile.
Her lips so sweet that monarchs kissed . . .

Sergeant: That's not it. . . . 'Her gown she wore was stained with gore.' . . . That's it – you missed that.

Man: You're right, sergeant, so it is; I missed it. (*Repeats line.*) But to think of a man like you knowing a song like that.

Sergeant: There's many a thing a man might know and might not have any wish for.

Man: Now, I daresay, sergeant, in your youth, you used to be sitting up on a wall, the way you are sitting up on this barrel now, and the other lads beside you, and you singing 'Granuaile'? . . .

Sergeant: I did then.

Man: And the 'Shan Bhean Bhocht'?* . . .

Sergeant: I did then.

Man: And the 'Green on the Cape?'

Sergeant: That was one of them.

Man: And maybe the man you are watching for tonight used to be sitting on the wall, when he was young, and singing those same songs. . . . It's a queer world. . . .

*'Shan Bhean Bhocht, i.e. Poor Old Woman, that is, Ireland.

Sergeant: Whisht! . . . I think I see something coming. . . .
It's only a dog.

Man: And isn't it a queer world? . . . Maybe it's one of the
boys you used to be singing with that time you will be arrest-
ing today or tomorrow, and sending into the dock. . . .

Sergeant: That's true indeed.

Man: And maybe one night, after you had been singing, if
the other boys had told you some plan they had, some plan
to free the country, you might have joined with them . . . and
maybe it is you might be in trouble now.

Sergeant: Well, who knows but I might? I had a great spirit
in those days.

Man: It's a queer world, sergeant, and it's little any mother
knows when she sees her child creeping on the floor what
might happen to it before it has gone through its life, or who
will be who in the end.

Sergeant: That's a queer thought now, and a true thought.
Wait now till I think it out. . . . If it wasn't for the sense I
have, and for my wife and family, and for me joining the
force the time I did, it might be myself now would be after
breaking gaol and hiding in the dark, and it might be him that's
hiding in the dark and that got out of gaol would be sitting
up where I am on this barrel. . . . And it might be myself
would be creeping up trying to make my escape from himself,
and it might be himself would be keeping the law, and myself would be breaking it, and myself would be trying maybe
to put a bullet in his head, or to take up a lump of a stone
the way you said he did . . . no, that myself did. . . . Oh!
(*Gasps. After a pause.*) What's that? (*Grasps man's
arm.*)

Man: (*Jumps off barrel and listens, looking out over water.*)   It's
nothing, sergeant.

Sergeant: I thought it might be a boat. I had a notion there
might be friends of his coming about the quays with a boat.

Man: Sergeant, I am thinking it was with the people you
were, and not with the law you were, when you were a young
man.

Sergeant: Well, if I was foolish then, that time's gone.

Man: Maybe, sergeant, it comes into your head sometimes, in spite of your belt and your tunic, that it might have been as well for you to have followed Granuaile.

Sergeant: It's no business of yours what I think.

Man: Maybe, sergeant, you'll be on the side of the country yet.

Sergeant: (*Gets off barrel.*)   Don't talk to me like that. I have my duties and I know them. (*Looks round.*)   That was a boat; I hear the oars.

(*Goes to the steps and looks down.*)

Man: (*Sings*) –

> O, then, tell me, Shawn O'Farrell,
>   Where the gathering is to be.
> In the old spot by the river
>   Right well known to you and me!

Sergeant: Stop that! Stop that, I tell you!

Man: (*Sings louder*) –

> One word more, for signal token,
>   Whistle up the marching tune,
> With your pike upon your shoulder,
>   At the Rising of the Moon.

Sergeant: If you don't stop that, I'll arrest you.

(*A whistle from below answers, repeating the air.*)

Sergeant: That's a signal. (*Stands between him and steps.*) You must not pass this way. . . . Step farther back. . . . Who are you? You are no ballad-singer.

Man: You needn't ask who I am; that placard will tell you. (*Points to placard.*)

Sergeant: You are the man I am looking for.

Man: (*Takes off hat and wig. Sergeant seizes them.*)   I am. There's a hundred pounds on my head. There is a friend of mine below in a boat. He knows a safe place to bring me to.

Sergeant: (*Looking still at hat and wig.*)   It's a pity! It's a pity. You deceived me. You deceived me well.

Man: I am a friend of Granuaile. There is a hundred pounds on my head.

Sergeant: It's a pity, it's a pity!

Man: Will you let me pass, or must I make you let me?

Sergeant: I am in the force. I will not let you pass.

Man: I thought to do it with my tongue. (*Puts hand in breast.*)   What is that?

(*Voice of Policeman X outside:*)   Here, this is where we left him.

Sergeant: It's my comrades coming.

Man: You won't betray me . . . the friend of Granuaile. (*Slips behind barrel.*)

(*Voice of Policeman B:*)   That was the last of the placards.

Policeman X: (*As they come in.*)   If he makes his escape it won't be unknown he'll make it.

(*Sergeant puts hat and wig behind his back.*)

Policeman B: Did any one come this way?

Sergeant: (*After a pause.*)   No one.

Policeman B: No one at all?

Sergeant: No one at all.

Policeman B: We had no orders to go back to the station; we can stop along with you.

Sergeant: I don't want you. There is nothing for you to do here.

Policeman B: You bade us to come back here and keep watch with you.

Sergeant: I'd sooner be alone. Would any man come this way and you making all that talk? It is better the place to be quiet.

Policeman B: Well, we'll leave you the lantern anyhow. (*Hands it to him.*)

Sergeant: I don't want it. Bring it with you.

Policeman B: You might want it. There are clouds coming up and you have the darkness of the night before you yet. I'll leave it over here on the barrel. (*Goes to barrel.*)

Sergeant: Bring it with you I tell you. No more talk.

Policeman B: Well, I thought it might be a comfort to you. I often think when I have it in my hand and can be flashing it about into every dark corner   (*doing so*)   that it's the same as being beside the fire at home, and the bits of bogwood blazing up now and again.

(*Flashes it about, now on the barrel, now on Sergeant.*)

Sergeant: (*Furious.*)   Be off the two of you, yourselves and
   your lantern!
   (*They go out. Man comes from behind barrel. He and Sergeant
   stand looking at one another.*)
Sergeant: What are you waiting for?
Man: For my hat, of course, and my wig. You wouldn't wish
   me to get my death of cold?
   (*Sergeant gives them.*)
Man: (*Going towards steps.*)   Well, good-night, comrade,
   and thank you. You did me a good turn tonight, and I'm
   obliged to you. Maybe I'll be able to do as much for you when
   the small rise up and the big fall down . . . when we all change
   places at the Rising   (*waves his hand and disappears*)   of the
   Moon.
Sergeant: (*Turning his back to audience and reading placard.*)
   A hundred pounds reward! A hundred pounds! (*Turns
   towards audience.*)   I wonder, now, am I as great a fool as I
   think I am?

CURTAIN

NOTES

WHEN I was a child and came with my elders to Galway for their salmon fishing in the river that rushes past the gaol, I used to look with awe at the window where men were hung, and the dark, closed gate. I used to wonder if ever a prisoner might by some means climb the high, buttressed wall and slip away in the darkness by the canal to the quays and find friends to hide him under a load of kelp in a fishing boat, as happens to my ballad-singing man. The play was considered offensive to some extreme Nationalists before it was acted, because it showed the police in too favourable a light, and a Unionist paper attacked it after it was acted because the policeman was represented 'as a coward and a traitor'; but after the Belfast police strike that same paper praised its 'insight into Irish character'. After all these ups and downs it passes unchallenged on both sides of the Irish Sea.

SPREADING THE NEWS

PERSONS

Bartley Fallon
Mrs Fallon
Jack Smith
Shawn Early
Tim Casey
James Ryan
Mrs Tarpey
Mrs Tully
A Policeman . . . . . . Jo Muldoon
A Removable Magistrate

SPREADING THE NEWS

Scene: The outskirts of a Fair. An Apple Stall. Mrs Tarpey sitting at it. Magistrate and Policeman enter.

Magistrate: So that is the Fair Green. Cattle and sheep and mud. No system. What a repulsive sight!

Policeman: That is so, indeed.

Magistrate: I suppose there is a good deal of disorder in this place?

Policeman: There is.

Magistrate: Common assault?

Policeman: It's common enough.

Magistrate: Agrarian crime, no doubt?

Policeman: That is so.

Magistrate: Boycotting? Maiming of cattle? Firing into houses?

Policeman: There was one time, and there might be again.

Magistrate: That is bad. Does it go any farther than that?

Policeman: Far enough, indeed.

Magistrate: Homicide, then! This district has been shamefully neglected! I will change all that. When I was in the Andaman Islands, my system never failed. Yes, yes, I will change all that. What has that woman on her stall?

Policeman: Apples mostly – and sweets.

Magistrate: Just see if there are any unlicensed goods underneath – spirits or the like. We had evasions of the salt tax in the Andaman Islands.

Policeman: (*Sniffing cautiously and upsetting a heap of apples.*) I see no spirits here – or salt.

Magistrate: (*To Mrs Tarpey.*) Do you know this town well, my good woman?

Mrs Tarpey: (*Holding out some apples.*) A penny the half-dozen, your honour.

Policeman: (*Shouting.*) The gentleman is asking do you know the town! He's the new magistrate!

Mrs Tarpey: (*Rising and ducking.*) Do I know the town? I do, to be sure.

Magistrate: (*Shouting.*) What is its chief business?

Mrs Tarpey: Business, is it? What business would the people here have but to be minding one another's business?

Magistrate: I mean what trade have they?

Mrs Tarpey: Not a trade. No trade at all but to be talking.

Magistrate: I shall learn nothing here.

(*James Ryan comes in, pipe in mouth. Seeing Magistrate he retreats quickly, taking pipe from mouth.*)

Magistrate: The smoke from that man's pipe had a greenish look; he may be growing unlicensed tobacco at home. I wish I had brought my telescope to this district. Come to the post-office, I will telegraph for it. I found it very useful in the Andaman Islands.

(*Magistrate and Policeman go out left.*)

Mrs Tarpey: Bad luck to Jo Muldoon, knocking my apples this way and that way. (*Begins arranging them.*) Showing off he was to the new magistrate.

(*Enter Bartley Fallon and Mrs Fallon.*)

Bartley: Indeed it's a poor country and a scarce country to be living in. But I'm thinking if I went to America it's long ago the day I'd be dead!

Mrs Fallon: So you might, indeed.

(*She puts her basket on a barrel and begins putting parcels in it, taking them from under her cloak.*)

Bartley: And it's a great expense for a poor man to be buried in America.

Mrs Fallon: Never fear, Bartley Fallon, but I'll give you a good burying the day you'll die.

Bartley: Maybe it's yourself will be buried in the graveyard of Cloonmara before me, Mary Fallon, and I myself that will be dying unbeknownst some night, and no one a-near me. And the cat itself may be gone straying through the country, and the mice squealing over the quilt.

Mrs Fallon: Leave off talking of dying. It might be twenty years you'll be living yet.

Bartley: (*With a deep sigh.*) I'm thinking if I'll be living at the end of twenty years, it's a very old man I'll be then!

Mrs Tarpey: (*Turns and sees them.*) Good morrow, Bartley Fallon; good morrow, Mrs Fallon. Well, Bartley, you'll find no cause for complaining today; they are all saying it was a good fair.

Bartley: (*Raising his voice.*) It was not a good fair, Mrs Tarpey. It was a scattered sort of a fair. If we didn't expect more, we got less. That's the way with me always; whatever I have to sell goes down and whatever I have to buy goes up. If there's ever any misfortune coming to this world, it's on myself it pitches, like a flock of crows on seed potatoes.

Mrs Fallon: Leave off talking of misfortunes, and listen to Jack Smith that is coming the way, and he singing.

(*Voice of Jack Smith heard singing*) –

I thought, my first love,
   There'd be but one house between you and me,
And I thought I would find
   Yourself coaxing my child on your knee.
Over the tide
   I would leap with the leap of a swan,
Till I came to the side
   Of the wife of the Red-haired man!

(*Jack Smith comes in; he is a red-haired man, and is carrying a hayfork.*)

Mrs Tarpey: That should be a good song if I had my hearing.

Mrs Fallon: (*Shouting.*) It's 'The Red-haired Man's Wife.'

Mrs Tarpey: I know it well. That's the song that has a skin on it!

(*She turns her back to them and goes on arranging her apples.*)

Mrs Fallon: Where's herself, Jack Smith?

Jack Smith: She was delayed with her washing; bleaching the clothes on the hedge she is, and she daren't leave them, with all the tinkers that do be passing to the fair. It isn't to the fair I came myself, but up to the Five Acre Meadow I'm going, where I have a contract for the hay. We'll get a share of it into tramps today. (*He lays down hayfork and lights his pipe.*)

Bartley: You will not get it into tramps today. The rain will be down on it by evening, and on myself too. It's seldom I ever started on a journey but the rain would come down on me before I'd find any place of shelter.

Jack Smith: If it didn't itself, Bartley, it is my belief you would carry a leaky pail on your head in place of a hat, the way you'd not be without some cause of complaining.

(*A voice heard, 'Go on, now, go on out o' that. Go on I say.'*)

Jack Smith: Look at that young mare of Pat Ryan's that is backing into Shaughnessy's bullocks with the dint of the crowd! Don't be daunted, Pat, I'll give you a hand with her.

(*He goes out, leaving his hayfork.*)

Mrs Fallon: It's time for ourselves to be going home. I have all I bought put in the basket. Look at there, Jack Smith's hayfork he left after him! He'll be wanting it. (*Calls.*) Jack Smith! Jack Smith! – He's gone through the crowd – hurry after him, Bartley, he'll be wanting it.

Bartley: I'll do that. This is no safe place to be leaving it. (*He takes up fork awkwardly and upsets the basket.*) Look at that now! If there is any basket in the fair upset, it must be our own basket! (*He goes out to right.*)

Mrs Fallon: Get out of that! It is your own fault, it is. Talk of misfortunes and misfortunes will come. Glory be! Look at my new egg-cups rolling in every part – and my two pound of sugar with the paper broke—

Mrs Tarpey: (*Turning from stall.*) God help us, Mrs Fallon, what happened your basket?

Mrs Fallon: It's himself that knocked it down, bad manners to him. (*Putting things up.*) My grand sugar that's destroyed, and he'll not drink his tea without it. I had best go back to the shop for more, much good may it do him! (*Enter Tim Casey.*)

Tim Casey: Where is Bartley Fallon, Mrs Fallon? I want a word with him before he'll leave the fair. I was afraid he might have gone home by this, for he's a temperate man.

Mrs Fallon: I wish he did go home! It'd be best for me if he went home straight from the fair green, or if he never came with me at all! Where is he, is it? He's gone up the road (*jerks elbow*) following Jack Smith with a hayfork. (*She goes out to left.*)

Tim Casey: Following Jack Smith with a hayfork! Did ever anyone hear the like of that. (*Shouts.*) Did you hear that news, Mrs Tarpey?

Mrs Tarpey: I heard no news at all.

Tim Casey: Some dispute I suppose it was that rose between Jack Smith and Bartley Fallon, and it seems Jack made off, and Bartley is following him with a hayfork!

Mrs Tarpey: Is he now? Well, that was quick work! It's not ten minutes since the two of them were here, Bartley going home and Jack going to the Five Acre Meadow; and I had my apples to settle up, that Jo Muldoon of the police had scattered, and when I looked round again Jack Smith was gone, and Bartley Fallon was gone, and Mrs Fallon's basket upset, and all in it strewed upon the ground – the tea here – the two pound of sugar there – the egg-cups there – Look, now, what a great hardship the deafness puts upon me, that I didn't hear the commencement of the fight! Wait till I tell James Ryan that I see below; he is a neighbour of Bartley's, it would be a pity if he wouldn't hear the news!

(*She goes out. Enter Shawn Early and Mrs Tully.*)

Tim Casey: Listen, Shawn Early! Listen, Mrs Tully, to the news! Jack Smith and Bartley Fallon had a falling out, and Jack knocked Mrs Fallon's basket into the road, and Bartley made an attack on him with a hayfork, and away with Jack, and Bartley after him. Look at the sugar here yet on the road!

Shawn Early: Do you tell me so? Well, that's a queer thing, and Bartley Fallon so quiet a man!

Mrs Tully: I wouldn't wonder at all. I would never think well of a man that would have that sort of a mouldering look. It's likely he has overtaken Jack by this.

(*Enter James Ryan and Mrs Tarpey.*)

James Ryan: That is great news Mrs Tarpey was telling me! I suppose that's what brought the police and the magistrate up this way. I was wondering to see them in it a while ago.

Shawn Early: The police after them? Bartley Fallon must have injured Jack so. They wouldn't meddle in a fight that was only for show!

Mrs Tully: Why wouldn't he injure him? There was many a man killed with no more of a weapon than a hayfork.

James Ryan: Wait till I run north as far as Kelly's bar to spread the news! (*He goes out.*)

Tim Casey: I'll go tell Jack Smith's first cousin that is standing there south of the church after selling his lambs. (*Goes out.*)

Mrs Tully: I'll go telling a few of the neighbours I see beyond to the west. (*Goes out.*)

Shawn Early: I'll give word of it beyond at the east of the green.

(*Is going out when Mrs Tarpey seizes hold of him.*)

Mrs Tarpey: Stop a minute, Shawn Early, and tell me did you see red Jack Smith's wife, Kitty Keary, in any place?

Shawn Early: I did. At her own house she was, drying clothes on the hedge as I passed.

Mrs Tarpey: What did you say she was doing?

Shawn Early: (*Breaking away.*)   Laying out a sheet on the hedge. (*He goes.*)

Mrs Tarpey: Laying out a sheet for the dead! The Lord have mercy on us! Jack Smith dead, and his wife laying out a sheet for his burying! (*Calls out.*) Why didn't you tell me that before, Shawn Early? Isn't the deafness the great hardship? Half the world might be dead without me knowing of it or getting word of it at all! (*She sits down and rocks herself.*)   O my poor Jack Smith! To be going to his work so nice and so hearty, and to be left stretched on the ground in the full light of the day!

(*Enter Tim Casey.*)

Tim Casey: What is it, Mrs Tarpey? What happened since?

Mrs Tarpey: O my poor Jack Smith!

Tim Casey: Did Bartley overtake him?

Mrs Tarpey: O the poor man!

Tim Casey: Is it killed he is?

Mrs Tarpey: Stretched in the Five Acre Meadow!

Tim Casey: The Lord have mercy on us! Is that a fact?

Mrs Tarpey: Without the rites of the Church or a ha'porth!

Tim Casey: Who was telling you?

Mrs Tarpey: And the wife laying out a sheet for his corpse. (*Sits up and wipes her eyes.*)   I suppose they'll wake him the same as another?

(*Enter Mrs Tully, Shawn Early, and James Ryan.*)

Mrs Tully: There is great talk about this work in every quarter of the fair.

Mrs Tarpey: Ochone! cold and dead. And myself maybe the last he was speaking to!

James Ryan: The Lord save us! Is it dead he is?

Tim Casey: Dead surely, and the wife getting provision for the wake.

Shawn Early: Well, now, hadn't Bartley Fallon great venom in him?

Mrs Tully: You may be sure he had some cause. Why would he have made an end of him if he had not? (*To Mrs Tarpey, raising her voice.*) What was it rose the dispute at all, Mrs Tarpey?

Mrs Tarpey: Not a one of me knows. The last I saw of them, Jack Smith was standing there, and Bartley Fallon was standing there, quiet and easy, and he listening to 'The Red-haired Man's Wife'.

Mrs Tully: Do you hear that, Tim Casey? Do you hear that, Shawn Early and James Ryan? Bartley Fallon was here this morning listening to red Jack Smith's wife, Kitty Keary that was! Listening to her and whispering with her! It was she started the fight so!

Shawn Early: She must have followed him from her own house. It is likely some person roused him.

Tim Casey: I never knew, before, Bartley Fallon was great with Jack Smith's wife.

Mrs Tully: How would you know it? Sure it's not in the streets they would be calling it. If Mrs Fallon didn't know of it, and if I that have the next house to them didn't know of it, and if Jack Smith himself didn't know of it, it is not likely you would know of it, Tim Casey.

Shawn Early: Let Bartley Fallon take charge of her from this out so, and let him provide for her. It is little pity she will get from any person in this parish.

Tim Casey: How can he take charge of her? Sure he has a wife of his own. Sure you don't think he'd turn souper and marry her in a Protestant church?

James Ryan: It would be easy for him to marry her if he brought her to America.

Shawn Early: With or without Kitty Keary, believe me it is for America he's making at this minute. I saw the new magistrate and Jo Muldoon of the police going into the post-office as I came up – there was hurry on them – you may be sure it was to telegraph they went, the way he'll be stopped in the docks at Queenstown!

Mrs Tully: It's likely Kitty Keary is gone with him, and not minding a sheet or a wake at all. The poor man, to be deserted by his own wife, and the breath hardly gone out yet from his body that is lying bloody in the field!

(*Enter Mrs Fallon.*)

Mrs Fallon: What is it the whole of the town is talking about? And what is it you yourselves are talking about? Is it about my man Bartley Fallon you are talking? Is it lies about him you are telling, saying that he went killing Jack Smith? My grief that ever he came into this place at all!

James Ryan: Be easy now, Mrs Fallon. Sure there is no one at all in the whole fair but is sorry for you!

Mrs Fallon: Sorry for me, is it? Why would anyone be sorry for me? Let you be sorry for yourselves, and that there may be shame on you for ever and at the day of judgment, for the words you are saying and the lies you are telling to take away the character of my poor man, and to take the good name off of him, and to drive him to destruction! That is what you are doing!

Shawn Early: Take comfort now, Mrs Fallon. The police are not so smart as they think. Sure he might give them the slip yet, the same as Lynchehaun.*

Mrs Tully: If they do get him, and if they do put a rope around his neck, there is no one can say he does not deserve it!

Mrs Fallon: Is that what you are saying, Bridget Tully, and is that what you think? I tell you it's too much talk you have, making yourself out to be such a great one, and to be running down every respectable person! A rope, is it? It isn't much of a rope was needed to tie up your own furniture the day you came into Martin Tully's house, and you never bringing

---

*James Lynchehaun was a criminal who was sheltered by the people of Achill Island and helped to escape to America. The incident contributed elements to Synge's *Playboy of the Western World*.

as much as a blanket, or a penny, or a suit of clothes with you and I myself bringing seventy pounds and two feather beds. And now you are stiffer than a woman would have a hundred pounds! It is too much talk the whole of you have. A rope is it? I tell you the whole of this town is full of liars and schemers that would hang you up for half a glass of whisky. (*Turning to go.*) People they are you wouldn't believe as much as daylight from without you'd get up to have a look at it yourself. Killing Jack Smith indeed! Where are you at all, Bartley, till I bring you out of this? My nice quiet little man! My decent comrade! He that is as kind and as harmless as an innocent beast of the field! He'll be doing no harm at all if he'll shed the blood of some of you after this day's work! That much would be no harm at all. (*Calls out.*) Bartley! Bartley Fallon! Where are you? (*Going out.*) Did anyone see Bartley Fallon?

(*All turn to look after her.*)

James Ryan: It is hard for her to believe any such a thing, God help her!

(*Enter Bartley Fallon from right, carrying hayfork.*)

Bartley: It is what I often said to myself, if there is ever any misfortune coming to this world it is on myself it is sure to come!

(*All turn round and face him.*)

Bartley: To be going about with this fork and to find no one to take it, and no place to leave it down, and I wanting to be gone out of this – Is that you, Shawn Early? (*Holds out fork.*) It's well I met you. You have no call to be leaving the fair for a while the way I have, and how can I go till I'm rid of this fork? Will you take it and keep it until such time as Jack Smith—

Shawn Early: (*Backing.*) I will not take it, Bartley Fallon, I'm very thankful to you!

Bartley: (*Turning to apple stall.*) Look at it now, Mrs Tarpey, it was here I got it; let me thrust it in under the stall. It will lie there safe enough, and no one will take notice of it until such time as Jack Smith—

Mrs Tarpey: Take your fork out of that! Is it to put trouble on me and to destroy me you want? Putting it there for the police to be rooting it out maybe. (*Thrusts him back.*)

Bartley: That is a very unneighbourly thing for you to do, Mrs Tarpey. Hadn't I enough care on me with that fork before this, running up and down with it like the swinging of a clock, and afeard to lay it down in any place! I wish I never touched it or meddled with it at all!

James Ryan: It is a pity, indeed, you ever did.

Bartley: Will you yourself take it, James Ryan? You were always a neighbourly man.

James Ryan: (*Backing.*)   There is many a thing I would do for you, Bartley Fallon, but I won't do that!

Shawn Early: I tell you there is no man will give you any help or any encouragement for this day's work. If it was something agrarian now—

Bartley: If no one at all will take it, maybe it's best to give it up to the police.

Tim Casey: There'd be a welcome for it with them surely! (*Laughter.*)

Mrs Tully: And it is to the police Kitty Keary herself will be brought.

Mrs Tarpey: (*Rocking to and fro.*)   I wonder now who will take the expense of the wake for poor Jack Smith?

Bartley: The wake for Jack Smith!

Tim Casey: Why wouldn't he get a wake as well as another? Would you begrudge him that much?

Bartley: Red Jack Smith dead! Who was telling you?

Shawn Early: The whole town knows of it by this.

Bartley: Do they say what way did he die?

James Ryan: You don't know that yourself, I suppose, Bartley Fallon? You don't know he was followed and that he was laid dead with the stab of a hayfork?

Bartley: The stab of a hayfork!

Shawn Early: You don't know, I suppose, that the body was found in the Five Acre Meadow?

Bartley: The Five Acre Meadow!

Tim Casey: It is likely you don't know that the police are after the man that did it?

Bartley: The man that did it!

Mrs Tully: You don't know, maybe, that he was made away with for the sake of Kitty Keary, his wife?

Bartley: Kitty Keary, his wife!
(*Sits down bewildered.*)

Mrs Tully: And what have you to say now, Bartley Fallon?

Bartley: (*Crossing himself.*) I to bring that fork here, and to find that news before me! It is much if I can ever stir from this place at all, or reach as far as the road!

Tim Casey: Look, boys, at the new magistrate, and Jo Muldoon along with him! It's best for us to quit this.

Shawn Early: That is so. It is best not to be mixed in this business at all.

James Ryan: Bad as he is, I wouldn't like to be an informer against any man.
(*All hurry away except Mrs Tarpey, who remains behind her stall. Enter magistrate and policeman.*)

Magistrate: I knew the district was in a bad state, but I did not expect to be confronted with a murder at the first fair I came to.

Policeman: I am sure you did not, indeed.

Magistrate: It was well I had not gone home. I caught a few words here and there that roused my suspicions.

Policeman: So they would, too.

Magistrate: You heard the same story from everyone you asked?

Policeman: The same story – or if it was not altogether the same, anyway it was no less than the first story.

Magistrate: What is that man doing? He is sitting alone with a hayfork. He has a guilty look. The murder was done with a hayfork!

Policeman: (*In a whisper.*) That's the very man they say did the act; Bartley Fallon himself!

Magistrate: He must have found escape difficult – he is trying to brazen it out. A convict in the Andaman Islands tried the same game, but he could not escape my system! Stand aside – Don't go far – have the handcuffs ready. (*He walks up to Bartley, folds his arms, and stands before him.*) Here, my man, do you know anything of John Smith?

Bartley: Of John Smith! Who is he, now?

Policeman: Jack Smith, sir – Red Jack Smith!

Magistrate: (*Coming a step nearer and tapping him on the shoulder.*)   Where is Jack Smith?

Bartley: (*With a deep sigh, and shaking his head slowly.*) Where is he, indeed?

Magistrate: What have you to tell?

Bartley: It is where he was this morning, standing in this spot, singing his share of songs – no, but lighting his pipe – scraping a match on the sole of his shoe —

Magistrate: I ask you, for the third time, where is he?

Bartley: I wouldn't like to say that. It is a great mystery, and it is hard to say of any man, did he earn hatred or love.

Magistrate: Tell me all you know.

Bartley: All that I know — Well, there are the three estates; there is Limbo, and there is Purgatory, and there is —

Magistrate: Nonsense! This is trifling! Get to the point.

Bartley: Maybe you don't hold with the clergy so? That is the teaching of the clergy. Maybe you hold with the old people. It is what they do be saying, that the shadow goes wandering, and the soul is tired, and the body is taking a rest – The shadow! (*Starts up.*)   I was nearly sure I saw Jack Smith not ten minutes ago at the corner of the forge, and I lost him again — Was it his ghost I saw, do you think?

Magistrate: (*To policeman.*)   Conscience-struck! He will confess all now!

Bartley: His ghost to come before me! It is likely it was on account of the fork! I to have it and he to have no way to defend himself the time he met with his death!

Magistrate: (*To policeman.*)   I must note down his words. (*Takes out notebook.*)   (*To Bartley.*)   I warn you that your words are being noted.

Bartley: If I had ha' run faster in the beginning, this terror would not be on me at the latter end! Maybe he will cast it up against me at the day of judgment — I wouldn't wonder at all at that.

Magistrate: (*Writing.*)   At the day of judgment —

Bartley: It was soon for his ghost to appear to me – is it coming after me always by day it will be, and stripping the clothes off in the night time ? – I wouldn't wonder at all at that, being as I am an unfortunate man!

Magistrate: (*Sternly.*) Tell me this truly. What was the motive of this crime ?

Bartley: The motive, is it ?

Magistrate: Yes, the motive; the cause.

Bartley: I'd sooner not say that.

Magistrate: You had better tell me truly. Was it money ?

Bartley: Not at all! What did poor Jack Smith ever have in his pockets unless it might be his hands that would be in them ?

Magistrate: Any dispute about land ?

Bartley: (*Indignantly.*) Not at all! He never was a grabber or grabbed from any one!

Magistrate: You will find it better for you if you tell me at once.

Bartley: I tell you I wouldn't for the whole world wish to say what it was – it is a thing I would not like to be talking about.

Magistrate: There is no use in hiding it. It will be discovered in the end.

Bartley: Well, I suppose it will, seeing that mostly everybody knows it before. Whisper here now. I will tell no lie; where would be the use ? (*Puts his hand to his mouth, and Magistrate stoops.*) Don't be putting the blame on the parish, for such a thing was never done in the parish before – it was done for the sake of Kitty Keary, Jack Smith's wife.

Magistrate: (*To policeman.*) Put on the handcuffs. We have been saved some trouble. I knew he would confess if taken in the right way.

(*Policeman puts on handcuffs.*)

Bartley: Handcuffs now! Glory be! I always said, if there was ever any misfortune coming to this place it was on myself it would fall. I to be in handcuffs! There's no wonder at all in that.

(*Enter Mrs Fallon, followed by the rest. She is looking back at them as she speaks.*)

Mrs Fallon: Telling lies the whole of the people of this town are; telling lies, telling lies as fast as a dog will trot! Speaking against my poor respectable man! Saying he made an end of

Jack Smith! My decent comrade! There is no better man and no kinder man in the whole of the five parishes! It's little annoyance he ever gave to anyone! (*Turns and sees him.*) What in the earthly world do I see before me? Bartley Fallon in charge of the police! Handcuffs on him! O Bartley, what did you do at all at all?

Bartley: O Mary, there has a great misfortune come upon me! It is what I always said, that if there is ever any misfortune —

Mrs Fallon: What did he do at all, or is it bewitched I am?

Magistrate: This man has been arrested on a charge of murder.

Mrs Fallon: Whose charge is that? Don't believe them! They are all liars in this place! Give me back my man!

Magistrate: It is natural you should take his part, but you have no cause of complaint against your neighbours. He has been arrested for the murder of John Smith, on his own confession.

Mrs Fallon: The saints of heaven protect us! And what did he want killing Jack Smith?

Magistrate: It is best you should know all. He did it on account of a love affair with the murdered man's wife.

Mrs Fallon: (*Sitting down.*) With Jack Smith's wife! With Kitty Keary! – Ochone, the traitor!

The Crowd: A great shame, indeed. He is a traitor, indeed.

Mrs Tully: To America he was bringing her, Mrs Fallon.

Bartley: What are you saying, Mary? I tell you —

Mrs Fallon: Don't say a word! I won't listen to any word you'll say! (*Stops her ears.*) O, isn't he the treacherous villain? Ohone go deo!

Bartley: Be quiet till I speak! Listen to what I say!

Mrs Fallon: Sitting beside me on the ass-car coming to the town, so quiet and so respectable, and treachery like that in his heart!

Bartley: Is it your wits you have lost or is it I myself that have lost my wits?

Mrs Fallon: And it's hard I earned you, slaving, slaving – and you grumbling, and sighing, and coughing, and discontented, and the priest wore out anointing you, with all the times you threatened to die!

Bartley: Let you be quiet till I tell you!

Mrs Fallon: You to bring such a disgrace into the parish. A thing that was never heard of before!

Bartley: Will you shut your mouth and hear me speaking?

Mrs Fallon: And if it was for any sort of a fine handsome woman, but for a little fistful of a woman like Kitty Keary, that's not four feet high hardly, and not three teeth in her head unless she got new ones! May God reward you, Bartley Fallon, for the black treachery in your heart and the wickedness in your mind, and the red blood of poor Jack Smith that is wet upon your hand!

(*Voice of Jack Smith heard singing*) –

> The sea shall be dry,
> > The earth under mourning and ban!
> Then loud shall he cry
> > For the wife of the red-haired man!

Bartley: It's Jack Smith's voice – I never knew a ghost to sing before — It is after myself and the fork he is coming!   (*Goes back. Enter Jack Smith.*)   Let one of you give him the fork and I will be clear of him now and for eternity!

Mrs Tarpey: The Lord have mercy on us! Red Jack Smith! The man that was going to be waked!

James Ryan: Is it back from the grave you are come?

Shawn Early: Is it alive you are, or is it dead you are?

Tim Casey: Is it yourself at all that's in it?

Mrs Tully: Is it letting on you were to be dead?

Mrs Fallon: Dead or alive, let you stop Kitty Keary, your wife, from bringing my man away with her to America!

Jack Smith: It is what I think, the wits are gone astray on the whole of you. What would my wife want bringing Bartley Fallon to America?

Mrs Fallon: To leave yourself, and to get quit of you she wants, Jack Smith, and to bring him away from myself. That's what the two of them has settled together.

Jack Smith: I'll break the head of any man that says that! Who is it says it?   (*To Tim Casey:*)   Was it you said it?   (*To Shawn Early:*)   Was it you?

All together: (*Backing and shaking their heads.*)   It wasn't I said it!

Jack Smith: Tell me the name of any man that said it!

All together: (*Pointing to Bartley*).   It was *him* that said it!

Jack Smith: Let me at him till I break his head!

(*Bartley backs in terror. Neighbours hold Jack Smith back.*)

Jack Smith: (*Trying to free himself.*)   Let me at him! Isn't he the pleasant sort of a scarecrow for any woman to be crossing the ocean with! It's back from the docks of New York he'd be turned (*trying to rush at him again*), with a lie in his mouth and treachery in his heart, and another man's wife by his side, and he passing her off as his own! Let me at him can't you.

(*Makes another rush, but is held back.*)

Magistrate: (*Pointing to Jack Smith.*) Policeman, put the handcuffs on this man. I see it all now. A case of false impersonation, a conspiracy to defeat the ends of justice. There was a case in the Andaman Islands, a murderer of the Mopsa tribe, a religious enthusiast —

Policeman: So he might be, too.

Magistrate: We must take both these men to the scene of the murder. We must confront them with the body of the real Jack Smith.

Jack Smith: I'll break the head of any man that will find my dead body!

Magistrate: I'll call more help from the barracks. (*Blows Policeman's whistle.*)

Bartley: It is what I am thinking, if myself and Jack Smith are put together in the one cell for the night, the handcuffs will be taken off him, and his hands will be free, and murder will be done that time surely!

Magistrate: Come on! (*They turn to the right.*)

NOTES

THE IDEA of this play first came to me as a tragedy. I kept seeing as in a picture people sitting by the roadside, and a girl passing to the market, gay and fearless. And then I saw her passing by the same place at evening, her head hanging, the heads of others turned from her, because of some sudden story that had risen out of a chance word, and had snatched away her good name.

But comedy and not tragedy was wanted at our theatre to put beside the high poetic work, *The King's Threshold, The Shadowy Waters, On Baile's Strand, The Well of the Saints*; and I let laughter have its way with the little play. I was delayed in beginning it for a while, because I could only think of Bartley Fallon as dull-witted or silly or ignorant, and the handcuffs seemed too harsh a punishment. But one day by the sea at Duras a melancholy man, who was telling me of the crosses he had gone through at home, said – 'But I'm thinking if I went to America, its long ago today I'd be dead. And its a great expense for a poor man to be buried in America.' Bartley was born at that moment, and, far from harshness, I felt I was providing him with a happy old age in giving him the lasting glory of that great and crowning day of misfortune.

It has been acted very often by other companies as well as our own, and the Boers have done me the honour of translating and pirating it.

QUEEN MARGARET COLLEGE LIBRARY

HYACINTH HALVEY

PERSONS

Hyacinth Halvey

James Quirke . . . . . . A BUTCHER

Fardy Farrell . . . . . A TELEGRAPH BOY

Sergeant Carden

Mrs Delane . . . . POSTMISTRESS AT CLOON

Miss Joyce . . . . THE PRIEST'S HOUSEKEEPER

HYACINTH HALVEY

Scene: Outside the Post Office at the little town of Cloon. Mrs Delane at Post Office door. Mr Quirke sitting on a chair at butcher's door. A dead sheep hanging beside it, and a thrush in a cage above. Fardy Farrell playing on a mouth organ. Train whistle heard.

Mrs Delane: There is the four o'clock train, Mr Quirke.

Mr Quirke: Is it now, Mrs Delane, and I not long after rising? It makes a man drowsy to be doing the half of his work in the night time. Going about the country, looking for little stags of sheep, striving to knock a few shillings together. That contract for the soldiers gives me a great deal to attend to.

Mrs Delane: I suppose so. It's hard enough on myself to be down ready for the mail car in the morning, sorting letters in the half dark. It's often I haven't time to look who are the letters from – or the cards.

Mr Quirke: It would be a pity you not to know any little news might be knocking about. If you did not have information of what is going on who should have it? Was it you, ma'am, was telling me that the new Sub-Sanitary Inspector would be arriving today?

Mrs Delane: Today it is he is coming, and it's likely he was in that train. There was a card about him to Sergeant Carden this morning.

Mr Quirke: A young chap from Carrow they were saying he was.

Mrs Delane: So he is, one Hyacinth Halvey; and, indeed, if all that is said of him is true, or if a quarter of it is true, he will be a credit to this town.

Mr Quirke: Is that so?

Mrs Delane: Testimonials he has by the score. To Father Gregan they were sent. Registered they were coming and going. Would you believe me telling you that they weighed up to three pounds?

Mr Quirke: There must be great bulk in them indeed.

Mrs Delane: It is no wonder he to get the job. He must have a great character so many persons to write for him as what there did.

Fardy: It would be a great thing to have a character like that.

Mrs Delane: Indeed, I am thinking it will be long before you will get the like of it, Fardy Farrell.

Fardy: If I had the like of that of a character it is not here carrying messages I would be. It's in Noonan's Hotel I would be, driving cars.

Mr Quirke: Here is the priest's housekeeper coming.

Mrs Delane: So she is; and there is the Sergeant a little while after her.

(*Enter Miss Joyce.*)

Mrs Delane: Good evening to you, Miss Joyce. What way is his Reverence today? Did he get any ease from the cough?

Miss Joyce: He did not indeed, Mrs Delane. He has it sticking to him yet. Smothering he is in the night time. The most thing he comes short in is the voice.

Mrs Delane: I am sorry, now, to hear that. He should mind himself well.

Miss Joyce: It's easy to say let him mind himself. What do you say to him going to the meeting tonight? (*Sergeant comes in.*) It's for his Reverence's *Freeman* I am come, Mrs Delane.

Mrs Delane: Here it is ready. I was just throwing an eye on it to see was there any news. Good evening, Sergeant.

Sergeant: (*Holding up a placard.*)   I brought this notice, Mrs Delane, the announcement of the meeting to be held tonight in the court-house. You might put it up here convenient to the window. I hope you are coming to it yourself?

Mrs Delane: I will come, and welcome. I would do more than that for you, Sergeant.

Sergeant: And you, Mr Quirke.

Mr Quirke: I'll come, to be sure. I forget what's this the meeting is about.

Sergeant: The Department of Agriculture is sending round a lecturer in furtherance of the moral development of the rural classes. (*Reads.*) 'A lecture will be given this evening in Cloon court-house, illustrated by magic lantern slides —' Those will not be in it; I am informed they were all broken in the first journey, the railway company taking them to be eggs. The subject of the lecture is 'The Building of Character.'

Mrs Delane: Very nice, indeed. I knew a girl lost her character, and she washed her feet in a blessed well after, and it dried up on the minute.

Sergeant: The arrangements have all been left to me, the Archdeacon being away. He knows I have a good intellect for things of the sort. But the loss of those slides puts a man out. The things people will not see it is not likely it is the thing they will believe. I saw what they call tableaux – standing pictures, you know – one time in Dundrum —

Mrs Delane: Miss Joyce was saying Father Gregan is supporting you.

Sergeant: I am accepting his assistance. No bigotry about me when there is a question of the welfare of any fellow-creatures. Orange and green will stand together tonight. I myself and the station-master on the one side; your parish priest in the chair.

Miss Joyce: If his Reverence would mind me he would not quit the house tonight. He is no more fit to go speak at a meeting than (*pointing to the one hanging outside Quirke's door*) that sheep.

Sergeant: I am willing to take the responsibility. He will have no speaking to do at all, unless it might be to bid them give the lecturer a hearing. The loss of those slides now is a great annoyance to me – and no time for anything. The lecturer will be coming by the next train.

Miss Joyce: Who is this coming up the street, Mrs Delane?

Mrs Delane: I wouldn't doubt it to be the new Sub-Sanitary Inspector. Was I telling you of the weight of the testimonials he got, Miss Joyce?

Miss Joyce: Sure, I heard the curate reading them to his Reverence. He must be a wonder for principles.

Mrs Delane: Indeed it is what I was saying to myself, he must be a very saintly young man.

(*Enter Hyacinth Halvey. He carries a small bag and a large, brown paper parcel. He stops and nods bashfully.*)

Hyacinth: Good evening to you. I was bid to come to the post office —

Sergeant: I suppose you are Hyacinth Halvey ? I had a letter about you from the Resident Magistrate.

Hyacinth: I heard he was writing. It was my mother got a friend he deals with to ask him.

Sergeant: He gives you a very high character.

Hyacinth: It is very kind of him indeed, and he not knowing me at all. But indeed all the neighbours were very friendly. Anything any one could do to help me they did it.

Mrs Delane: I'll engage it is the testimonials you have in your parcel ? I know the wrapping paper, but they grew in bulk since I handled them.

Hyacinth: Indeed I was getting them to the last. There was not one refused me. It is what my mother was saying, a good character is no burden.

Fardy: I would believe that indeed.

Sergeant: Let us have a look at the testimonials.

(*Hyacinth Halvey opens parcel, and a large number of envelopes fall out.*)

Sergeant: (*Opening and reading one by one.*) 'He possesses the fire of the Gael, the strength of the Norman, the vigour of the Dane, the stolidity of the Saxon' —

Hyacinth: It was the Chairman of the Poor Law Guardians wrote that.

Sergeant: 'A magnificent example to old and young —'

Hyacinth: That was the Secretary of the De Wet Hurling Club—

Sergeant: 'A shining example of the value conferred by an eminently careful and high class education'—

Hyacinth: That was the National Schoolmaster.

Sergeant: 'Devoted to the highest ideals of his Mother-land to such an extent as is compatible with a hitherto non-parliamentary career'—

Hyacinth: That was the Member for Carrow.

Sergeant: 'A splendid exponent of the purity of the race'—

Hyacinth: The Editor of the *Carrow Champion.*

Sergeant: 'Admirably adapted for the efficient discharge of all possible duties that may in future be laid upon him'—

Hyacinth: The new Station-master.

Sergeant: 'A champion of every cause that can legitimately benefit his fellow-creatures'— Why, look here, my man, you are the very one to come to our assistance tonight.

Hyacinth: I would be glad to do that. What way can I do it?

Sergeant: You are a newcomer – your example would carry weight – you must stand up as a living proof of the beneficial effect of a high character, moral fibre, temperance – there is something about it here I am sure— (*Looks.*) I am sure I saw 'unparalleled temperance' in some place—

Hyacinth: It was my mother's cousin wrote that – I am no drinker, but I haven't the pledge taken—

Sergeant: You might take it for the purpose.

Mr Quirke: (*Eagerly.*) Here is an anti-treating button. I was made a present of it by one of my customers – I'll give it to you (*sticks it in Hyacinth's coat*) and welcome.

Sergeant: That is it. You can wear the button on the platform – or a bit of blue ribbon – hundreds will follow your example – I know the boys from the Workhouse will—

Hyacinth: I am in no way wishful to be an example—

Sergeant: I will read extracts from the testimonials. 'There he is,' I will say, 'an example of one in early life who by his own unaided efforts and his high character has obtained a profitable situation' – (*Slaps his side.*) I know what I'll do. I'll engage a few corner-boys from Noonan's bar, just as they are, greasy and sodden, to stand in a group – there will be the contrast – The sight will deter others from a similar fate – That's the way to do a tableau – I knew I could turn out a success.

Hyacinth: I wouldn't like to be a contrast—

Sergeant: (*Puts testimonials in his pocket.*) I will go now and engage those lads – sixpence each, and well worth it – Nothing like an example for the rural classes.

(*Goes off, Hyacinth feebly trying to detain him.*)

Mrs Delane: A very nice man indeed. A little high up in himself, may be. I'm not one that blames the police. Sure they have their own bread to earn like every other one. And indeed it is often they will let a thing pass.

Mr Quirke: (*Gloomily.*) Sometimes they will, and more times they will not.

Miss Joyce: And where will you be finding a lodging, Mr Halvey?

Hyacinth: I was going to ask that myself, ma'am. I don't know the town.

Miss Joyce: I know of a good lodging, but it is only a very good man would be taken into it.

Mrs Delane: Sure there could be no objection there to Mr Halvey. There is no appearance on him but what is good, and the Sergeant after taking him up the way he is doing.

Miss Joyce: You will be near to the Sergeant in the lodging I speak of. The house is convenient to the barracks.

Hyacinth: (*Doubtfully.*) To the barracks?

Miss Joyce: Alongside of it and the barrack yard behind. And that's not all. It is opposite to the priest's house.

Hyacinth: Opposite, is it?

Miss Joyce: A very respectable place, indeed, and a very clean room you will get. I know it well. The curate can see into it from his window.

Hyacinth: Can he now?

Fardy: There was a good many, I am thinking, went into that lodging and left it after.

Miss Joyce: (*Sharply.*) It is a lodging you will never be let into or let stop in, Fardy. If they did go they were a good riddance.

Fardy: John Hart, the plumber, left it—

Miss Joyce: If he did it was because he dared not pass the police coming in, as he used, with a rabbit he was after snaring in his hand.

Fardy: The schoolmaster himself left it.

Miss Joyce: He needn't have left it if he hadn't taken to card-playing. What way could you say your prayers, and shadows shuffling and dealing before you on the blind?

Hyacinth: I think maybe I'd best look around a bit before I'll settle in a lodging—

Miss Joyce: Not at all. *You* won't be wanting to pull down the blind.

Mrs Delane: It is not likely *you* will be snaring rabbits.

Miss Joyce: Or bringing in a bottle and taking an odd glass the way James Kelly did.

Mrs Delane: Or writing threatening notices, and the police taking a view of you from the rear.

Miss Joyce: Or going to roadside dances or running after good-for-nothing young girls—

Hyacinth: I give you my word I'm not so harmless as you think.

Mrs Delane: Would you be putting a lie on these, Mr Halvey? (*Touching testimonials.*) I know well the way *you* will be spending the evenings, writing letters to your relations—

Miss Joyce: Learning O'Growney's exercises—

Mrs Delane: Sticking post cards in an album for the convent bazaar.

Miss Joyce: Reading the *Catholic Young Man*—

Mrs Delane: Playing the melodies on a melodeon—

Miss Joyce: Looking at the pictures in the *Lives of the Saints.* I'll hurry on and engage the room for you.

Hyacinth: Wait. Wait a minute—

Miss Joyce: No trouble at all. I told you it was just opposite. (*Goes.*)

Mr Quirke: I suppose I must go upstairs and ready myself for the meeting. If it wasn't for the contract I have for the soldiers' barracks and the Sergeant's good word, I wouldn't go anear it. (*Goes into shop.*)

Mrs Delane: I should be making myself ready too. I must be in good time to see you being made an example of, Mr Halvey. It is I myself was the first to say it; you will be a credit to the town. (*Goes.*)

Hyacinth: (*In a tone of agony.*) I wish I had never seen Cloon.

Fardy: What is on you?

Hyacinth: I wish I had never left Carrow. I wish I had been drowned the first day I thought of it, and I'd be better off.

Fardy: What is it ails you?

Hyacinth: I wouldn't for the best pound ever I had be in this place today.

Fardy: I don't know what you are talking about.

Hyacinth: To have left Carrow, if it was a poor place, where I had my comrades, and an odd spree, and a game of cards – and a coursing match coming on, and I promised a new greyhound from the city of Cork. I'll die in this place, the way I am. I'll be too much closed in.

Fardy: Sure it mightn't be as bad as what you think.

Hyacinth: Will you tell me, I ask you, what way I can undo it ?

Fardy: What is it you are wanting to undo ?

Hyacinth: Will you tell me what way can I get rid of my character ?

Fardy: To get rid of it, is it ?

Hyacinth: That is what I said. Aren't you after hearing the great character they are after putting on me ?

Fardy: That is a good thing to have.

Hyacinth: It is not. It's the worst in the world. If I hadn't it, I wouldn't be like a prize mangold at a show with every person praising me.

Fardy: If I had it, I wouldn't be like a head in a barrel, with every person making hits at me.

Hyacinth: If I hadn't it, I wouldn't be shoved into a room with all the clergy watching me and the police in the back yard.

Fardy: If I had it, I wouldn't be but a message-carrier now, and a clapper scaring birds in the summer time.

Hyacinth: If I hadn't it, I wouldn't be wearing this button and brought up for an example at the meeting.

Fardy: (*Whistles.*) Maybe you're not, so, what those papers make you out to be ?

Hyacinth: How would I be what they make me out to be ? Was there ever any person of that sort since the world was a world, unless it might be Saint Antony of Padua looking down from the chapel wall ? If it is like that I was, isn't it in Mount Melleray I would be, or with the Friars at Esker ? Why would I be living in the world at all, or doing the world's work ?

Fardy: (*Taking up parcel.*) Who would think, now, there would be so much lies in a small place like Carrow?

Hyacinth: It was my mother's cousin did it. He said I was not reared for labouring – he gave me a new suit and bid me never to come back again. I daren't go back to face him – the neighbours knew my mother had a long family – bad luck to them the day they gave me these. (*Tears letters and scatters them.*) I'm done with testimonials. They won't be here to bear witness against me.

Fardy: The Sergeant thought them to be great. Sure he has the samples of them in his pocket. There's not one in the town but will know before morning that you are the next thing to an earthly saint.

Hyacinth: (*Stamping.*) I'll stop their mouths. I'll show them I can be a terror for badness. I'll do some injury. I'll commit some crime. The first thing I'll do I'll go and get drunk. If I never did it before I'll do it now. I'll get drunk – then I'll make an assault – I tell you I'd think as little of taking a life as of blowing out a candle.

Fardy: If you get drunk you are done for. Sure that will be held up after as an excuse for any breaking of the law.

Hyacinth: I will break the law. Drunk or sober I'll break it. I'll do something that will have no excuse. What would you say is the worst crime that any man can do?

Fardy: I don't know. I heard the Sergeant saying one time it was to obstruct the police in the discharge of their duty—

Hyacinth: That won't do. It's a patriot I would be then, worse than before, with my picture in the weeklies. It's a red crime I must commit that will make all respectable people quit minding me. What can I do? Search your mind now.

Fardy: It's what I heard the old people saying there could be no worse crime than to steal a sheep—

Hyacinth: I'll steal a sheep – or a cow – or a horse – if that will leave me the way I was before.

Fardy: It's maybe in gaol it will leave you.

Hyacinth: I don't care – I'll confess – I'll tell why I did it – I give you my word I would as soon be picking oakum or breaking stones as to be perched in the daylight the same as that bird, and all the town chirruping to me or bidding me chirrup—

Fardy: There is reason in that, now.

Hyacinth: Help me, will you?

Fardy: Well, if it is to steal a sheep you want, you haven't far to go.

Hyacinth: (*Looking round wildly.*) Where is it? I see no sheep.

Fardy: Look around you.

Hyacinth: I see no living thing but that thrush—

Fardy: Did I say it was living? What is that hanging on Quirke's rack?

Hyacinth: It's (*fingers it*) a sheep, sure enough—

Fardy: Well, what ails you that you can't bring it away?

Hyacinth: It's a dead one—

Fardy: What matter if it is?

Hyacinth: If it was living I could drive it before me—

Fardy: You could. Is it to your own lodging you would drive it? Sure, everyone would take it to be a pet you brought from Carrow.

Hyacinth: I suppose they might.

Fardy: Miss Joyce sending in for news of it and it bleating behind the bed.

Hyacinth: (*Distracted.*) Stop! stop!

Mrs Delane: (*From upper window.*) Fardy! Are you there, Fardy Farrell?

Fardy: I am, ma'am.

Mrs Delane: (*From window.*) Look and tell me is that the telegraph I hear ticking?

Fardy: (*Looking in at door.*) It is, ma'am.

Mrs Delane: Then botheration to it, and I not dressed or undressed. Wouldn't you say, now, it's to annoy me it is calling me down. I'm coming! I'm coming! (*Disappears.*)

Fardy: Hurry on, now! hurry! She'll be coming out on you. If you are going to do it, do it, and if you are not, let it alone.

Hyacinth: I'll do it! I'll do it!

Fardy: (*Lifting the sheep on his back.*) I'll give you a hand with it.

Hyacinth: (*Goes a step or two and turns round.*) You told me no place where I could hide it.

Fardy: You needn't go far. There is the church beyond at the side of the Square. Go round to the ditch behind the wall – there's nettles in it.

Hyacinth: That'll do.

Fardy: She's coming out – run! run!

Hyacinth: (*Runs a step or two.*) It's slipping!

Fardy: Hoist it up! I'll give it a hoist! (*Halvey runs out.*)

Mrs Delane: (*Calling out.*) What are you doing Fardy Farrell? Is it idling you are?

Fardy: Waiting I am, ma'am, for the message—

Mrs Delane: Never mind the message yet. Who said it was ready? (*Going to door.*) Go ask for the loan of – no, but ask news of – Here, now go bring that bag of Mr Halvey's to the lodging Miss Joyce has taken—

Fardy: I will, ma'am. (*Takes bag and goes out.*)

Mrs Delane: (*Coming out with a telegram in her hand.*) Nobody here? (*Looks round and calls cautiously.*) Mr Quirke! Mr Quirke! James Quirke!

Mr Quirke: (*Looking out of his upper window with soap-suddy face.*) What is it, Mrs Delane!

Mrs Delane: (*Beckoning.*) Come down here till I tell you.

Mr Quirke: I cannot do that. I'm not fully shaved.

Mrs Delane: You'd come if you knew the news I have.

Mr Quirke: Tell it to me now. I'm not so supple as I was.

Mrs Delane: Whisper now, have you an enemy in any place?

Mr Quirke: It's likely I may have. A man in business—

Mrs Delane: I was thinking you had one.

Mr Quirke: Why would you think that at this time more than any other time?

Mrs Delane: If you could know what is in this envelope you would know that, James Quirke.

Mr Quirke: Is that so? And what, now, is there in it?

Mrs Delane: Who do you think now is it addressed to?

Mr Quirke: How would I know that, and I not seeing it?

Mrs Delane: That is true. Well, it is a message from Dublin Castle to the Sergeant of Police!

Mr Quirke: To Sergeant Carden, is it?

Mrs Delane: It is. And it concerns yourself.

Mr Quirke: Myself, is it? What accusation can they be bringing against me? I'm a peaceable man.

Mrs Delane: Wait till you hear.

Mr Quirke: Maybe they think I was in that moonlighting case—

Mrs Delane: That is not it—

Mr Quirke: I was not in it – I was but in the neighbouring field – cutting up a dead cow, that those never had a hand in—

Mrs Delane: You're out of it—

Mr Quirke: They had their faces blackened. There is no man can say I recognized them.

Mrs Delane: That's not what they're saying—

Mr Quirke: I'll swear I did not hear their voices or know them if I did hear them.

Mrs Delane: I tell you it has nothing to do with that. It might be better for you if it had.

Mr Quirke: What is it, so?

Mrs Delane: It is an order to the Sergeant bidding him immediately to seize all suspicious meat in your house. There is an officer coming down. There are complaints from the Shannon Fort Barracks.

Mr Quirke: I'll engage it was that pork.

Mrs Delane: What ailed it for them to find fault?

Mr Quirke: People are so hard to please nowadays, and I recommended them to salt it.

Mrs Delane: They had a right to have minded your advice.

Mr Quirke: There was nothing on that pig at all but it went mad on poor O'Grady that owned it.

Mrs Delane: So I heard, and went killing all before it.

Mr Quirke: Sure, it's only in the brain madness can be. I heard the doctor saying that.

Mrs Delane: He should know.

Mr Quirke: I give you my word I cut the head off it. I went to the loss of it, throwing it to the eels in the river. If they had salted the meat, as I advised them, what harm would it have done to any person on earth?

Mrs Delane: I hope no harm will come on poor Mrs Quirke and the family.

Mr Quirke: Maybe it wasn't that but some other thing—

Mrs Delane: Here is Fardy. I must send the message to the Sergeant. Well, Mr Quirke, I'm glad I had the time to give you a warning.

Mr Quirke: I'm obliged to you, indeed. You were always very neighbourly, Mrs Delane. Don't be too quick now sending the message. There is just one article I would like to put away out of the house before the Sergeant will come. (*Enter Fardy.*)

Mrs Delane: Here now, Fardy – that's not the way you're going to the barracks. Anyone would think you were scaring birds yet. Put on your uniform. (*Fardy goes into office.*) You have this message to bring to the Sergeant of Police. Get your cap now, it's under the counter.

(*Fardy reappears, and she gives him telegram.*)

Fardy: I'll bring it to the station. It's there he was going.

Mrs Delane: You will not, but to the barracks. It can wait for him there.

(*Fardy goes off. Mr Quirke has appeared at door.*)

Mr Quirke: It was indeed a very neighbourly act, Mrs Delane, and I'm obliged to you. There is just *one* article to put out of the way. The Sergeant may look about him then and welcome. It's well I cleared the premises on yesterday. A consignment to Birmingham I sent. The Lord be praised isn't England a terrible country with all it consumes?

Mrs Delane: Indeed you always treat the neighbours very decent, Mr Quirke, not asking them to buy from you.

Mr Quirke: Just one article. (*Turns to rack.*) That sheep I brought in last night. It was for a charity indeed I bought it from the widow woman at Kiltartan Cross. Where would the poor make a profit out of their dead meat without me? Where now is it? Well, now, I could have swore that that sheep was hanging there on the rack when I went in—

Mrs Delane: You must have put it in some other place.

Mr Quirke: (*Going in and searching and coming out.*) I did not; there is no other place for me to put it. Is it gone blind I am, or is it not in it, it is?

Mrs Delane: It's not there now, anyway.

Mr Quirke: Didn't you take notice of it there yourself this morning?

Mrs Delane: I have it in my mind that I did; but it's not there now.

Mr Quirke: There was no one here could bring it away?

Mrs Delane: Is it me myself you suspect of taking it, James Quirke?

Mr Quirke: Where is it at all? It is certain it was not of itself it walked away. It was dead, and very dead, the time I bought it.

Mrs Delane: I have a pleasant neighbour indeed that accuses me that I took his sheep. I wonder, indeed, you to say a thing like that! I to steal your sheep or your rack or anything that belongs to you or to your trade! Thank you, James Quirke. I am much obliged to you indeed.

Mr Quirke: Ah, be quiet, woman; be quiet—

Mrs Delane: And let me tell you, James Quirke, that I would sooner starve and see everyone belonging to me starve than to eat the size of a thimble of any joint that ever was on your rack or that ever will be on it, whatever the soldiers may eat that have no other thing to get, or the English that devour all sorts, or the poor ravenous people that's down by the sea! (*She turns to go into shop.*)

Mr Quirke: (*Stopping her.*)   Don't be talking foolishness, woman. Who said you took my meat? Give heed to me now. There must some other message have come. The Sergeant must have got some other message.

Mrs Delane: (*Sulkily.*)   If there is any way for a message to come that is quicker than to come by the wires, tell me what it is and I'll be obliged to you.

Mr Quirke: The Sergeant was up here making an excuse he was sticking up that notice. What was he doing here, I ask you?

Mrs Delane: How would I know what brought him?

Mr Quirke: It is what he did; he made as if to go away – he turned back again and I shaving – he brought away the sheep – he will have it for evidence against me—

Mrs Delane: (*Interested.*)   That might be so.

Mr Quirke: I would sooner it to have been any other beast nearly ever I had upon the rack.

Mrs Delane: Is that so?

Mr Quirke: I bade the Widow Early to kill it a fortnight ago – but she would not, she was that covetous!

Mrs Delane: What was on it?

Mr Quirke: How would I know what was on it? Whatever was on it, it was the will of God put it upon it – wasted it was, and shivering and refusing its share.

Mrs Delane: The poor thing.

Mr Quirke: Gone all to nothing – wore away like a flock of thread. It did not weigh as much as a lamb of two months.

Mrs Delane: It is likely the Inspector will bring it to Dublin?

Mr Quirke: The ribs of it streaky with the dint of patent medicines—

Mrs Delane: I wonder is it to the Petty Sessions you'll be brought or is it to the Assizes?

Mr Quirke: I'll speak up to them. I'll make my defence. What can the Army expect at fippence a pound?

Mrs Delane: It is likely there will be no bail allowed?

Mr Quirke: Would they be wanting me to give them good quality meat out of my own pocket? Is it to encourage them to fight the poor Indians and Africans they would have me? It's the Anti-Enlisting Societies should pay the fine for me.

Mrs Delane: It's not a fine will be put on you, I'm afraid. It's five years in gaol you will be apt to be getting. Well, I'll try and be a good neighbour to poor Mrs Quirke.

(*Mr Quirke, who has been stamping up and down, sits down and weeps. Halvey comes in and stands on one side.*)

Mr Quirke: Hadn't I heart-scalding enough before, striving to rear five weak children?

Mrs Delane: I suppose they will be sent to the Industrial Schools?

Mr Quirke: My poor wife—

Mrs Delane: I'm afraid the workhouse—

Mr Quirke: And she out in an ass-car at this minute helping me to follow my trade.

Mrs Delane: I hope they will not arrest her along with you.

Mr Quirke: I'll give myself up to justice. I'll plead guilty!
I'll be recommended to mercy!

Mrs Delane: It might be best for you.

Mr Quirke: Who would think so great a misfortune could
come upon a family through the bringing away of one sheep!

Hyacinth: (*Coming forward.*) Let you make yourself easy.

Mr Quirke: Easy! It's easy to say let you make yourself easy.

Hyacinth: I can tell you where it is.

Mr Quirke: Where what is?

Hyacinth: The sheep you are fretting after.

Mr Quirke: What do you know about it?

Hyacinth: I know everything about it.

Mr Quirke: I suppose the Sergeant told you?

Hyacinth: He told me nothing.

Mr Quirke: I suppose the whole town knows it, so?

Hyacinth: No one knows it, as yet.

Mr Quirke: And the Sergeant didn't see it?

Hyacinth: No one saw it or brought it away but myself.

Mr Quirke: Where did you put it at all?

Hyacinth: In the ditch behind the church wall. In among the
nettles it is. Look at the way they have me stung. (*Holds
out hands.*)

Mr Quirke: In the ditch! The best hiding place in the town.

Hyacinth: I never thought it would bring such great trouble
upon you. You can't say anyway I did not tell you.

Mr Quirke: You yourself that brought it away and that hid it!
I suppose it was coming in the train you got information
about the message to the police.

Hyacinth: What now do you say to me?

Mr Quirke: Say! I say I am as glad to hear what you said as
if it was the Lord telling me I'd be in heaven this minute.

Hyacinth: What are you going to do to me?

Mr Quirke: Do, is it? (*Grasps his hand.*) Any earthly thing
you would wish me to do. I will do it.

Hyacinth: I suppose you will tell—

Mr Quirke: Tell! It's I that will tell when all is quiet. It is I
will give you the good name through the town!

Hyacinth: I don't well understand.

Mr Quirke: (*Embracing him.*) The man that preserved me!

Hyacinth: That preserved you?

Mr Quirke: That kept me from ruin!

Hyacinth: From ruin?

Mr Quirke: That saved me from disgrace!

Hyacinth: (*To Mrs Delane.*) What is he saying at all?

Mr Quirke: From the Inspector!

Hyacinth: What is he talking about?

Mr Quirke: From the magistrates!

Hyacinth: He is making some mistake.

Mr Quirke: From the Winter Assizes!

Hyacinth: Is he out of his wits?

Mr Quirke: Five years in gaol!

Hyacinth: Hasn't he the queer talk?

Mr Quirke: The loss of the contract!

Hyacinth: Are my own wits gone astray?

Mr Quirke: What way can I repay you?

Hyacinth: (*Shouting.*) I tell you I took the sheep—

Mr Quirke: You did, God reward you!

Hyacinth: I stole away with it—

Mr Quirke: The blessing of the poor on you!

Hyacinth: I put it out of sight—

Mr Quirke: The blessing of my five children—

Hyacinth: I may as well say nothing—

Mrs Delane: Let you be quiet now, Quirke. Here's the Sergeant coming to search the shop—

(*Sergeant comes in; Quirke leaves go of Halvey, who arranges his hat, etc.*)

Sergeant: The Department to blazes!

Mrs Delane: What is it is putting you out?

Sergeant: To go to the train to meet the lecturer, and there to get a message through the guard that he was unavoidably detained in the South, holding an inquest on the remains of a drake.

Mrs Delane: The lecturer, is it?

Sergeant: To be sure. What else would I be talking of? The lecturer has failed me, and where am I to go looking for a person that I would think fitting to take his place?

Mrs Delane: And that's all? And you didn't get any message but the one?

Sergeant: Is that all? I am surprised at you, Mrs Delane. Isn't it enough to upset a man, within three quarters of an hour of the time of the meeting? Where, I would ask you, am I to find a man that has education enough and wit enough and character enough to put up speaking on the platform on the minute?

Mr Quirke: (*Jumps up.*)   It is I myself will tell you that.

Sergeant: You!

Mr Quirke: (*Slapping Halvey on the back.*)   Look at here, Sergeant. There is not one word was said in all those papers about this young man before you but it is true. And there could be no good thing said of him that would be too good for him.

Sergeant: It might not be a bad idea.

Mr Quirke: Whatever the paper said about him, Sergeant, I can say more again. It has come to my knowledge – by chance – that since he came to this town that young man has saved a whole family from destruction.

Sergeant: That is much to his credit – helping the rural classes—

Mr Quirke: A family and a long family, big and little, like sods of turf – and they depending on a – on one that might be on his way to dark trouble at this minute if it was not for his assistance. Believe me, he is the most sensible man, and the wittiest, and the kindest, and the best helper of the poor that ever stood before you in this square. Is not that so, Mrs Delane?

Mrs Delane: It is true indeed. Where he gets his wisdom and his wit and his information from I don't know, unless it might be that he is gifted from above.

Sergeant: Well, Mrs Delane, I think we have settled that question. Mr Halvey, you will be the speaker at the meeting. The lecturer sent these notes – you can lengthen them into a speech. You can call to the people of Cloon to stand out, to begin the building of their character. I saw a lecturer do it one time at Dundrum. 'Come up here,' he said, 'Dare to be a Daniel,' he said—

Hyacinth: I can't – I won't—

Sergeant: (*Looking at papers and thrusting them into his hand.*)

You will find it quite easy. I will conduct you to the platform
– these papers before you and a glass of water – That's
settled. (*Turns to go.*) Follow me on to the court-house in
half an hour – I must go to the barracks first – I heard there
was a telegram— (*Calls back as he goes.*) Don't be late, Mrs
Delane. Mind, Quirke, you promised to come.

Mrs Delane: Well, it's time for me to make an end of
settling myself – and indeed, Mr. Quirke, you'd best do
the same.

Mr Quirke: (*Rubbing his cheek.*) I suppose so. I had best keep
on good terms with him for the present. (*Turns.*) Well,
now, I had a great escape this day.

(*Both go in as Fardy reappears whistling.*)

Hyacinth: (*Sitting down.*) I don't know in the world what
has come upon the world that the half of the people of it
should be cracked!

Fardy: Weren't you found out yet?

Hyacinth: Found out, is it? I don't know what you mean by
being found out.

Fardy: Didn't he miss the sheep?

Hyacinth: He did, and I told him it was I took it – and what
happened I declare to goodness I don't know— Will you
look at these? (*Holds out notes.*)

Fardy: Papers! Are they more testimonials?

Hyacinth: They are what is worse. (*Gives a hoarse laugh.*)
Will you come and see me on the platform – these in my
hand – and I speaking – giving out advice. (*Fardy whistles.*)
Why didn't you tell me, the time you advised me to steal a
sheep, that in this town it would qualify a man to go preaching, and the priest in the chair looking on.

Fardy: The time I took a few apples that had fallen off a stall,
they did not ask me to hold a meeting. They welted me well.

Hyacinth: (*Looking round.*) I would take apples if I could
see them. I wish I had broke my neck before I left Carrow
and I'd be better off! I wish I had got six months the time
I was caught setting snares – I wish I had robbed a
church.

Fardy: Would a Protestant church do?

Hyacinth: I suppose it wouldn't be so great a sin.

Fardy: It's likely the Sergeant would think worse of it—
Anyway, if you want to rob one, it's the Protestant church
is the handiest.

Hyacinth: (*Getting up.*) Show me what way to do it?

Fardy: (*Pointing.*) I was going around it a few minutes
ago, to see might there be e'er a dog scenting the sheep, and
I noticed the window being out.

Hyacinth: Out, out and out?

Fardy: It was, where they are putting coloured glass in it for
the distiller—

Hyacinth: What good does that do me?

Fardy: Every good. You could go in by that window if you
had some person to give you a hoist. Whatever riches there
is to get in it then, you'll get them.

Hyacinth: I don't want riches. I'll give you all I will find if
you will come and hoist me.

Fardy: Here is Miss Joyce coming to bring you to your
lodging. Sure, I brought your bag to it, the time you were
away with the sheep—

Hyacinth: Run! Run!

(*They go off. Enter Miss Joyce.*)

Miss Joyce: Are you here, Mrs Delane? Where, can you tell
me, is Mr Halvey?

Mrs Delane: (*Coming out dressed.*) It's likely he is gone on to
the court-house. Did you hear he is to be in the chair and to
make an address to the meeting?

Miss Joyce: He is getting on fast. His Reverence says he will
be a good help in the parish. Who would think, now, there
would be such a godly young man in a little place like
Carrow!

(*Enter Sergeant in a hurry, with telegram.*)

Sergeant: What time did this telegram arrive, Mrs Delane?

Mrs Delane: I couldn't be rightly sure, Sergeant. But sure it's
marked on it, unless the clock I have is gone wrong.

Sergeant: It is marked on it. And I have the time I got it
marked on my own watch.

Mrs Delane: Well, now, I wonder none of the police would
have followed you with it from the barracks – and they with
so little to do—

Sergeant: (*Looking in at Quirke's shop.*)   Well, I am sorry to do what I have to do, but duty is duty.

(*He ransacks shop. Mrs Delane looks on. Mr Quirke puts his head out of window.*)

Mr Quirke: What is that going on inside?   (*No answer.*)   Is there any one inside, I ask?   (*No answer.*)   It must be that dog of Tannian's – wait till I get at him.

Mrs Delane: It is Sergeant Carden, Mr Quirke. He would seem to be looking for something—

(*Mr Quirke appears in shop. Sergeant comes out, makes another dive, taking up sacks, etc.*)

Mr Quirke: I'm greatly afraid I am just out of meat, Sergeant – and I'm sorry now to disoblige you, and you not being in the habit of dealing with me—

Sergeant: I should think not, indeed.

Mr Quirke: Looking for a tender little bit of lamb, I suppose you are, for Mrs Carden and the youngsters?

Sergeant: I am not.

Mr Quirke: If I had it now, I'd be proud to offer it to you, and make no charge. I'll be killing a good kid tomorrow. Mrs Carden might fancy a bit of it—

Sergeant: I have had orders to search your establishment for unwholesome meat, and I am come here to do it.

Mr Quirke: (*Sitting down with a smile.*)   Is that so? Well, isn't it a wonder the schemers does be in the world.

Sergeant: It is not the first time there have been complaints.

Mr Quirke: I suppose not. Well, it is on their own head it will fall at the last!

Sergeant: I have found nothing so far.

Mr Quirke: I suppose not, indeed. What is there you could find, and it not in it?

Sergeant: Have you no meat at all upon the premises?

Mr Quirke: I have, indeed, a nice barrel of bacon.

Sergeant: What way did it die?

Mr Quirke: It would be hard for me to say that. American it is. How would I know what way they do be killing the pigs out there? Machinery, I suppose, they have – steam hammers—

Sergeant: Is there nothing else here at all?

Mr Quirke: I give you my word, there is no meat living or dead in this place, but yourself and myself and that bird above in the cage.

Sergeant: Well, I must tell the Inspector I could find nothing. But mind yourself for the future.

Mr Quirke: Thank you, Sergeant. I will do that. (*Enter Fardy. He stops short.*)

Sergeant: It was you delayed that message to me, I suppose ? You'd best mend your ways or I'll have something to say to you. (*Seizes and shakes him.*)

Fardy: That's the way everyone does be faulting me. (*Whimpers.*)

(*The Sergeant gives him another shake. A half-crown falls out of his pocket.*)

Miss Joyce: (*Picking it up.*)   A half-a-crown! Where, now, did you get that much, Fardy ?

Fardy: Where did I get it, is it !

Miss Joyce: I'll engage it was in no honest way you got it.

Fardy: I picked it up in the street—

Miss Joyce: If you did, why didn't you bring it to the Sergeant or to his Reverence ?

Mrs Delane: And some poor person, may be, being at the loss of it.

Miss Joyce: I'd best bring it to his Reverence. Come with me, Fardy, till he will question you about it.

Fardy: It was not altogether in the street I found it—

Miss Joyce: There, now! I knew you got it in no good way! Tell me, now.

Fardy: It was playing pitch and toss I won it—

Miss Joyce: And who would play for half-crowns with the like of you, Fardy Farrell ? Who was it, now ?

Fardy: It was – a stranger—

Miss Joyce: Do you hear that ? A stranger! Did you see e'er a stranger in this town, Mrs Delane, or Sergeant Carden, or Mr Quirke ?

Mr Quirke: Not a one.

Sergeant: There was no stranger here.

Mrs Delane: There could not be one here without me knowing it.

Fardy: I tell you there was.

Miss Joyce: Come on, then, and tell who was he to his Reverence.

Sergeant: (*Taking other arm.*) Or to the bench.

Fardy: I did get it, I tell you, from a stranger.

Sergeant: Where is he, so?

Fardy: He's in some place – not far away.

Sergeant: Bring me to him.

Fardy: He'll be coming here.

Sergeant: Tell me the truth and it will be better for you.

Fardy: (*Weeping.*) Let me go and I will.

Sergeant: (*Letting go.*) Now – who did you get it from?

Fardy: From that young chap came today, Mr Halvey.

All: Mr Halvey!

Mr Quirke: (*Indignantly.*) What are you saying, you young ruffian you? Hyacinth Halvey to be playing pitch and toss with the like of you!

Fardy: I didn't say that.

Miss Joyce: You did say it. You said it now.

Mr Quirke: Hyacinth Halvey! The best man that ever came into this town!

Miss Joyce: Well, what lies he has!

Mr Quirke: It's my belief the half-crown is a bad one. Maybe it's to pass it off it was given to him. There were tinkers in the town at the time of the fair. Give it here to me. (*Bites it.*) No, indeed, it's sound enough. Here, Sergeant, it's best for you to take it.

(*Gives it to Sergeant, who examines it.*)

Sergeant: Can it be? Can it be what I think it to be?

Mr Quirke: What is it? What do you take it to be?

Sergeant: It is, it is. I know it. I know this half-crown—

Mr Quirke: That is a queer thing, now.

Sergeant: I know it well. I have been handling it in the church for the last twelvemonth—

Mr Quirke: Is that so?

Sergeant: It is the nest-egg half-crown we hand round in the collection plate every Sunday morning. I know it by the dint on the Queen's temples and the crooked scratch under her nose.

Mr Quirke: (*Examining it.*)   So there is, too.

Sergeant: This is a bad business. It has been stolen from the church.

All: O! O! O!

Sergeant: (*Seizing Fardy.*)   You have robbed the church!

Fardy: (*Terrified.*)   I tell you I never did!

Sergeant: I have the proof of it.

Fardy: Say what you like! I never put a foot in it!

Sergeant: How did you get this, so?

Miss Joyce: I suppose from the *stranger*?

Mrs Delane: I suppose it was Hyacinth Halvey gave it to you, now?

Fardy: It was so.

Sergeant: I suppose it was he robbed the church?

Fardy: (*Sobs.*)   You will not believe me if I say it.

Mr Quirke: O! the young vagabond! Let me get at him!

Mrs Delane: Here he is himself now!

(*Hyacinth comes in. Fardy releases himself and creeps behind him.*)

Mrs Delane: It is time you to come, Mr Halvey, and shut the mouth of this young schemer.

Miss Joyce: I would like you to hear what he says of you, Mr Halvey. Pitch and toss, he says.

Mr Quirke: Robbery, he says.

Mrs Delane: Robbery of a church.

Sergeant: He has had a bad name long enough. Let him go to a reformatory now.

Fardy: (*Clinging to Hyacinth.*)   Save me, save me! I'm a poor boy trying to knock out a way of living; I'll be destroyed if I go to a reformatory.   (*Kneels and clings to Hyacinth's knees.*)

Hyacinth: I'll save you easy enough.

Fardy: Don't let me be gaoled!

Hyacinth: I am going to tell them.

Fardy: I'm a poor orphan—

Hyacinth: Will you let me speak?

Fardy: I'll get no more chance in the world—

Hyacinth: Sure I'm trying to free you—

Fardy: It will be tasked to me always.

Hyacinth: Be quiet, can't you.

Fardy: Don't you desert me!

Hyacinth: Will you be silent?

Fardy: Take it on yourself.

Hyacinth: I will if you'll let me.

Fardy: Tell them you did it.

Hyacinth: I am going to do that.

Fardy: Tell them it was you got in at the window.

Hyacinth: I will! I will!

Fardy: Say it was you robbed the box.

Hyacinth: I'll say it! I'll say it!

Fardy: It being open!

Hyacinth: Let me tell, let me tell.

Fardy: Of all that was in it.

Hyacinth: I'll tell them that.

Fardy: And gave it to me.

Hyacinth: (*Putting hand on his mouth and dragging him up.*) Will you stop and let me speak?

Sergeant: We can't be wasting time. Give him here to me.

Hyacinth: I can't do that. He must be let alone.

Sergeant: (*Seizing him.*) He'll be let alone in the lock-up.

Hyacinth: He must not be brought there.

Sergeant: I'll let no man get him off.

Hyacinth: I will get him off.

Sergeant: You will not!

Hyacinth: I will.

Sergeant: Do you think to buy him off?

Hyacinth: I will buy him off with my own confession.

Sergeant: And what will that be?

Hyacinth: It was I robbed the church.

Sergeant: That is likely indeed!

Hyacinth: Let him go, and take me. I tell you I did it.

Sergeant: It would take witnesses to prove that.

Hyacinth: (*Pointing to Fardy.*) He will be witness.

Fardy: O! Mr Halvey, I would not wish to do that. Get me off and I will say nothing.

Hyacinth: Sure you must. You will be put on oath in the court.

Fardy: I will not! I will not! All the world knows I don't understand the nature of an oath!

Mr Quirke: (*Coming forward*).   Is it blind ye all are?

Mrs Delane: What are you talking about?

Mr Quirke: Is it fools ye all are?

Miss Joyce: Speak for yourself.

Mr Quirke: Is it idiots ye all are?

Sergeant: Mind who you're talking to.

Mr Quirke: (*Seizing Hyacinth's hands.*)   Can't you see? Can't you hear? Where are your wits? Was ever such a thing seen in this town?

Mrs Delane: Say out what you have to say.

Mr Quirke: A walking saint he is!

Mrs Delane: Maybe so.

Mr Quirke: The preserver of the poor! Talk of the holy martyrs! They are nothing at all to what he is! Will you look at him! To save that poor boy he is going! To take the blame on himself he is going! To say he himself did the robbery he is going! Before the magistrate he is going! To gaol he is going! Taking the blame on his own head! Putting the sin on his own shoulders! Letting on to have done a robbery! Telling a lie – that it may be forgiven him – to his own injury! Doing all that I tell you to save the character of a miserable slack lad, that rose in poverty.

(*Murmur of admiration from all.*)

Mr Quirke: Now, what do you say?

Sergeant: (*Pressing his hand.*)   Mr Halvey, you have given us all a lesson. To please you, I will make no information against the boy. (*Shakes him and helps him up.*)   I will put back the half-crown in the poor-box next Sunday. (*To Fardy.*) What have you to say to your benefactor?

Fardy: I'm obliged to you, Mr Halvey. You behaved very decent to me, very decent indeed. I'll never let a word be said against you if I live to be a hundred years.

Sergeant: (*Wiping eyes with a blue handkerchief.*)   I will tell it at the meeting. It will be a great encouragement to them to build up their character. I'll tell it to the priest and he taking the chair—

Hyacinth: O stop, will you—

Mr Quirke: The chair. It's in the chair he himself should be. It's in a chair we will put him now. It's to chair him through

the streets we will. Sure he'll be an example and a blessing
to the whole of the town. (*Seizes Halvey and seats him in
chair.*) Now, Sergeant, give a hand. Here, Fardy.
(*They all lift the chair with Halvey in it, wildly protesting.*)

Mr Quirke: Come along now to the court-house. Three cheers
for Hyacinth Halvey! Hip! hip! hoora!
(*Cheers heard in the distance as the curtain drops.*)

NOTES

I WAS pointed out one evening a well-brushed well-dressed man in the stalls, and was told gossip about him, perhaps not all true, which made me wonder if that appearance and behaviour as of extreme respectability might not now and again be felt a burden.

After a while he translated himself in my mind into Hyacinth; and as one must set one's original a little way off to get a translation rather than a tracing, he found himself in Cloon, where, as in other parts of our country, 'charácter' is built up or destroyed by a password or an emotion, rather than by experience and deliberation.

The idea was more of a universal one than I knew at the first, and I have had but uneasy appreciation from some apparently blameless friends.

THE WORKHOUSE WARD

PERSONS

Mike McInerney ⎱
Michael Miskell ⎰ · · · · · · PAUPERS
Mrs Donohoe · · · · · A COUNTRYWOMAN

THE WORKHOUSE WARD

Scene: A ward in Cloon Workhouse. The two old men in their beds.

Michael Miskell: Isn't it a hard case, Mike McInerney, myself and yourself to be left here in the bed, and it the feast day of Saint Colman, and the rest of the ward attending on the Mass.

Mike McInerney: Is it sitting up by the hearth you are wishful to be, Michael Miskell, with cold in the shoulders and with speckled shins? Let you rise up so, and you well able to do it, not like myself that has pains the same as tin-tacks within in my inside.

Michael Miskell: If you have pains within in your inside there is no one can see it or know of it the way they can see my own knees that are swelled up with the rheumatism, and my hands that are twisted in ridges the same as an old cabbage stalk. It is easy to be talking about soreness and about pains, and they maybe not to be in it at all.

Mike McInerney: To open me and to analyse me you would know what sort of a pain and a soreness I have in my heart and in my chest. But I'm not one like yourself to be cursing and praying and tormenting the time the nuns are at hand, thinking to get a bigger share than myself of the nourishment and of the milk.

Michael Miskell: That's the way you do be picking at me and faulting me. I had a share and a good share in my early time, and it's well you know that, and the both of us reared in Skehanagh.

Mike McInerney: You may say that, indeed, we are both of us reared in Skehanagh. Little wonder you to have good nourishment the time we were both rising, and you bringing away my rabbits out of the snare.

Michael Miskell: And you didn't bring away my own eels, I suppose, I was after spearing in the Turlough? Selling them

85

to the nuns in the convent you did, and letting on they to be
your own. For you were always a cheater and a schemer,
grabbing every earthly thing for your own profit.

Mike McInerney: And you were no grabber yourself, I suppose, till your land and all you had grabbed wore away from
you!

Michael Miskell: If I lost it itself, it was through the crosses I
met with and I going through the world. I never was a ram-
bler and a card-player like yourself, Mike McInerney, that
ran through all and lavished it unknown to your mother!

Mike McInerney: Lavished it, is it? And if I did was it you
yourself led me to lavish it or some other one? It is on my
own floor I would be today and in the face of my family, but
for the misfortune I had to be put with a bad next door
neighbour that was yourself. What way did my means go
from me is it? Spending on fencing, spending on walls,
making up gates, putting up doors, that would keep your hens
and your ducks from coming in through starvation on my
floor, and every four-footed beast you had from preying and
trespassing on my oats and my mangolds and my little lock
of hay!

Michael Miskell: O to listen to you! And I striving to please
you and to be kind to you and to close my ears to the abuse
you would be calling and letting out of your mouth. To
trespass on your crops is it? It's little temptation there was
for my poor beasts to ask to cross the mering. My God
Almighty! What had you but a little corner of a field!

Mike McInerney: And what do you say to my garden that
your two pigs had destroyed on me the year of the big tree
being knocked, and they making gaps in the wall.

Michael Miskill: Ah, there does be a great deal of gaps
knocked in a twelvemonth. Why wouldn't they be knocked
by thunder, the same as the tree, or some storm that came up
from the west?

Mike McInerney: It was the west wind, I suppose, that devoured
my green cabbage? And that rooted up my Champion
potatoes? And that ate the gooseberries themselves from off
the bush?

Michael Miskell: What are you saying? The two quietest pigs ever I had, no way wicked and well ringed. They were not ten minutes in it. It would be hard for them eat strawberries in that time, let alone gooseberries that's full of thorns.

Mike McInerney: They were not quiet, but very ravenous pigs you had that time, as active as a fox they were, killing my young ducks. Once they had blood tasted you couldn't stop them.

Michael Miskell: And what happened myself the fair day of Esserkelly, the time I was passing your door? Two brazened dogs that rushed out and took a piece of me. I never was the better of it or of the start I got, but wasting from then till now!

Mike McInerney: Thinking you were a wild beast they did, that had made his escape out of the travelling show, with the red eyes of you and the ugly face of you, and the two crooked legs of you that wouldn't hardly stop a pig in a gap. Sure any dog that had any life in it at all would be roused and stirred seeing the like of you going the road!

Michael Miskell: I did well taking out a summons against you that time. It is a great wonder you not to have been bound over through your lifetime, but the laws of England is queer.

Mike McInerney: What ailed me that I did not summons yourself after you stealing away the clutch of eggs I had in the barrel, and I away in Ardrahan searching out a clocking hen.

Michael Miskell: To steal your eggs is it? Is that what you are saying now? (*Holds up his hands.*) The Lord is in heaven, and Peter and the saints, and yourself that was in Ardrahan that day put a hand on them as soon as myself! Isn't it a bad story for me to be wearing out my days beside you the same as a spancelled goat. Chained I am and tethered I am to a man that is ramsacking his mind for lies!

Mike McInerney: If it is a bad story for you, Michael Miskell, it is a worse story again for myself. A Miskell to be next and near me through the whole of the four quarters of the year. I never heard there to be any great name on the Miskells as there was on my own race and name.

Michael Miskell: You didn't, is it? Well, you could hear it if you had but ears to hear it. Go across to Lisheen Crannagh and down to the sea and to Newtown Lynch and the mills of Duras and you'll find a Miskell, and as far as Dublin!

Mike McInerney: What signifies Crannagh and the mills of Duras? Look at all my own generations that are buried at the Seven Churches. And how many generations of the Miskells are buried in it? Answer me that!

Michael Miskell: I tell you but for the wheat that was to be sowed there would be more side cars and more common cars at my father's funeral (God rest his soul!) than at any funeral ever left your own door. And as to my mother, she was a Cuffe from Claregalway, and it's she had the purer blood!

Mike McInerney: And what do you say to the banshee? Isn't she apt to have knowledge of the ancient race? Was ever she heard to screech or to cry for the Miskells? Or for the Cuffes from Claregalway? She was not, but for the six families, the Hyneses, the Foxes, the Faheys, the Dooleys, the McInerneys. It is of the nature of the McInerneys she is I am thinking, crying them the same as a king's children.

Michael Miskell: It is a pity the banshee not to be crying for yourself at this minute, and giving you a warning to quit your lies and your chat and your arguing and your contrary ways; for there is no one under the rising sun could stand you. I tell you you are not behaving as in the presence of the Lord!

Mike McInerney: Is it wishful for my death you are? Let it come and meet me now and welcome so long as it will part me from yourself! And I say, and I would kiss the book on it, I to have one request only to be granted, and I leaving it in my will, it is what I would request, nine furrows of the field, nine ridges of the hills, nine waves of the ocean to be put between your grave and my own grave the time we will be laid in the ground!

Michael Miskell: Amen to that! Nine ridges, is it? No, but let the whole ridge of the world separate us till the Day of Judgment! I would not be laid anear you at the Seven Churches, I to get Ireland without a divide!

Mike McInerney: And after that again! I'd sooner than ten pound in my hand, I to know that my shadow and my ghost will not be knocking about with your shadow and your ghost, and the both of us waiting our time. I'd sooner be delayed in Purgatory! Now, have you anything to say?

Michael Miskell: I have everything to say, if I had but the time to say it!

Mike McInerney: (*Sitting up.*)   Let me up out of this till I'll choke you!

Michael Miskell: You scolding pauper you!

Mike McInerney: (*Shaking his fist at him.*)   Wait a while!

Michael Miskell: (*Shaking his fist.*)   Wait a while yourself!

(*Mrs Donohoe comes in with a parcel. She is a countrywoman with a frilled cap and a shawl. She stands still a minute. The two old men lie down and compose themselves.*)

Mrs Donohoe: They bade me come up here by the stair. I never was in this place at all. I don't know am I right. Which now of the two of ye is Mike McInerney?

Mike McInerney: Who is it is calling me by my name?

Mrs Donohoe: Sure amn't I your sister, Honor McInerney that was, that is now Honor Donohoe.

Mike McInerney: So you are, I believe. I didn't know you till you pushed anear me. It is time indeed for you to come see me, and I in this place five year or more. Thinking me to be no credit to you, I suppose, among that tribe of the Donohoes. I wonder they to give you leave to come ask am I living yet or dead?

Mrs Donohoe: Ah, sure, I buried the whole string of them. Himself was the last to go. (*Wipes her eyes.*)   The Lord be praised he got a fine natural death. Sure we must go through our crosses. And he got a lovely funeral; it would delight you to hear the priest reading the Mass. My poor John Donohoe! A nice clean man, you couldn't but be fond of him. Very severe on the tobacco he was, but he wouldn't touch the drink.

Mike McInerney: And is it in Curranroe you are living yet?

Mrs Donohoe: It is so. He left all to myself. But it is a lonesome thing the head of a house to have died!

Mike McInerney: I hope that he has left you a nice way of living?

Mrs Donohoe: Fair enough, fair enough. A wide lovely house I have; a few acres of grass land . . . the grass does be very sweet that grows among the stones. And as to the sea, there is something from it every day of the year, a handful of periwinkles to make kitchen, or cockles maybe. There is many a thing in the sea is not decent, but cockles is fit to put before the Lord!

Mike McInerney:　You have all that! And you without ere a man in the house?

Mrs Donohoe:　It is what I am thinking, yourself might come and keep me company. It is no credit to me a brother of my own to be in this place at all.

Mike McInerney:　I'll go with you! Let me out of this! It is the name of the McInerneys will be rising on every side!

Mrs Donohoe:　I don't know. I was ignorant of you being kept to the bed.

Mike McInerney:　I am not kept to it, but maybe an odd time when there is a colic rises up within me. My stomach always gets better the time there is a change in the moon. I'd like well to draw anear you. My heavy blessing on you, Honor Donohoe, for the hand you have held out to me this day.

Mrs Donohoe:　Sure you could be keeping the fire in, and stirring the pot with the bit of Indian meal for the hens, and milking the goat and taking the tacklings off the donkey at the door; and maybe putting out the cabbage plants in their time. For when the old man died the garden died.

Mike McInerney:　I could to be sure, and be cutting the potatoes for seed. What luck could there be in a place and a man not to be in it? Is that now a suit of clothes you have brought with you?

Mrs Donohoe:　It is so, the way you will be tasty coming in among the neighbours at Curranroe.

Mike McInerney:　My joy you are! It is well you earned me! Let me up out of this! (*He sits up and spreads out the clothes and tries on coat.*)　That not is a good frieze coat . . . and a hat in the fashion . . . (*He puts on hat.*)

Michael Miskell:　(*Alarmed.*)　And is it going out of this you are, Mike McInerney?

Mike McInerney:　Don't you hear I am going? To Curranroe I am going. Going I am to a place where I will get every good thing!

Michael Miskell: And is it to leave me here after you you will?

Mike McInerney: (*In a rising chant.*) Every good thing! The goat and the kid are there, the sheep and the lamb are there, the cow does be running and she coming to be milked! Ploughing and seed sowing, blossom at Christmas time, the cuckoo speaking through the dark days of the year! Ah, what are you talking about? Wheat high in hedges, no talk about the rent! Salmon in the rivers as plenty as turf! Spending and getting and nothing scarce! Sport and pleasure, and music on the strings! Age will go from me and I will be young again. Geese and turkeys for the hundreds and drink for the whole world!

Michael Miskell: Ah, Mike, is it truth you are saying, you to go from me and to leave me with rude people and with townspeople, and with people of every parish in the union, and they having no respect for me or no wish for me at all!

Mike McInerney: Whist now and I'll leave you . . . my pipe (*hands it over*); and I'll engage it is Honor Donohoe won't refuse to be sending you a few ounces of tobacco an odd time, and neighbours coming to the fair in November or in the month of May.

Michael Miskell: Ah, what signifies tobacco? All that I am craving is the talk. There to be no one at all to say out to whatever thought might be rising in my innate mind! To be lying here and no conversable person in it would be the abomination of misery!

Mike McInerney: Look now, Honor . . . It is what I often heard said, two to be better than one. . . . Sure, if you had an old trouser was full of holes . . . or a skirt . . . wouldn't you put another in under it that might be as tattered as itself, and the two of them together would make some sort of a decent show?

Mrs Donohoe: Ah, what are you saying? There is no holes in that suit I brought you now, but as sound it is as the day I spun it for himself.

Mike McInerney: It is what I am thinking, Honor . . . I do be weak an odd time . . . any load I would carry, it preys upon my side . . . and this man does be weak an odd time

with the swelling in his knees . . . but the two of us together
it's not likely it is at the one time we would fail. Bring the
both of us with you, Honor, and the height of the castle of
luck on you, and the both of us together will make one good
hardy man!

Mrs Donohoe: I'd like my job! Is it queer in the head you are
grown asking me to bring in a stranger off the road?

Michael Miskell: I am not, ma'am, but an old neighbour I am.
If I had forecasted this asking I would have asked it myself.
Michael Miskell I am, that was in the next house to you in
Skehanagh!

Mrs Donohoe: For pity's sake! Michael Miskell is it? That's
worse again. Yourself and Mike that never left fighting and
scolding and attacking one another! Sparring at one another
like two young pups you were, and threatening one another
after like two grown dogs!

Mike McInerney: All the quarrelling was ever in the place it
was myself did it. Sure his anger rises fast and goes away like
the wind. Bring him out with myself now, Honor Donohoe,
and God bless you.

Mrs Donohoe: Well, then, I will not bring him out, and I will
not bring yourself out, and you not to learn better sense. Are
you making yourself ready to come?

Mike McInerney: I am thinking, maybe . . . it is a mean thing
for a man that is shivering into seventy years to go changing
from place to place.

Mrs Donohoe: Well, take your luck or leave it. All I asked was
to save you from the hurt and the harm of the year.

Mike McInerney: Bring the both of us with you or I will not
stir out of this.

Mrs Donohoe: Give me back my fine suit so   (*begins gathering
up the clothes*),   till I'll go look for a man of my own!

Mike McInerney: Let you go so, as you are so unnatural and
so disobliging, and look for some man of your own, God help
him! For I will not go with you at all!

Mrs Donohoe: It is too much time I lost with you, and dark
night waiting to overtake me on the road. Let the two of you
stop together, and the back of my hand to you. It is I will
leave you there the same as God left the Jews!

(*She goes out. The old men lie down and are silent for a moment.*)

Michael Miskell: Maybe the house is not so wide as what she says.

Mike McInerney: Why wouldn't it be wide?

Michael Miskell: Ah, there does be a good deal of middling poor houses down by the sea.

Mike McInerney: What would you know about wide houses? Whatever sort of a house you had yourself it was too wide for the provision you had into it.

Michael Miskell: Whatever provision I had in my house it was wholesome provision and natural provision. Herself and her periwinkles! Periwinkles is a hungry sort of food.

Mike McInerney: Stop your impudence and your chat or it will be the worse for you. I'd bear with my own father and mother as long as any man would, but if they'd vex me I would give them the length of a rope as soon as another!

Michael Miskell: I would never ask at all to go eating periwinkles. . .

Mike McInerney: (*Sitting up.*)   Have you anyone to fight me?

Michael Miskell: (*Whimpering.*)   I have not, only the Lord!

Mike McInerney: Let you leave putting insults on me so, and death picking at you!

Michael Miskell: Sure I am saying nothing at all to displease you. It is why I wouldn't go eating periwinkles, I'm in dread I might swallow the pin.

Mike McInerney: Who in the world wide is asking you to eat them? You're as tricky as a fish in the full tide!

Michael Miskell: Tricky is it! Oh, my curse and the curse of the four and twenty men upon you!

Mike McInerney: That the worm may chew you from skin to marrow bone!   (*Seizes his pillow.*)

Michael Miskell: (*Seizing his own pillow.*)   I'll leave my death on you, you scheming vagabond!

Mike McInerney: By cripes! I'll pull out your pin feathers! (*Throwing pillow.*)

Michael Miskell: (*Throwing pillow.*)   You tyrant! You big bully you!

Mike McInerney: (*Throwing pillow and seizing mug.*) Take this so, you stobbing ruffian you!
(*They throw all within their reach at one another, mugs, prayer books, pipes, etc.*)

CURTAIN

NOTES

I HEARD of an old man in the workhouse who had been disabled many years before by, I think, a knife thrown at him by his wife in some passionate quarrel.

One day I heard the wife had been brought in there, poor and sick. I wondered how they would meet, and if the old quarrel was still alive, or if they who knew the worst of each other would be better pleased with one another's company than with that of strangers.

I wrote a scenario of the play, Dr Douglas Hyde, getting in plot what he gave back in dialogue, for at that time we thought a dramatic movement in Irish would be helpful to our own as well as to the Gaelic League. Later I tried to rearrange it for our own theatre, and for three players only, but in doing this I found it necessary to write entirely new dialogue, the two old men in the original play obviously talking at an audience in the wards, which is no longer there.

I sometimes think the two scolding paupers are a symbol of ourselves in Ireland – 'it is better to be quarrelling than to be lonesome.' The Rajputs, that great fighting race, when they were told they had been brought under the Pax Britannica and must give up war, gave themselves to opium in its place, but Connacht has not yet planted its poppy gardens.

THE GAOL GATE

PERSONS

THE GAOL GATE

Scene: Outside the gate of Galway Gaol. Two countrywomen, one in a long, dark cloak, the other with a shawl over her head, have just come in. It is just before dawn.

Mary Cahel: I am thinking we are come to our journey's end, and that this should be the gate of the gaol.

Mary Cushin: It is certain it could be no other place. There was surely never in the world such a terrible great height of a wall.

Mary Cahel: He that was used to the mountain to be closed up inside of that! What call had he to go moonlighting or to bring himself into danger at all?

Mary Cushin: It is no wonder a man to grow faint-hearted and he shut away from the light. I never would wonder at all at anything he might be driven to say.

Mary Cahel: There were good men were gaoled before him never gave in to anyone at all. It is what I am thinking, Mary, he might not have done what they say.

Mary Cushin: Sure, you heard what the neighbours were calling the time their own boys were brought away. 'It is Denis Cahel,' they were saying, 'that informed against them in the gaol.'

Mary Cahel: There is nothing that is bad or is wicked but a woman will put it out of her mouth, and she seeing them that belong to her brought away from her sight and her home.

Mary Cushin: Terry Fury's mother was saying it, and Pat Ruane's mother and his wife. They came out calling it after me, 'It was Denis swore against them in the gaol!' The sergeant was boasting, they were telling me, the day he came searching Daire-caol, it was he himself got his confession with drink he had brought him in the gaol.

Mary Cahel: They might have done that, the ruffians, and the boy have no blame on him at all. Why should it be cast up against him, and his wits being out of him with drink?

Mary Cushin: If he did give their names up itself, there was maybe no wrong in it at all. Sure, it's known to all the village it was Terry that fired the shot.

Mary Cahel: Stop your mouth now and don't be talking. You haven't any sense worth while. Let the sergeant do his own business with no help from the neighbours at all.

Mary Cushin: It was Pat Ruane that tempted them on account of some vengeance of his own. Every creature knows my poor Denis never handled a gun in his life.

Mary Cahel: (*Taking from under her cloak a long blue envelope.*) I wish we could know what is in the letter they are after sending us through the post. Isn't it a great pity for the two of us to be without learning at all?

Mary Cushin: There are some of the neighbours have learning, and you bade me not bring it anear them. It would maybe have told us what way he is or what time he will be quitting the gaol.

Mary Cahel: There is wonder on me, Mary Cushin, that you would not be content with what I say. It might be they put down in the letter that Denis informed on the rest.

Mary Cushin: I suppose it is all we have to do so, to stop here for the opening of the door. It's a terrible long road from Slieve Echtge we were travelling the whole of the night.

Mary Cahel: There was no other thing for us to do but to come and to give him a warning. What way would he be facing the neighbours, and he to come back to Daire-caol?

Mary Cushin: It is likely they will let him go free, Mary, before many days will be out. What call have they to be keeping him? It is certain they promised him his life.

Mary Cahel: If they promised him his life, Mary Cushin, he must live it in some other place. Let him never see Daire-caol again, or Daroda or Druimdarod.

Mary Cushin: O, Mary, what place will we bring him to, and we driven from the place that we know? What person that is sent among strangers can have one day's comfort on earth?

Mary Cahel: It is only among strangers, I am thinking, he could be hiding his story at all. It is best for him to go to America, where the people are as thick as grass.

Mary Cushin: What way could he go to America and he having no means in his hand? There's himself and myself to make the voyage and the little one-een at home.

Mary Cahel: I would sooner to sell the holding than to ask for the price paid for blood. There'll be money enough for the two of you to settle your debts and to go.

Mary Cushin: And what would yourself be doing and we to go over the sea? It is not among the neighbours you would wish to be ending your days.

Mary Cahel: I am thinking there is no one would know me in the workhouse at Oughterard. I wonder could I go in there, and I not to give them my name?

Mary Cushin: Ah, don't be talking foolishness. What way could I bring the child? Sure he's hardly out of the cradle; he'd be lost out there in the States.

Mary Cahel: I could bring him into the workhouse, I to give him some other name. You could send for him when you'd be settled or have some place of your own.

Mary Cushin: It is very cold at the dawn. It is time for them open the door. I wish I had brought a potato or a bit of a cake or of bread.

Mary Cahel: I'm in dread of it being opened and not knowing what we will hear. The night that Denis was taken he had a great cold and a cough.

Mary Cushin: I think I hear some person coming. There's a sound like the rattling of keys. God and His Mother protect us! I'm in dread of being found here at all!

(*The gate is opened, and the Gatekeeper is seen with a lantern in his hand.*)

Gatekeeper: What are you doing here, women? It's no place to be spending the night time.

Mary Cahel: It is to speak with my son I am asking, that is gaoled these eight weeks and a day.

Gatekeeper: If you have no order to visit him it's as good for you to go away home.

Mary Cahel: I got this letter ere yesterday. It might be it is giving me leave.

Gatekeeper: If that's so he should be under the doctor, or in the hospital ward.

Mary Cahel: It's no wonder if he's down with the hardship, for he had a great cough and a cold.

Gatekeeper: Give me here the letter to read it. Sure it never was opened at all.

Mary Cahel: Myself and this woman have no learning. We were loth to trust any other one.

Gatekeeper: It was posted in Galway the twentieth, and this is the last of the month.

Mary Cahel: We never thought to call at the post office. It was chance brought it to us in the end.

Gatekeeper: (*Having read letter.*) You poor unfortunate women, don't you know Denis Cahel is dead? You'd a right to come this time yesterday if you wished any last word at all.

Mary Cahel: (*Kneeling down.*) God and His Mother protect us and have mercy on Denis's soul!

Mary Cushin: What is the man after saying? Sure it cannot be Denis is dead?

Gatekeeper: Dead since the dawn of yesterday, and another man now in his cell. I'll go see who has charge of his clothing if you're wanting to bring it away.

(*He goes in. The dawn has begun to break.*)

Mary Cahel: There is lasting kindness in Heaven when no kindness is found upon earth. There will surely be mercy found for him, and not the hard judgment of men! But my boy that was best in the world, that never rose a hair of my head, to have died with his name under blemish, and left a great shame on his child! Better for him have killed the whole world than to give any witness at all! Have you no word to say, Mary Cushin? Am I left here to keen him alone?

Mary Cushin: (*Who has sunk on to the step before the door, rocking herself and keening.*) Oh, Denis, my heart is broken you to have died with the hard word upon you! My grief you to be alone now that spent so many nights in company!

What way will I be going back through Gort and through Kilbecanty? The people will not be coming out keening you, they will say no prayer for the rest of your soul!

What way will I be the Sunday and I going up the hill to

the Mass? Every woman with her own comrade, and Mary
Cushin to be walking her lone!

What way will I be the Monday and the neighbours turning their heads from the house? The turf Denis cut lying on
the bog, and no well-wisher to bring it to the hearth!

What way will I be in the night time, and none but the dog
calling after you? Two women to be mixing a cake, and not a
man in the house to break it!

What way will I sow the field, and no man to drive the
furrow? The sheaf to be scattered before springtime that
was brought together at the harvest!

I would not begrudge you, Denis, and you leaving praises
after you. The neighbours keening along with me would be
better to me than an estate.

But my grief your name to be blackened in the time of the
blackening of the rushes! Your name never to rise up again
in the growing time of the year! (*She ceases keening and
turns towards the old woman.*)   But tell me, Mary, do you
think would they give us the body of Denis? I would lay
him out with myself only; I would hire some man to dig the
grave.

(*The Gatekeeper opens the gate and hands out some clothes.*)

Gatekeeper: There now is all he brought in with him; the
flannels and the shirt and the shoes. It is little they are worth
altogether; those mountainy boys do be poor.

Mary Cushin: They had a right to give him time to ready
himself the day they brought him to the magistrates. He to
be wearing his Sunday coat, they would see he was a decent
boy. Tell me where will they bury him, the way I can follow
after him through the street? There is no other one to show
respect to him but Mary Cahel, his mother, and myself.

Gatekeeper: That is not to be done. He is buried since yesterday in the field that is belonging to the gaol.

Mary Cushin: It is a great hardship that to have been done,
and not one of his own there to follow after him at all.

Gatekeeper: Those that break the law must be made an
example of. Why would they be laid out like a well behaved
man? A long rope and a short burying, that is the order for
a man that is hanged.

Mary Cushin: A man that was hanged! O Denis, was it they
that made an end of you and not the great God at all? His
curse and my own curse upon them that did not let you die
on the pillow! The curse of God be fulfilled that was on
them before they were born! My curse upon them that
brought harm on you, and on Terry Fury that fired the shot!

Mary Cahel: (*Standing up.*)   And the other boys, did they
hang them along with him, Terry Fury and Pat Ruane that
were brought from Daire-caol?

Gatekeeper: They did not, but set them free twelve hours ago.
It is likely you may have passed them in the night time.

Mary Cushin: Set free is it, and Denis made an end of? What
justice is there in the world at all?

Gatekeeper: He was taken near the house. They knew his
footmark. There was no witness given against the rest worth
while.

Mary Cahel: Then the sergeant was lying and the people
were lying when they said Denis Cahel had informed in the
gaol?

Gatekeeper: I have no time to be stopping here talking. The
judge got no evidence and the law set them free.

(*He goes in and shuts gate after him.*)

Mary Cahel: (*Holding out her hands.*)   Are there any people
in the streets at all till I call on them to come hither? Did
they ever hear in Galway such a thing to be done, a man to
die for his neighbour?

Tell it out in the streets for the people to hear, Denis Cahel
from Slieve Echtge is dead. It was Denis Cahel from Daire-
caol that died in the place of his neighbour!

It is he was young and comely and strong, the best reaper
and the best hurler. It was not a little thing for him to die,
and he protecting his neighbour!

Gather up, Mary Cushin, the clothes for your child;
they'll be wanted by this one and that one. The boys crossing
the sea in the springtime will be craving a thread for a
memory.

One word to the judge and Denis was free, they offered
him all sorts of riches. They brought him drink in the gaol,
and gold, to swear away the life of his neighbour!

Pat Ruane was no good friend to him at all, but a foolish, wild companion; it was Terry Fury knocked a gap in the wall and sent in the calves to our meadow.

Denis would not speak, he shut his mouth, he would never be an informer. It is no lie he would have said at all giving witness against Terry Fury.

I will go through Gort and Kilbecanty and Druimdarod and Daroda; I will call to the people and the singers at the fairs to make a great praise for Denis!

The child he left in the house that is shook, it is great will be his boast in his father! All Ireland will have a welcome before him, and all the people in Boston.

I to stoop on a stick through half a hundred years, I will never be tired with praising! Come hither, Mary Cushin, till we'll shout it through the roads, Denis Cahel died for his neighbour!

(*She goes off to the left, Mary Cushin following her.*)

CURTAIN

NOTES

I WAS TOLD a story someone had heard, of a man who had gone to welcome his brother coming out of gaol, and heard he had died there before the gates had been opened for him.

I was going to Galway, and at the Gort station I met two cloaked and shawled countrywomen from the slopes of Slieve Echtge, who were obliged to go and see some law official in Galway, because of some money left them by a kinsman in Australia. They had never been in a train or to any place farther than a few miles from their own village, and they felt astray and terrified 'like blind beasts in a bog' they said, and I took care of them through the day.

An agent was fired at on the road from Athenry, and some men were taken up on suspicion. One of them was a young carpenter from my old home, and in a little time a rumour was put about that he had informed against the others in Galway gaol. When the prisoners were taken across the bridge to the court-house he was hooted by the crowd. But at the trial it was found that he had not informed, that no evidence had been given at all; and bonfires were lighted for him as he went home.

These three incidents coming within a few months wove themselves into this little play, and within three days it had written itself, or been written. I like it better than any in the volume, and I have never changed a word of it.

DERVORGILLA

PERSONS

Dervorgilla	. . . .	ONCE QUEEN OF BREFFNY
Flann	. . . . . .	AN OLD SERVANT
Mona	. . . .	HIS WIFE
Owen	. . . .	A YOUNG MAN
Other Young Men		
Mamie	. . . .	A GIRL
Other Girls		
A Wandering Songmaker		

Time – 1193. *Scene, outside the Abbey of Mellifont, near Drogheda.*

DERVORGILLA

Scene: *A green lawn outside a garden wall. Flann is arranging a chair with cloaks and cushions. Mona standing beside him.*

Mona: Put a cloak there on the ground, Flann. It would not serve the lady, the damp of the earth to be rising up about her feet.

Flann: What ails her coming abroad at all, and the length of time she never asked to come outside the walls?

Mona: The young lads wanting to get prizes and to show off at their sports, it is that enticed her entirely. More sports there will be in it today than the most of them saw in their lifetime.

Flann: Fighting and killings and robbery, that is the sport they were brought up to, and that is all the sport that was in it for the last two-score years.

Mona: The Lord be with the good old times, when a woman suckling her child would be safe crossing Ireland from sea to sea! No wonder our own poor lady to be vexed and torn in the night-time. It seemed to me she had a very shook appearance this morning.

Flann: There is no occasion for her to be fretting or lonesome, and the way her name is up through the whole of the province.

Mona: Why wouldn't it be up, after the way she fed old and young through the bad times, giving means and cattle to those the English had robbed.

Flann: It is royal she is in giving as in race. Look at all the weight of gold the Abbey got from her, and the golden vessels upon the high altar.

Mona: No wonder the people to be saying she will surely get the name of a saint; the darling queen-woman of the Abbey of Mellifont.

Flann: God grant it, God grant it. We have her secret well kept so far as this. It would be a queer thing if it would not be kept to the end.

(*Shouts are heard.*)

Mona: It is the lads shouting for their own champions that are after beating the men of Assaroe.

(*Owen and other lads come in.*)

Owen: Is the lady herself coming out, Flann? Has she got good prizes in her hand?

Flann: Good and too good. The lady is too much bothered with the whole of you, stretching out her hand to you the way she does.

Another lad: Show us the prizes.

Another lad: Are they there in the basket, Flann? Give them over here to me.

Flann: Let you behave yourselves now and have manners, or you will get nothing at all.

Owen: It is little we would get if you had the giving of it, Flann! Here, Mamie, come and see the grand things Flann is keeping under his cloak!

(*They all hustle Flann. Mamie runs in.*)

Mamie: Do you see what is there beyond? Beyond upon the hill?

Owen: A troop of men on horses. I suppose it is to race the horses they are come.

Mamie: It is not, it is not; but a troop of English soldiers they are. Bows they have and swords. I am in dread of them. I went hiding in the scrub as they passed. Is there any fear, Flann, they will be coming to this place?

Flann: Sure the lady herself is coming outside the gate. Would I let her do that, there to be danger in it? I tell you the place she is, is as safe as a burrow under rocks.

Mona: Let you stop your chat. Here she is now, coming to the gate.

Mamie: I would never be in dread where she is. There are some say she has power from beyond the world, for there is no one knows her name or her race.

Flann: Whisht, the whole of ye!

(*They stand back and Dervorgilla comes in leaning upon her*

stick. Flann and Mona lead her to her chair and she stands for
a moment.)

Dervorgilla: God save you, children.

All: God save you, lady.

Dervorgilla: His blessing be upon you, and my blessing, and
the blessing of the summer-time. Let me see that the doings
of the great men are not forgotten, and that you can be as
good runners, and as good hurlers, and as good at hitting the
mark, as your old fathers were.

All: We will, we will.

Owen: You will be proud, lady, to see what the men of Ulster
can do against the men of Leinster and of Meath.

Dervorgilla: That is so, I will be proud. For though I am an
old woman given to praying, I can take pride yet in strength
of body and readiness of hand; for I saw such things long
ago in kings' houses.

Owen: There is no fear of us at all! We will not be put down;
we will gain the day! Come on, lads, some of the sports
might be over. Come along, Mamie, and be looking at us
from the bank of the embroiderers. (*They go out.*)

Dervorgilla: It is many years since we had a day like this of
sport and of mirth-making. It seems as if those were wrong
who said the English would always bring trouble on us;
there may be a good end to the story after all.

Flann: There will be a good end, to be sure. A bad behaved
race the people of this country are. It is the strong hand of
the English is the best thing to be over them.

Dervorgilla: England is a rich, powerful country to be joined to.

Flann: We should surely grow rich ourselves joined with her,
the same as a girl of the ducks and the ashes that would be
married to a great lord's son.

Dervorgilla: I can go in peace if I know I have left peace after
me, and content, but sometimes I am afraid. I had a dream
last night, a troublesome dream— What is that ? I hear a cry.
(*Mamie runs in with a dead bird.*)

Mamie: Oh, look, lady, it is a crane. It is dead, they have shot
it!

Dervorgilla: The fowlers should have spared all life on a day
of mirth like this.

Mamie: It was one of the English bowmen; he shot it in the air. It fell at my feet. It died there at my feet.

Dervorgilla: It vexes me, that to have happened on such a day as this.

Flann: Get out of that now, Mamie. You should have more sense than to be bringing in a thing of the kind. Look now, there has blood dropped upon the lady's cloak. Bring it out of this and throw it in some place where it will be in no one's way. I wonder at you annoying the lady, and the way she is spending her means upon you all. (*Mamie goes out.*)

Dervorgilla: (*Looking at cloak which Mona is wiping.*) It has brought to my mind other blood that was spilled, and that I, I myself, have to answer for.

Flann: You think entirely too much of it, lady, taking on yourself the weight of the bringing in of the English. It was the quarrelling of the provinces with one another brought them in.

Dervorgilla: No, no. It was I brought them in for good or for evil, by my own sin and the wars that were stirred up for my sake.

Flann: No, but it was in the prophecies that they would come. Didn't Blessed Caillen see them coming over the sea, and he at the brink of death waiting for the angels of God? There is no use at all trying to go against the prophecies.

Dervorgilla: You are always trying to flatter and to comfort me, but surely I brought trouble upon Ireland, as well as on all I had to do with. Diarmuid, King of Leinster, that was my lover, perished like a beast fallen by the roadside, without sacrament, without repentance. It was I brought that curse upon him.

Flann: (*Mutters.*) It was he himself earned that curse; God knows he earned it well.

Dervorgilla: Was it not I brought the curse upon O'Rourke, King of Breffny, the husband I left and betrayed? The head I made bow with shame was struck off and sent to the English King. The body I forsook was hung on the walls shamefully, by the feet, like a calf after slaughter. It is certain there is a curse on all that have to do with me. What I have done can never be undone. How can I be certain of the forgiveness of God?

Mona: Be easy now. Who would be forgiven if you would not be forgiven? Sure the Lord has seen your prayers and your crying, and your great giving and your holy life.

Dervorgilla: Four years I have lived and four-score, and for half my life I ran my own way, and through the other half of my life I have paid the penalty. For every day or night of pride or of pleasure, I have spent a day and a night of prayer and of pain. Will not that bring forgiveness? Is not that paying the penalty?

Mona: Indeed, and surely you have made it up with God. Surely you are forgiven and well forgiven! It is God Himself will open to you the gate of heaven!

Dervorgilla: But the people, the people; will they ever forgive what I have done?

Mona: They have enough to do to be minding themselves. What call would they have to go draw it down upon you at all?

Dervorgilla: I dreamt last night that the people knew me, that they knew my story and my sin; that they knew it was for my sake the wars were stirred up and the Gall brought into Ireland. They seemed to curse and to threaten me. They stooped like this, to take up stones to throw at me, knowing me at last to be Dervorgilla!

(*A voice is heard singing.*)

Mona: Whisht! Listen.

Dervorgilla: What is that? Who is that coming?

Flann: A beggar – some wandering lad. He has a great appearance of poverty. Will I go get something for him? There is no comfort at all, comforts you like giving to the poor. Look now the way his shoes are broken!

Dervorgilla: I can help the poor, still. God gives me leave to do that. Thank God I have leave yet to be a giver of gifts. Go bring me shoes for him, and a cloak, and some silver money.

Flann: Where is the use spoiling him with silver? Shoes are enough, shoes are enough. What call has a lad of his age to go begging; that is a trade of life should be left to give employment to the old.

(*He goes out. A ragged lad comes in. He is carrying a sort of rough fiddle.*)

Dervorgilla: Where do you come from, boy?

Songmaker: From the province of Connacht I am come. Connacht yesterday, Armagh tomorrow. Today it is Mellifont has got hold of me.   (*Sings*) –

> Yesterday travelling Connacht,
>   Drogheda has me today;
> My back to the empty pockets,
> My face to the place will pay!

Dervorgilla: You are young to be wandering.

Songmaker: Where would I be stopping? This day five year the thatch I was reared under was burned by the Gall, and all I had of kindred scattered. I rambled Ireland since that time, just roving around.   (*Sings*) –

> Just roving around
>   To my grief and my sorrow,
> Under a rock today,
>   Under a bush tomorrow.

It will be a long time till the Pope of Rome will get a hearth tax on my account, from the tax-gatherers of the King of England.

Dervorgilla: Have you no trade that you can follow?

Songmaker: The best, the best. I have in me the makings of a poet – and a good poet – according to the treatment I would be given – one day sweet, another day sour.   (*Sings*) –

> Syrupy sweet today,
>   Sour as sloes tomorrow;
> Sweet to the lads that pay,
>   Sour to the lads that borrow!

It is a sweet poem I would wish to be making in this grand place.

Dervorgilla: You have no right to the name of a poet; you have not learned it in the schools.

Songmaker: I did learn it well. Wasn't my grandfather a poet, and I reared up by him on the brink of a running stream? I know the rules well. Believe me, the mensuration of verses is a very ticklish thing.

Dervorgilla: The old poets had knowledge from the well of wisdom. They could tell and foretell many things.

Songmaker: It is often the people far and near would draw to my grandfather to question him. Let them come to him, sick or sour, he had an answer for all of them, or a cure.

Dervorgilla: Did you ever hear him say to any one that asked him, if a sin once committed could be forgiven?

Songmaker: It wants no poet's knowledge to know that. Can a sin be forgiven, is it? Why not, or who would people heaven?

Dervorgilla: But – did you ever hear him say if it can be undone? Can a wrong once done ever be undone? Suppose there was some person who had done a great wrong, had brought, maybe, a bad neighbour into the house, or a hard stranger in among kindred – it might be a race, an army into a country. Could that person ever gain forgiveness, praying and sorrowing?

Songmaker: Well, God is good. But to bring in a bad neighbour is a hard thing to get over. It was a bad neighbour in the next house, drove St Patrick back from Rome to Ireland.

Dervorgilla: But if that neighbour, that stranger, that race, should turn kind and honest, or could be sent back, and all be as before, would not forgiveness be gained by that?

Songmaker: Wait, now, till I think. There was something my grandfather, God rest his soul, used to be saying. He had great wisdom, I tell you, being silly-like and blind. Wait, now, till I see can I sound it out right. Talking, the neighbours were, about St Martin's mitten. It was St Martin made a throw of his mitten at the mice one time they had him annoyed, nibbling at the oatenmeal in the mill; and, in the throwing, it turned to be a cat, and scattered them. That was the first cat that ever was in Ireland.

Mona: To be sure; to be sure; so it was. St Martin's mitten was the first cat. Everybody knows that.

Songmaker: But it is what my grandfather said, that if all the saints in Ireland had wished it, and if St Martin himself had wished it along with them, it would fail them to have turned that cat to be a mitten again, or the English to be quiet neighbours again, furry and innocent, and having no claws!

Flann: (*Bringing cloak and shoes.*)   Give thanks now to the lady that is giving you more than you deserve.   (*Hands him the things and some money.*)

Songmaker: My blessing down upon you, lady, whoever you are. Faith, you have a strong pocket! The house you are in is no empty house, or any bad house at all.   (*He sits down on the ground and begins to lace on shoes, singing*) –

I am after being given two grand steppers,
　　Matching one another like two swallows on the wind,
Made from the skin of the Brown Bull of Cuailgne,
　　Or the cow Argus minded, he that was not blind.

It's the roads of the world will be proud to see them,
　　It's a great ornament they will be, far and near;
She that gave them never learned to be a niggard,
　　Though the Gall are among us this four and twenty year!

(*Owen, Mamie, and the rest run in.*)

Owen: I have the prize won! I was best over the leaps. I have taken the sway!

Mamie: My worked border was the best! Everyone gave in to that!

Another Lad: I leaped very high; I leaped as high as that!

Another: It was I won at the hurley! I took the goal from the men of Meath!

Dervorgilla: You have all done well. I am proud of you, children. I can give you all prizes. Flann, give me the prizes. (*He hands them to her and she gives them one by one.*) Here, Mamie, is a necklace from the Eastern world. You have earned it well by your worked border. Make the borders of your house beautiful. Keep within its borders all God has given you in charge. (*To Owen.*) Here is a silver cup. (*To another.*) Here is a cloak with a brooch. (*To another.*) Here, you are the youngest, you must have a prize. Take this hurl, this silver ball. Practice with them well and you will be first yet. (*They all stoop and kiss her hand as she gives the presents.*)

Flann: Give a good shout now for the lady. (*They all shout, the singer joins.*)

Owen: Who is that? A stranger? He has not the look of our own people. Is he come to make sport for us?

Dervorgilla: He is a maker of songs. He has the sweet voice of the Connacht men. They have the soft sea mist in their mouths.

Owen: Give out a song now, till we'll hear what you can do.

Songmaker: Give me the key so. There can be no singing without a key.

Owen: What do you call a key?

Songmaker: Three keys there are; you should know that. It is only love or drink or friendship can unlock a song.

Dervorgilla: Give him a cup of wine.

Flann: Will nothing do him but wine? Wine that is too good and too strong. (*Gives him a cup, Songmaker drinks.*)

Songmaker: What will you have now for a song? Destructions, cattle preys, courtships, feats of battle?

Owen: No, no; we are tired of those.

Songmaker: Well, I'll rhyme you out a verse about Finn and the Danish wedding.

Owen: Those old songs of Finn and his men are only for winter nights, and the feet among the sods. Give us out a new song.

Songmaker: It is best keep to the old ones. The old ones are merry, but the new ones are sorrowful.

Owen: The sorrowful songs are sometimes the best. They tell of the death of the big men and of the quarrelling of kings.

Songmaker: Well, if it is a sorrowful song you want, it is easy to find it, for there was not made these forty years any song or any story in Ireland that was not sorrowful. And if it is the quarrellings of kings you want, I will tell you of a quarrelling brought such trouble into Ireland, that if a grain of it could be blown through a pipe in amongst the angels of heaven, it would bring a dark mist over their faces. (*Rocks himself.*) I tell you, that if the half of all the tears, shed through that quarrelling, could be sent through a pipe into hell, the flames would be put out, and the hearth of it black-flooded with otters!

Owen: That must be the story of the coming of the Gall into Ireland.

Flann: That trouble is surely lessening. There are no more killings. It is best to put away old griefs out of mind. Think now of some other thing. Something happened in Spain or in France.

Dervorgilla: Do not meddle with him, Flann. It is not the telling of the story makes the story. Let me hear what is the common voice.

(*Songmaker sings*) –

It is pitiful and sharp today are the wounds of Ireland,
From Galway of white flaggy stones to Cork of the white strand;
The branches that were full of leaves and honey on the leaves,
Are torn and stripped and shortened by the stranger to our grief.

It is long, O Royal Ireland, you were mannerly and kind,
A nursing mother to your sons, fair, hospitable, wise;
Now you are wine spilled from a cup beneath the strangers' feet,
The English-speaking troop today have trodden down our wheat.

The wild white fawn has lost the shape was comely in the wood,
Since the foreign crow came nesting in the yew-tree overhead,
Since the red East wind brought to our hurt the troop of foreign rogues,
We are drifted like the wretched fur of a cat upon a bog!

Flann: Where is the use of yelping and yowling like a hound that has lost the pack? Get out of this, if that screeching of a banshee is all that you can do.

Dervorgilla: I have given him leave to sing his songs. Let him travel his own road. Let him take his own way.

Songmaker: It is hard for me to tell my story and that one not giving me leave to tell it. There must be a preparation for everything and a beginning. Wouldn't you hear the wind making its cry about the house before you would hear the hammering of the rain upon the stones? Give me time now, and I will give out the story of a man that has left a name will never be forgotten here, and that is Diarmuid MacMurrough, King of Leinster, that first called the English into Ireland. (*Sings*) –

Through Diarmuid's bad sway we are wasted today,
It was he brought away the Queen of Breffny;
And when O'Rourke raised Connacht against him,
Gave the English pay to come to Ireland.

It were better for all that are under the Gall,
If death made a call and he in the cradle;
Bind him down very strong and bruise him long,
The way he can wrong us no more for ever.

His great body is down under the stone
Chased by the hounds were before the world;
It was Peter's own frown closed the door before him,
It is Diarmuid is bound in cold Hell for ever!

Dervorgilla: That is enough, that is enough! Why should you heap up blame upon one that is dead? King Diarmuid's lips are closed now with clay. It is a shameful thing, a cowardly thing, to make attacks upon a man that cannot answer. Are you not satisfied to let God be the judge?

Songmaker: I had no intention to give offence. To dispraise Diarmuid and the English, I thought that would give satisfaction in this place, the same as it does in Connacht.

Dervorgilla: Those that have a good heart and a high nature try to find excuses for the dead.

Songmaker: So they would, so they would. It is finding excuses we should be for the dead. There is an excuse for every one; the Blessed Mother knows that, and she sitting every Saturday as the attorney for poor souls. Making out a case for them she does be.

Dervorgilla: There is no one who might not be freed from blame, if his case and what led to his wrongdoing were put down.

Songmaker: I'll make out a case for him. I can tell out what led King Diarmuid into his sin and his treachery; and that is the thing brings mostly all mischief into the world, the changeable wagging nature of a woman. (*Sings*) –

He cares little for life, puts trust in a wife,
It is long it is known they go with the wind;
A queer thing a woman was joined with O'Rourke
To show herself kind to a pet from Leinster.

The rat in the larder, the fire in the thatch,
The guest to be fattening, the children famished;
If 'twas Diarmuid's call that brought in the Gall,
Let the weight of it fall upon Dervorgilla!

(*Dervorgilla tries to rise and cannot. Mona supports her, Flann offers her wine. She lies back as if faint. They attend to her, their backs to the rest. The singer crosses to the young men, who give him money.*)

Mamie: I often heard of Dervorgilla that left the King of Breffny for Diarmuid, and started the war, but I never heard what happened to her after.

Owen: There is no one knows that. Some say King Roderick put her under locks in a cell at Clonmacnoise.

Songmaker: More likely she hanged herself, after setting the whole of the country in an uproar.

Owen: If she did they had a right to bury her with a hound on her false heart, the same as Diarmuid himself was buried.

Songmaker: No, but Diarmuid's father was buried with the hound. Excuse or no excuse, a bad race they are, a bad race.

Flann: (*To Songmaker.*)   Quit off now out of this place before I will make you quit it. Take yourself and your rags and your venomous tongue out of this.

Songmaker: Let you leave me alone. Is that the way you are laying hands upon a poet?

Dervorgilla: Leave him go, Flann. You are judging him now. God is the Judge; let him go.

Songmaker: Look at the way you have me tore! It is where I'll go on to that troop of English on the hill beyond. I'll sound my songs for them. I will get better treatment from them itself, than I am getting from you. If it wasn't for respect for the lady, it's a great overthrow I'd make of you. I'll go to the English.   (*He goes off, singing as he goes.*)

Since the Gall have the sway, it's for them I will play
There's none would lay blame on a boy that's a beggar,
But a queer thing a woman was joined to O'Rourke,
To show herself kind to a fox from Leinster!

Owen: The English look to be friendly enough. They are drinking beer from the barrels. They are cheering the horses that go over the bank. Come along, boys, and see the big leaps.

Mamie: Take care now, it would not be safe to go near the bowmen. Didn't you see the way they made an end of that crane a while ago?

Owen: Flann said they would do no harm. I would like well to get a near view of the big bows. Come along, Mamie.

Mamie: I will not. I will go into the garden of the Abbey.

(*She goes in through gate, Owen and young men go out.*)

Dervorgilla: (*Raising herself up.*) Oh, my sin, my sin has come upon my head! Why did I come out from the Abbey walls? A cell is the only fitting place for me! I should never have come out into the light of the day!

Flann: Ah, what does it signify? What is it all but a vagabond's song that was born in a minute, and will vanish away like a wisp of smoke.

Dervorgilla: The dream of the night was true. It is coming true. My sin is remembered – I shall be known – I saw it all – they stooped to pick up stones – there was no forgiveness when they knew me to be Dervorgilla!

Flann: That is a thing they will never know and that they have no way to know. Sure, in the Abbey itself there is no one knows it outside the Order.

Dervorgilla: It will be discovered, some one will see me.

Flann: Ah, there are few living in any place that ever saw you in the old days. And if they should see you now itself, how would they know those holy withered cheeks to belong to the lovely lady that set kings fighting in her bloom? And many happenings have happened since then, and it is likely the Queen of Breffny is forgotten. Sure, you heard them saying that Dervorgilla is dead.

Dervorgilla: I will go in. Bring me back into the shelter of the walls.

Flann: It might be best. There will be no drunken poets and schemers of the sort going in there to annoy you. It is too open-handed you are to them all, that is what makes them so stubborn and so high-minded. Gather up the pillows, Mona, till we'll bring the lady in.

Mona: It's best, it's best. Ah, don't be fretting, dear. There is no one on earth knows your secret and your name but myself, that was reared with you, and this man that is my own comrade. And you know well, and I swear to you, the both of us would be dragged through briars, and ground under millstones, before we would consent to say out your name to any person at all. I would sooner my tongue to be turned to a stone here and now, than you to be uneasy the way you are.

Dervorgilla: There is no hiding it, no hiding it. Dreams come true. Who was there today to tell it, and that beggar told the story. He will be singing it from troop to troop. The English will hear it, the runners will hear it, it will be blazed before night through the provinces, it will set them thinking of me, and talking.

Flann: The devil skelp him! It would be no harm at all to come from behind and give him a tip of a hurl on the head to quiet his impudence and his talk. There is strength in my hand yet, and weight in my stick.

Dervorgilla: No, no, I will not have anyone hurt for my sake. I will have no other blood upon my head. But follow him, Flann. Go after him and put him under bonds to go away, to leave the province, to give up his singing. Give him money, all this money, that he may live in some far-away place, without singing and wandering.

Flann: (*Taking the purse.*) I will do that. Wait three minutes and I'll be coming back to bring you within the walls. I'll put him under heavy oaths to quit this, to go do his croaking with the crows of Scotland. That they may make an end of him with their beaks, and be pecking the eyes out of him, and lining their nests with every hair of his head! (*He goes off.*)

Dervorgilla: It is of no use, dreams cannot lie, my punishment must come. I knew it all the time, even within the walls. I tried to make it up with good works. It was of no use, my name in men's mouths.

Mona: What signifies one beggar's song? It is not on you the blame should be laid. It was not you went to Diarmuid

MacMurrough. It was not you followed after him to Leinster. It was he came and brought you away. There are many say it was by force. There are many that are saying that. That is the way it will be written in the histories.

Dervorgilla: If Diarmuid MacMurrough had taken me by force, do you think I would have lived with him for one day only? My hands were strong then. I had my courage then. I was free to make an end of myself or of him. Will the generations think better of me, thinking me to have been taken as a prey, like the Connacht hag's basket, or the Munster hag's speckled cow? Does the marten that is torn from the woods lull itself in its master's arms?

Mona: Maybe so, maybe so. I used to be better pleased myself hearing them say it, than putting the blame on yourself of leaving O'Rourke.

Dervorgilla: O'Rourke was a good man, and a brave man, and a kinder man than Diarmuid, but it was with Diarmuid my heart was. It is to him I was promised before ever I saw O'Rourke, and I loved him better than ever my own lord, and he me also, and this was long! I loved him, I loved him! Why did they promise me to him and break the promise? Why was every one against him then and always, every one against Diarmuid? Why must they be throwing and ever-throwing sharp reproaches upon his name? Had a man loved by a king's daughter nothing in him to love? A man great of body, hardy in fight, hoarse with shouts of battle. He had liefer be dreaded than loved! It was he cast down the great, it was the dumb poor he served! Every proud man against him and he against every proud man. Oh, Diarmuid, I did not dread you. It was I myself led you astray! Let the curse and the vengeance fall upon me and me only, for the great wrong and the treachery done by both of us to Ireland! (*A loud cry is heard. Both look towards where it comes from.*)

Mona: Listen, listen!

Dervorgilla: What is it? What is that cry?

Mona: It is like the heavy shout does be given out over a man that has been struck down by his enemies. (*The shout is heard nearer.*)

Dervorgilla: What is it!

Mona: (*Looking out.*) The young men are coming back. Their heads are drooping.

Dervorgilla: God grant no trouble may have fallen upon them.

Mona: There is trouble, and heavy trouble upon them, sure enough.

(*Mamie comes in from the garden, young men come in.*)

Dervorgilla: What is it, my children? What has happened?

Owen: The truce has been broken. The wasp we thought drowsy has found its sting. The hand of the Gall has again been reddened.

Mona: Tell it out, tell it out, what is it has happened at all?

Owen: Get ready for the burying of Flann of Breffny, the lady's steward and distributor, and your good comrade.

Mona: Ah! that is foolishness. It cannot be true. He was here but a minute ago, standing on this spot.

Owen: It is true.

Dervorgilla: How did he die? Tell me all.

Owen: He came where that Connachtman was doing his tricks for the English troop. They asked a song of him; he was going to give it out. Flann tried to bring him away. The bowmen had mugs of beer in their hands; they were laughing at the tricks; they wanted the song. They called out to Flann to leave him to make fun for them, but Flann tried to bring him away. He spoke in his ear; he put his hand over his mouth. They were rightly vexed then, and one of them called out: 'There, spoil-sport, is a spoiling of all sport for you,' and he drew his bow and sent an arrow through Flann's body, that he fell like a stone, without a word. Then they turned their horses, and one of them said it was a pity, but another said their dinners would be spoiling in Drogheda. And so they rode away in a hurry.

Dervorgilla: Another. Death has come upon another. (*Holds out her hands.*) Come to me, my poor Mona, my friend.

Mona: Is it Flann is dead? Flann, my husband? He had a year less than I myself had. It was not his time to die. Who is there to close my own eyes now? He always said he would close my eyes.

Dervorgilla: Your trouble is no greater than my trouble. It was for my sake and in following my bidding he died.

Mona: It was the Gall killed his two brothers and destroyed the house and trampled down the field of oats. What did they want killing him? Wasn't it enough to have destroyed his oats?

Dervorgilla: Come into the Abbey and prepare for him there.

Mona: So near to the chapel, and not a priest to overtake him before he died. That was no death for a Christian man.

Dervorgilla: Candles will be lighted, and many Masses said for his soul.

Mona: And it was with the sword itself he was killed, that's natural. His brothers were killed with the sword. But an arrow! Not one of the family was killed with that before. That is not a thing you would be hearing in the ballads.

Owen: Will you go where the body is? There are some that are laying it out?

Mona: I will, I will. Bring me to my decent comrade; and bring me to that singer was here. I will lay it upon him to make a great cursing to put upon the Gall, a great heavy curse upon all that had to do with the Gall. (*She is going off, but turns back to Dervorgilla.*) But it is not on yourself I will let them put a curse, or lay on you any blame at all. You know well I never put blame on you, or said a sharp word of you, the time you were in Breffny with O'Rourke, or the time you were in Leinster with Diarmuid MacMurrough, and I myself following you from place to place. You know well, and the man that is stretched cold and dumb knows, I never said a hard word or an unkind word or a bad word of you yourself, Dervorgilla. (*She goes out babbling.*) Oh, no, no; I would never do such a thing as that!

Owen: (*To the others.*) Dervorgilla! Oh, did you hear her say it is Dervorgilla?

Dervorgilla: (*Stands up with difficulty.*) Since you were born and before you were born I have been here, kneeling and praying, kneeling and praying, fasting and asking forgiveness of God. I think my father God has forgiven me. They tell me my mother the Church has forgiven me. That old man had forgiven me, and he had suffered by the Gall. The old – the old – that old woman, even in her grief, she called out no word against me. You are young. You will surely forgive me, for you are young. (*They are all silent. Then Owen comes over and lays down his cup at her feet, then turns and walks slowly away.*) It is not your hand has done this, but the righteous hand of God that has moved your hand. (*Other lads lay down their gifts.*) I take this shame for the shame in the west I put on O'Rourke of Breffny, and the death I brought upon him by the hand of the Gall. (*The youngest boy who has hesitated, comes and lays down his hurl and silver ball, and goes away, his head drooping.*) I take this reproach for the reproach in the east I brought upon Diarmuid, King of Leinster, thrusting upon him wars and attacks and battles, till for his defence and to defend Leinster, he called in the strangers that have devoured Ireland. (*The young men have all gone. Mamie comes as if to lay down her gift, but draws back. Dervorgilla turns to her.*) Do not be afraid to give back my gifts, do not separate yourself from your companions for my sake. For there is little of my life but is spent, and there has come upon me this day all the pain of the world and its anguish, seeing and knowing that a deed once done has no undoing, and the lasting trouble my unfaithfulness has brought upon you and your children for ever. (*Mamie lays down her necklace and goes away sadly.*) There is kindness in your unkindness, not leaving me to go and face Michael and the Scales of Judgment wrapped in comfortable words, and the praises of the poor, and the lulling of psalms, but from the swift, unflinching, terrible judgment of the young! (*She sinks slowly to the ground holding to the chair. The stage begins to darken; the voice of the Songmaker is heard coming nearer, singing*) –

> The rat in the cupboard, the fire in the lap;
> The guest to be fattening, the children fretting;
> My curse upon all that brought in the Gall,
> Upon Diarmuid's call, and on Dervorgilla!

CURTAIN

NOTES

DERVORGILLA, daughter of the King of Meath, wife of O'Rourke, King of Breffny, was taken away, willingly or unwillingly, by Diarmuid MacMurrough, King of Leinster, in the year 1152. O'Rourke and his friends invaded Leinster in revenge, and in the wars which followed, Diarmuid, driven from Ireland, appealed for help to Henry II of England, and was given an army under Strongbow, to whom Diarmuid promised Leinster as reward. It is so the English were first brought into Ireland. Dervorgilla, having outlived O'Rourke and Diarmuid and Henry and Strongbow, is said to have died at the Abbey of Mellifont, near Drogheda, in the year 1193, aged 85.

That is how the story is told in the histories. And I have heard in Kiltartan: 'Dervorgilla was a red-haired woman, and it was she put the great curse on Ireland, bringing in the English through MacMurrough, that she went to from O'Rourke. It was to Henry the Second MacMurrough went, and he sent Strongbow, and they stopped in Ireland ever since. But who knows but another race might be worse, such as the Spaniards that were scattered along the whole coast of Connacht at the time of the Armada? And the laws are good enough. I heard it said the English will be dug out of their graves one day for the sake of their law. As to Dervorgilla, she was not brought away by force, she went to MacMurrough herself. For there are men in the world that have a coaxing way, and sometimes women are weak.'

THE WHITE COCKADE

PERSONS

Patrick Sarsfield . . . . . EARL OF LUCAN
King James II
Carter . . . . . SECRETARY TO KING JAMES
A Poor Lady
Matt Kelleher . . . OWNER OF AN INN AT DUNCANNON
Mary Kelleher . . . . . . HIS WIFE
Owen Kelleher . . . . HIS SON
First Sailor
Second Sailor
First Williamite
Second Williamite
A Captain and other Williamites

ACT I

Scene: An Inn kitchen at Duncannon. Owen Kelleher lying on the hearth playing jackstones. Mrs Kelleher rubbing a bit of meat. A barrel beside her.

Owen: One – and one – and five – that's scatters.

Mrs Kelleher: Leave playing jackstones, Owen, and give me a hand with the meat.

Owen: Two – and two – and one – that's doubles. There is time enough. Sure it's not today it's wanted.

Mrs Kelleher: What's put off till harvest is put off for ever. It's better to catch the pig by the leg when you get her. The French ship might be going before we have the barrels ready, and some other might get the profit.

Owen: The ship didn't get orders yet from King James. The sailors were not sure was it to Dublin he would bid them go, or to some other place. It is time for us to be hearing news of him. I have a mind to go ask it.

Mrs Kelleher: Come over and rub a bit of the meat, and leave thinking about King James. We hear enough talk of him, listening to poor Lady Dereen.

Owen: You have not enough of salt to pack the meat till my father will bring it back from Ross.

Mrs Kelleher: The lamb teaching its mother to bleat! If I have not itself, I have what serves for rubbing it. (*She pushes back dresser from before a side door.*)   Be moving now, and come down to the cellar till we bring up another leg of the pork.

Owen: (*Going on playing.*)   One – and one – and one – crow's nest.

Mrs Kelleher: (*Going through door to cellar.*)   I give you my word it is as hard to make you stir as to make a hedgehog run.

(*Owen whistles 'The White Cockade'.*)

Mrs Kelleher: (*Coming back with another bit of meat.*)   It is yourself finds the hob a good harbourage!

Owen: It is not worth my while to be bringing it up bit by bit – if it was to bring up the whole of it now—

Mrs Kelleher: I suppose not! I wonder now what is worth your while if it is not to mind the place and the inn that will be coming to yourself some day. It is a poor hen that can't scratch for itself!

Owen: There might be something worth doing outside this place.

Mrs Kelleher: (*Scornfully.*)   There might! It's the hills far off that are green!

Owen: It is beyond the hills that I would like to be going. There is no stir at all in this place.

Mrs Kelleher: What is it at all you are wanting or talking about ?

Owen: There used to be great fighters in Ireland in the old times.

Mrs Kelleher: If there were, they had no other trade! Every crane according to its thirst. Believe me, if they had found as good a way of living as what you have, they would not have asked to go rambling. I know well it is an excuse you are making, with your talk of fighting and your songs, not to be doing the work that is at your hand. You are as lazy as the tramp that will throw away his bag. You would have got the sluggard's prize from Aristotle of the books!

Owen: Well, it's good to be best at something.

Mrs Kelleher: If you saw a car and a horse coming at you, you would not stir out of the rut! You would spend your night on the floor sooner than go up a ladder to the loft! Stir! You would not stir yourself to turn the crispy side of a potato if you had but the one bite only!

Owen: One – and four – high castles.

Mrs Kelleher: I tell you a day will come when you will grow to the ground the way you will never reach to heaven!

Owen: It is time for you to leave off faulting me. There is some one coming to the door.

Mrs Kelleher: (*Looking out of door.*)   It is the poor Lady. She wasn't here this good while. It is a pity she to have gone spending all for the King the way she did, and to go in beggary and misery ever after.

(*Owen sings*) –

> The cuckoo has no word to say,
> Sharp grief has put her under rent,
> The heavy cloud is on the Gael,
> But comely James will bring content!

Mrs Kelleher: I believe it is herself put the half of those songs in your head. (*Pulls dresser over door.*) It is best shut this door. There is no use too many eyes seeing it.

(*Old Lady comes in. Her hand is over her eyes as if half-blind. She wears ragged clothes that have once been handsome.*)

Mrs Kelleher: You are welcome, my poor Lady Dereen.

Lady: I thank you, Mary Kelleher. I have always found a welcome in this house, and a shelter from the heat and the rain.

Mrs Kelleher: Who should get a welcome here if you wouldn't get it, Lady? And I born and reared on your own estate before you lost it through the wars.

Lady: I have had great losses, but now I will have great gains. I lost all through Charles; I will get all back through James. My eyes are tired watching for the sun to rise in the east. The sun of our success is rising at last!

Mrs Kelleher: It is time for success to come to yourself, Lady, indeed. I remember the time you had great riches.

Lady: I did not grudge anything, my lord did not grudge anything to Charles Stuart, our King. I shall be rich again now; I never lost my faith.

Mrs Kelleher: Well, I would never have faith myself in the thing I wouldn't see.

Lady: I lost all through Charles; I will get all back through James!

Mrs Kelleher: That you may, Lady. I would sooner you have kept it when you had it. A wren in the fist is better than a crane on loan. It's hard getting butter out of a dog's mouth.

Lady: The Stuart has been under the mists of night. The sun is rising that will scatter them. The whole country is going out to help him. The young men are leaving the scythes in the meadows; the old men are leaving the stations and the blessed wells. Give me some white thing – some feathers – I have to make cockades for the King's men.

Mrs Kelleher: (*Giving her feathers from the dresser.*)   Look at that now! These come as handy as a gimlet. I was plucking ducks yesterday for the captain of the French ship.

Lady: (*Taking feathers and beginning to fasten them together with shaking hands.*)   James, our own King, will bring prosperity to us all.

Mrs Kelleher: So long as we get it, I wouldn't mind much what King brings it. One penny weighs as good as another, whatever King may have his head upon it. If you want to grow old, you must use hot and cold.

Lady: Is it nothing to you, Mary Kelleher, that the broken altars of the Faith will be built up again?

Mrs Kelleher: God grant it! Though, indeed, myself I am no great bigot. I would always like to go to a Protestant funeral. You would see so many well-dressed people at it.

Lady: (*Beginning to make another cockade.*)   I must be quick, very quick. There will be a hard battle fought. William, the Dutchman, has brought trained men from all the countries of Europe. James has gone out to meet him.

Mrs Kelleher: Is it going to fight a battle he is? It is likely he will have sent orders to the French ship, so. It is to take his orders it was here. The dear knows where it might be to-morrow, and the pigs we have killed left on our hands! Only for you giving me no help the way you did, Owen, the meat would be nearer ready now than what it is. Look at him now, Lady; maybe he'll mind what you will say. Bid him leave lying on the floor at midday.

Lady: It is time you should get up, boy; there is plenty of work to do.

Mrs Kelleher: That is what I am saying. Work for all hands.

Lady: Work for all and no time to lose.

Mrs Kelleher: That is what I am saying. What is put off till harvest—

Lady: It is not right for a young man with strong hands to be taking his ease. (*Owen gets up and stands awkwardly.*)

Mrs Kelleher: And his mother not sparing herself.

Lady: You lying there, while there is a friend out under the heat of the day fighting our battle.

Mrs Kelleher: My poor man! So he is. Striving to bring the salt.

Lady: (*Giving Owen a cockade.*) Take that White Cockade. Go out, go northward. Join the King's army, go and fight for the King!

Mrs Kelleher: To fight for the King, is it?

Lady: Hurry, hurry, you may be in time to strike a blow for him! (*Sings with a feeble voice*) –

> Our heart's desire, our pleasant James,
> Our treasure and our only choice!

Mrs Kelleher: Look here now, Lady, have sense. I have but the one son only, and it is sending him away from me you would be?

Lady: Our King has no son; he has false daughters. We must give our sons to the King!

Mrs Kelleher: It is my opinion we must keep them to mind ourselves. What profit would he get joining the King's army? It is not the one thing to go to town and come from it.

Lady: (*Putting hand on her arm.*) It would be a pity to disappoint so great a friend.

Mrs Kelleher: That is true, but reason is reason. I have but the one son to help me; and it is what I say: you can't whistle and eat oatmeal; the gull can't attend the two strands; words won't feed the friars. How will Owen mind this place, and he maybe shot as full of holes as a riddle?

Owen: When you have your minds made up if it's to go fighting I am, or to go rubbing the bacon I am, it will be time enough for me to stir myself.

Lady: Do you grudge your service? Will you betray the King as the English betrayed him? O my heart leaps up with my pleasant Stuart!

Owen: I would like well to go serve the King; but I don't know how could I do it.

Lady: You say that because of idleness. It is through idleness you have come to have a coward's heart, the heart of a linnet, of a trader, a poor, weak spirit, a heart of rushes.

Mrs Kelleher: You are too hard now, Lady, upon the boy.

Leave him alone. There is no man knows which is best, hurry or delay. It's often it's not better to be first than last. Many a tattered colt makes a handsome horse. The first thread is not of the piece. It's not the big men cut all the harvest. When the time comes, the child comes. Every good comes by waiting.

Lady: King James in the country wanting all his helpers!

Mrs Kelleher: Let every herring hang by its own tail.

Lady: It is for our comfort he has come.

Mrs Kelleher: He might. It's to please itself the cat purrs.

Lady: (*Putting hand on Owen's shoulder.*)   The Stuart in the field!

Mrs Kelleher: (*Seizing other shoulder.*)   The meat in the cellar!

Lady: Our hero in danger!

Mrs Kelleher: Our bacon in danger!

Lady: Our prince under mists!

Mrs Kelleher: Our meat under mildew!

Lady: Oh! The great Stuart!

Mrs Kelleher: (*Striking it.*)   The empty barrel!

(*Owen turns from one to the other, undecided. Voices are heard singing a French song.*)

Lady: Is that the army of the King?

Mrs Kelleher: It is what is worse. It's the French sailors coming for the meat and it not ready.

(*Two sailors come in singing*) –

> Madame, si vous voulez danser
> Vite je vous prie de commencer
> Avec l'air des Français,
> Avec l'air de la Cour.

First Sailor: We are come, Madame, for the pork and the bacon.

Second Sailor: And de sau-sa-ges.

Mrs Kelleher: I haven't them ready yet.

First Sailor: We must sail this night before morning.

Mrs Kelleher: Did you get any orders from King James?

First Sailor: We did not get them. He is fighting in the north, at some river. We go to Dublin. If he succeed, we carry news

to France. If he is beaten, he will want help from France. We
sail at sunrise when the tide is high.

Mrs Kelleher: Well, look now; I will have the meat for you
before that.

First Sailor: All right. There is moon. We will come to the
pier before sunrise, after the midnight.

Mrs Kelleher: There is a quick way. Maybe you don't know
the outer door to the cellar ?

Second Sailor: I do know it. I did put wine in there last week –
no duty; no douane. (*Puts finger on nose.*)

(*Matt Kelleher comes bursting in. He throws a bag of salt on the
floor.*)

Mrs Kelleher: Here is himself, and he running like a hare
before hounds. Give me here the salt.

Matt: Salt! salt! salt! Who would be talking of salt ?

Mrs Kelleher: The ship is going.

Matt: Where is the use of salt on such a day as this, unless it
might be to make a man drouthy ?

Mrs Kelleher: I tell you I was as idle without it as a smith
without bellows.

Matt: To make a man drouthy! To give him a good thirst, the
way he will drink to the King! Where are the glasses ?

Mrs Kelleher: Indeed, if signs are signs, I think you yourself
have been drinking to the King!

Matt: We will all drink to the King! Where are the glasses ?

Mrs Kelleher: Quiet yourself now. You are too good a cus-
tomer to yourself; putting on the mill the straw of the kiln.

Matt: Would you begrudge me so much as one glass on a day
like this ?

Mrs Kelleher: What has happened on this day more than any
other day ?

Matt: This day has brought news of the battle, I tell you – of
the great battle at the Boyne!

First Sailor: The Boyne – that is it! That is the same story we
heard.

Matt: Where would you hear your story ? It was away in Ross
I got mine. There was news brought to the barracks there.

Mrs Kelleher: Tell me now, was the battle fought in earnest ?

Matt: Fought is it ? It is it that was fought! A great battle –

the ground that was hard turning soft, and the ground that was soft turning hard, under the trampling of feet! The sea coming in on the land, and the land going out into the sea! Fire from the edges of every sword! The blood falling like a shower in harvest time! The air black with ravens; the river reddened with blood! Sarsfield going through the field the same as fire through furze.

Mrs Kelleher: What there is good comes out in the blood. Sure he is of the race of Conall Cearnach. What would an apple be like but an apple? What would the cat's son do but kill mice?

Matt: King James raging like a lion in every gap!

Lady: Oh! I knew it! I knew it! The brave Stuart!

Mrs Kelleher: And who was it, will you tell me, that won in the fight?

Matt: Sure, amn't I telling you, if you would listen? The man has won that should win, great King James!

Lady: I knew the sun would rise at last for victory!

Matt: You will get your rights now, Lady. We'll all get our rights.   (*Sings*) –

> Three times the fairest of the Scots,
> The blossomed branch, the Phoenix rare,
> Our secret love, our only choice,
> The shining candle of the war!

Lady: My lord spent all upon Charles, James will pay all back again!

Matt: He will, he will! You will get your estates, Lady, and your white halls! We will drink the cellar dry the day you get your estates. There will be red wine of Spain running through your white halls!

Lady: I have his promise! I have the King's seal to his promise!
    (*She takes a large seal and folded parchment from a bag hanging at her side and shows it.*)

Matt: It is a good seal – a grand seal. Drink a health, I say, to the King's seal! Let me go down to the cellar for spirits – no, but for wine!
    (*He pushes back dresser. Mrs Kelleher pulls him from the door.*)

Mrs Kelleher: You will not go down. Thirst makes thirst!

Matt: (*To sailors.*) Go down there, I say. Bring up a bottle – two bottles – plenty of bottles!

(*They go down.*)

Lady: I will go to Dublin. I will go to his Court. I will show him the promise and the seal.

Matt: You will, ma'am. He can't deny the seal.

Lady: I will put on my silks and my velvets. I will have jewels about my neck. I will bid my waiting-women to spread out my dress.

(*Makes a gesture as if spreading out a train.*)

Matt: It is you will look well, Lady, as you did in the old times, with your silks and your jewels.

Lady: I will come to the door. The coach will stop – the young lords will hand me out of it – my own young kinsmen will be there.

Matt: I will go see you in the coach, Lady. It is myself will open the door!

Lady: They will bring me to the throne-room. I will leave my cloak at the door. I will walk up to the throne!

(*She walks a few steps.*)

Matt: (*Walking crookedly.*) I will walk up myself. I would like well to see the King on his throne.

Lady: (*Curtsying.*) A curtsy to the right to the Queen – a curtsy to the left to the princesses.

Matt: (*Curtsying.*) That is it, that is it! We will curtsy to the princesses.

Lady: The King will smile at me. I will take out the King's seal. (*Touches it.*) I will kneel and kiss his hand.

Matt: I will kneel – no, I will not. (*Stumbles and kneels.*) There, I did now in spite of myself. Here, Mary, help me up again.

Mrs Kelleher: Stop where you are, Kelleher, and be ashamed of yourself. When wine goes in, wit goes out.

Owen: (*Helping the lady up.*) All will go well with you now, Lady, since the King has gained the day.

Mrs Kelleher: Maybe he was not the winner after all. It is often we heard news from Ross that wouldn't be true after.

Matt: Why wouldn't he win? He has the prayers of the people with him.

Lady: He has God with him.

Owen: He has Sarsfield with him.

Lady: Oh! who will go to the King? who will go for news of the King?

Owen: I will go.

Lady: Yes, go, go! Here, take these to give to the King's men. (*She gives him cockades.*)

Mrs Kelleher: Do not go until we are sure is the battle over. The last of a feast is better than the first of a fight.

Owen: I will go now. I delayed long enough. I wish I had gone in time for the fighting.

Mrs Kelleher: Well, since he is the winner – a friend in Court is better than a coin in the pocket – it might be for profit.
(*Owen begins washing hands and face in a basin. Puts on coat. Sailors bring up an armful of bottles from the cellar.*)

Matt: (*Still on the floor, seizing a bottle.*)   Here's to the King's health, I say!
(*The sailors give him glasses; he opens bottle, fills them, and they hand them round.*)

Lady: (*Touching glass with her lips, and throwing it down.*)   The King and the King's right!

Mrs Kelleher: The King and the Catholics in fashion!

Owen: The King that fought the battle!

Sailors: The King and France!

Matt: The King and wine without duty!

All Together: King James and Ireland!

All: (*Singing*) –

> O well-tuned harp of silver strings,
> O strong green oak, O shining Mars,
> Our hearts' desire, fair James our King,
> Our great Cuchulain in the war!

CURTAIN

ACT II

SCENE I

Scene: A wood. James sitting on a camp stool. He is richly dressed, and wears an Order. Carter standing beside him. Sarsfield pointing with sword to a map on the ground.

Sarsfield: If your Majesty will look at the plan I have marked on this map, you will see how we can make up for the defeat of the Boyne. The news we have had of William's march makes it very simple. He will be in our hands by morning. You know what we have to do tonight. Tomorrow we shall be dictating terms from Limerick.

James: Yes, yes, you told me all that. I wonder if this wood is quite safe. (*Looks round.*)

Sarsfield: If our army had to fall back, it fell back in good order. We have guns, stores, horses. We have plenty of troops to strengthen Athlone. We can keep the mass of the enemy from passing the Shannon.

James: I hope the bridge we crossed that last little river by has been broken so that no one can follow us.

Sarsfield: Kilkenny must be strengthened too. Waterford is loyal. Munster and Connacht are safe. Our success will give us back Dublin. In half an hour our horses will be rested. We must be at Clonmel before midnight.

James: But there is a troop of William's men somewhere about. We might fall into their hands.

Sarsfield: They are in small divisions. We and a few men will be more than a match for them.

James: Of course, of course; but we must not risk our lives.

Carter: Not a doubt of it! The King's life must not be put in danger!

Sarsfield: Danger! Who says that? Who said it at the Boyne? Was it you that drove the King from the battle? Bad advisers! Bad advisers! He who says 'danger' is a bad adviser.

141

Carter: I did nothing – it was His Majesty's own doing.

James: Yes, yes, of course. I am more than a soldier. I have the whole kingdom to think of.

Carter: Not a doubt of it. But you and I, Sarsfield, have only ourselves to think of.

Sarsfield: You and I – maybe – this dust (*striking himself*) – that dust of yours – has the King's livery made us of the one baking? No, no; there is some leaven in this dough. (*To the King.*) Rouse yourself, sir. Put your hand to the work.

James: I suppose I must carry out this plan of a surprise.

Sarsfield: That is right, sir. Carry it out and the Boyne will be forgotten.

James: Is that some noise? (*Starts.*)

Sarsfield: It is but the trampling of our own horses.

James: Just go, Sarsfield, and see to the breaking of that bridge. If we are caught here by those murderous Dutch, your plans will be ended with a rope or a scaffold.

Sarsfield: I will send orders on to Clonmel. The Boyne will be forgotten! – forgotten! (*Goes out.*)

James: I hope Sarsfield knows what he is talking about.

Carter: H'm – he may.

James: If we are sure of winning—

Carter: Just so.

James: He says we are sure.

Carter: He does.

James: I hope there will be not much more fighting.

Carter: Or any.

James: That would be best; if they would give in without a fight.

Carter: Best indeed.

James: But if there is danger—

Carter: There is always danger.

James: Of another battle—

Carter: Or a surprise.

James: I would prefer to be elsewhere. It is all very well for those who have a taste for fighting. I had it once myself – when I was a boy. But it has gone from me now with the taste for green apples.

Carter: Not a doubt of it.

James: A King's life does not belong to himself.

Carter: He must not let it be taken.

James: He must not let it be risked.

Carter: That is what I meant.

James: Now if we had come to the sea—

Carter: We would be handy to it.

James: If there were a French ship—

Carter: And a fair wind.

James: We might – what is that?

(*Owen's voice heard singing 'The White Cockade'.*)

Carter: It is a friend – he is singing 'The White Cockade'.

Owen: (*Comes in singing*) –

> The heavy cloud is on the Gael,
> But comely James will bring content.

James: Where are you going, boy?

Owen: I am going looking for news of King James. (*Sits down and wipes his face.*)   I'm after wringing my shirt twice, with respects to you. I would not have walked so far for any one living but the King! And it is bad news of him I am after getting.

James: Then the defeat is known. What did you hear?

Owen: I heard a great clattering of horses, and then I heard a fife and drum – a tune they were playing like this. (*Whistles 'Lillibulero'.*)

James: The rebels are here! It is 'Lillibulero'!

Owen: Then I saw a troop of men and of horses.

James: Were they Dutch?

Owen: They were not. They were as good speakers as myself. Men from the north they were, and they were giving out as they passed that William had gained the day, and that King James was running, and if they got him, they would give his legs rest for a while.

James: Heavens! What a terrible threat!

Carter: Terrible, indeed! Is there no place where we could be safe?

Owen: If you belong to King James, you would be safe where I come from, and that is the inn at the harbour of Duncannon.

James: The harbour! Do many ships come in there?

Owen: There do not. But there is one in it presently.

James: An English ship?

Owen: It is not, but a ship from France. But if it is itself, it is not long it will be in it. It will be sailing at sunrise. There will be a boat coming from it after midnight, for the meat my mother has promised.

James: I must go to Duncannon! Look here, boy, would it be safe if I – if the King himself were to go there tonight?

Owen: Now that he is down, I think there is not one in the place but would carry a hurt dog if it belonged to King James.

James: But tell me – if – I only say *if* the King should come and should be seen by anyone – is there any chance he would be known?

Owen: Every chance. Sure, he is well known by the songs.

James: By the songs?

Owen: (*Singing*) –

> Curled locks like Angus of the Sidhe,
> Friendly, brave, bright, loving, fair;
> High hawk that gains the mastery,
> Cupid in peace, a Mars in war!

James: (*To Carter.*)   It will be safer not to go till after dark. We must go quietly – we must leave our men and horses at a distance.

Carter: That will be best.

James: You must keep the inn clear, boy. You must keep the French boat till I come – till the King comes. He will knock at the door before midnight.

Owen: Believe me he will get a good welcome! If it was known he was coming there would be a candle lighted in every harbour.

James: No, no candles.

Owen: I may as well be going now to make all ready.

   (*Goes out singing*) –

> Three times the fairest of the Scots,
> My prince and my heart-secret, James,
> Our treasure and our only choice –
> The darling Caesar of the Gael!

James: That was a good chance. We can go on board at once, and slip away to France. I have done with this detestable Ireland.

(*Kicks the ground.*)

Carter: And I. (*Kicks the ground.*)

James: It might be as well—

Carter: Well?

James: Not to mention anything—

Carter: I won't.

James: That is, nothing more than the sending of dispatches to – there he is coming.

(*Puts his finger to his lips. Carter nods. Sarsfield comes in.*)

Sarsfield: I have sent orders to Clonmel, sir. A thousand of our men will have gathered there to meet us at midnight.

James: I have changed my mind. I have had messages. I knew France would not desert me. There is a ship at Duncannon. I have dispatches to send to King Louis. I will go to Duncannon tonight, and not to Clonmel.

Sarsfield: We cannot afford that delay, sir. We should loose the chance of surprising the Dutch troop.

James: That is enough, General Sarsfield. You will obey orders.

Sarsfield: Are they, sir, what is best for Ireland?

James: Yes, yes, of course. She is a very good rod to beat England with.

Sarsfield: Whatever use you may put her to, sir, you are bound to do your best for her now.

James: Yes, yes, of course.

Sarsfield: The troops coming to us must not be left to scatter again. They believe yet in the King. They are sure he will not betray them again—

James: I am not betraying them. I am getting them help from France. You need say no more. When I think well of fighting I will fight; when I think well of retreating I will retreat.

(*He walks to the end of the stage and looks at himself in a hand-mirror.*)

Carter: Not a doubt of it! I hope General Sarsfield will loyally follow your Majesty's orders.

Sarsfield: Obey them? And what about Ireland – the lasting

cry ? Am I giving heed to the lasting cry of luckless Ireland ?
Am I listening to that ?

Carter: You have sworn to obey the King.

Sarsfield: Just so, just so, we have sworn. – He is our King –
we have taken the oath. Well, is not a feather in the hat as
good a cry as another ? A feather in a hat, a King in a song:

> The darling Caesar of the Gael,
> The great Cuchulain of the War!

(*Fife and drum heard playing 'Lillibulero'.*)

James: (*Rushing back.*) That is Lillibulero! Oh, the rebels
are coming!

Sarsfield: It is that troop we knew of. They are not many. We
have enough men to stand against them.

(*Music heard, right.*)

James: They are coming very close!

Carter: Here, sir, let us hide in the wood!   (*They run left.*)

James: They are coming this way!

(*They cross to the right. Music follows.*)

Carter: Is it an army or an echo ? (*They run left again.*)

James: (*Clinging to Sarsfield.*) It is all around us!

Sarsfield: (*Taking up cloak which James has dropped.*) I can
offer your Majesty's ears the protection of this cloak.

(*Holds out cloak over them, as music dies away.*)

Scene II

*Scene: Inn kitchen, much as before, but without the barrel;
night-time, candles burning. Owen standing as if just to come in.
Matt and Mrs Kelleher with back to audience listening to him.
Old Lady sitting, her head in her hands, rocking herself.*

Mrs Kelleher: The King beaten! Sure they said first he had
won. Well, the bottom comes out of every riddle at the last!

Matt: I had it in mind there was some great misfortune
coming upon us. I was trying to hearten myself through the
whole of the morning. I give you my word, now, I am as
sorry as if there was one dead belonging to me!

Owen: Did you hear me, Lady, what I was telling ?

Lady: (*Sitting up.*) If it was true, it was a dark story, a dark sorrowful story!

(*She gets up and looks out of door into the darkness.*)

Owen: King James is beaten surely.

Lady: The King beaten, and the moon in the skies not darkened!

Owen: Beaten and wandering.

Lady: The King beaten and the fish not dead in the rivers!

Owen: Beaten and wandering and hunted.

(*Matt Kelleher gives a groan at the end of each sentence.*)

Lady: The King beaten and the leaves on the trees not withered! (*She turns from the door.*) The sun is a liar that rose in the east for victory. What was the sun doing that day? Where was God? Where was Sarsfield?

(*She walks up and down, wringing her hands.*)

Mrs Kelleher: It is what I was often saying, there is nought in this world but a mist.

Lady: Where were the people that were wise and learned? Where were the troop readying their spears? Where are they till they smooth out this knot for me? (*Takes Owen by the shoulders.*) Why did not the hills fall upon the traitors? Why did not the rivers rise against them?

Mrs Kelleher: Sit down now, Lady, for a while. It's no wonder you be fretting, and your lands and your means gone like froth on the stream. Sure the law of borrowing, is the loan to be broken.

Lady: I will not sit under a roof and my King under clouds. It is not the keening of one plain I hear, but of every plain. The sea and the waves crying through the harbour! The people without a lord but the God of glory! Where is he? Where is my royal Stuart? I will go out crying after the King! (*She goes out.*)

Mrs Kelleher: But is it surely true, Owen, that the King is coming to this house?

Owen: Sure and certain sure.

Mrs Kelleher: If we had but known, to have killed a sheep or a kid itself! I declare I would think more of him now than when he had all at his command.

Owen: It is likely, indeed, he found no good table in the wood.

Mrs Kelleher: The man without dinner is two to supper. Well, the cakes are baked, and eggs we have in plenty, and pork if we had but the time to boil it, and a bit of corned beef. Indeed if I had twenty times as much, I wouldn't begrudge it to the King.

Matt: (*Looking at bottles.*)   There is good wine for him anyway. The Frenchmen knew the best corner.

Mrs Kelleher: Mind yourself, now.

Matt: (*Indignantly.*)   Do you think I would take so much as one drop from what I have put on one side for the rightful King?

Mrs Kelleher: Give me a hand to get down the best delft. It's well I had the barrels packed out of the way. It's getting on for midnight. He might be here any time.

(*Trampling of horses heard, and fife and drum playing 'Lillibulero'.*)

Matt: What is that? Is it the King that is coming?

Owen: It is not; but King William's men that are looking for the King.

Mrs Kelleher: Keep them out of this! Foxes in the hencoop!

Owen: It is here they are coming, sure enough.

(*Music comes nearer. Mrs Kelleher hurriedly puts food in cupboard and flings a sack over bottles. Door is opened; two men of William's army come in. They have fife and drum.*)

First Williamite: That is good! I smell supper.

Second Williamite: We are lucky to find an inn so handy.

First Williamite: I knew where the inn was. I told the Newry troop to come meet us here.   (*Turns to door.*)   Here, you lads, go and spread yourselves here and there through the town: don't go far; I will fire two shots when you are wanted. (*Voices outside.*)   'All right.' 'We'll do that, sir.'

Second Williamite: I don't think King James is in these parts at all.

First Williamite: There is a French ship in the harbour. He might be making for her.

Second Williamite: We will stop here anyway. We have a good view of the pier in the moonlight.

Mrs Kelleher: I am loath to disoblige you, gentlemen, but you can't stop here tonight.

First Williamite: Why do you say that? Inns were made to stop in.

Mrs Kelleher: This is not an inn now – not what you would rightly call an inn – we gave up business of late – we were stumbling under the weight of it, like two mice under a stack.

First Williamite: I wouldn't think so small a place would be so great a burden.

Mrs Kelleher: A hen itself is heavy if you carry it far. It's best to give up in time. A good run is better than a bad battle. We got no comfort for ourselves – who is nearest the church is not nearest the altar.

First Williamite: Quiet this woman, some of you. Where is the man of the house? The hen doesn't crow when there's a cock in the yard – you see, ma'am, I have proverbs myself.

Mrs Kelleher: (*To Matt.*) We must keep them out of the way. (*To Williamites.*) There are no beds for you to get. The beds are damp. Aren't they, Matt?

Matt: Damp, indeed – rotten with damp.

Owen: Damp and soaked with the drip from the roof.

First Williamite: Beds! Are we asking for beds? It is not often we feel a blanket over us, thanks to King James. These chairs will do us well.

Mrs Kelleher: You don't know what lay on those chairs last night!

First Williamite: What was that?

Mrs Kelleher: A corpse – wasn't it, Matt?

Matt: It was – a dead corpse.

Owen: Cold and dead.

First Williamite: (*Contemptuously.*) Corpses! I was own brother to a corpse in the last scrimmage. A knock I got on the head. Sit down.

Mrs Kelleher: It is likely you don't know what sickness did this one die of. Of smallpox – didn't it, Matt?

Matt: It did. Of a pitted smallpox.

Owen: And it left lying there without a coffin.

First Williamite: It would be worse news if it had got a wake that had left the house bare.

Mrs Kelleher: Bare! This is the house that is bare!   I have a bad husband, haven't I, Matt?

Matt: What's that you are saying?

Mrs Kelleher: A while drunk, a while in fury, tearing the strings and going mad!   (*Giving him a nudge.*)   And a son that is a gambler.   (*Owen starts, but she nudges him.*)   Two hands scattering, and but one saving. They spent all we had. There is nothing for you to find in the house, I tell you. It's hard to start a hare out of an empty bush!

Second Williamite: (*Taking sack off bottles.*)   Here is something that looks better than holy water.
(*Takes up bottle and uncorks it.*)

First Williamite: (*Opening cupboard.*)   I see the scut of a hare in this bush!   (*Takes out meat.*)

Second Williamite: (*Drinking.*)   Faith you have a strong cellar.   (*Hands on bottle and opens another.*)   Here, innkeeper, have a glass of your own still – drink now to the King.

Matt: I will not. I will not touch one drop from those bottles that are for—

Second Williamite: Drink, man; drink till you are in better humour.

Matt: (*Taking glass.*)   Well, if I do, I call for all to witness that I was forced to it! Four against one, and forced! (*Drinks and holds glass out again.*)   And anyway, if I do (*drinks*)   it's not to your master I am drinking but to King James!

First Williamite: Little I care! I'd drink to any of them myself, if I had no other way to get it. Dutch or Scotch, there's no great difference. If we had a King of our own, that would be another story.

Second Williamite: You have taken your job under William.

First Williamite: And amn't I doing the job, drinking the wine of a Jacobite? To fight for William by day, and to drink King James's wine by night, isn't that doing double service?

Owen: (*To Mrs Kelleher.*)   I will go and turn back those that were coming.

Mrs Kelleher: Do, and God be with you. (*He goes to the door.*)

First Williamite: Stop here youngster, and drink to the King.

Owen: I will not.

First Williamite: Well, stop and drink against the King.

Owen: I must go. (*Puts hand on latch.*)

First Williamite: (*Holding him.*) You have nothing to do that is so easy as this.

Owen: I have colts that are astray to put back on the right road.

First Williamite: A fine lad like you to be running after colts, and King William wanting soldiers! Come, join our troop and we'll make a corporal of you.

Owen: Leave me alone. I have my own business to mind.

Second Williamite: The drill would take that stoop out of your shoulders.

First Williamite: It would, and straighten his back. Wait I drill you! I'll give you your first lesson. I'll have you as straight as a thistle before morning. See here now: left, right; left, right; right about face. (*He holds him while the other swings him round.*)

Second Williamite: Give him the balance-step first. Now, youngster, balance step without gaining ground. (*Crooks up Owen's leg.*) See now, this way; stand straight or you will fall over like a sack of potatoes. I should get promotion now; I am training recruits for King William.

Matt: (*Who is by the window.*) Let him go, let him go. There are some persons coming. I hear them. Who now would be coming here so late as midnight?

Second Williamite: Are these our men?

First Williamite: They are not, our men will be riding.

Owen: (*Passionately.*) Let me go.

Second Williamite: You are not through your drill yet. Here now— (*A knocking at the door.*)

Matt: Customers, maybe. Wait till I open the door.

Owen: (*To Mrs Kelleher.*) Don't let him open it!

Mrs Kelleher: (*Seizing him.*) Leave opening the door, Matt Kelleher!

Matt: Let me alone! I will open it. It's my business to open the door. (*He breaks from her.*)

Mrs Kelleher: Stop, I tell you! What are you doing?

(*Whispers.*)   Don't you know that it might be King James.

Matt: King James! The King outside in the night and we not opening the door! Leave the doorway clear! A welcome, a great welcome to King James!

(*Williamites start up and seize muskets. Kelleher flings the door open. James comes in, followed by Carter and Sarsfield.*)

Owen: (*Shouting.*)   Are you come, strangers, to join King William's men?

First Williamite: They are wearing the white cockade!

Second Williamite: They belong to James, sure enough.

Matt: (*Seizing James's hand.*)   My thousand welcomes to you! And tell me, now, which of you is King James?

James: (*Going back a step.*)   This is a trap!

Carter: Not a doubt of it!

First Williamite: Fire, fire quick! Bring back our troop!

(*They raise their muskets. Sarsfield rushes past James, seizes the muskets which they are raising so that they are pointed at his own body.*)

Sarsfield: Fire! Yes, here I am! Call back your comrades to bury the King!

Matt: Shame! Shame! Would you kill the King?

First Williamite: We have orders to take him, alive or dead.

Sarsfield: Back, back, put down your muskets! Damn you! Are these Dutch manners?

First Williamite: You are our prisoner. We must call our troop.

Sarsfield: (*Pushing them back angrily.*)   Dutch manners! I swear I will not go to prison on an empty stomach! Supper, host, supper! Is a man to be sent empty to his death, even if he be a King?

First Williamite: We have orders. We are King William's men.

Sarsfield: Whoever you are, I will sup here tonight. Hurry host, hurry. What have you there? Here is a follower of mine who is always hungry. (*Pointing to Carter.*) What have you here? Beef – good – and bread.

(*Williamites go and stand at door with muskets ready.*)

Matt: (*Bewildered.*)   I have, indeed – that is, I had. I had all ready. These traitors came – it failed me to get them out.

Mrs Kelleher: Leave talking. You have done enough harm for this night. With your wine muddled wits you have brought your King to his death. (*She puts plates on table.*)

Sarsfield: (*To Carter.*) Give me a chair. Here (*To James.*) are my gloves. (*He sits down.*) You may sit there. (*They sit down, James keeping his face in shadow, and muffled in cloak. They begin eating. To Carter.*) You, I know, are ready for your supper.

Carter: Not a doubt of it! (*He eats greedily.*)

Matt: (*Falling on his knees.*) O forgive me, forgive! To betray my King! Oh! oh! oh! It's the drink that did it.

Sarsfield: That will do. I forgive, I forgive.

Matt: Take my life! O take my life! I have brought destruction on my King!

Sarsfield: Get up, old fool. Here, ma'am, those bottles.

Matt: (*Getting up.*) I wish I had died of thirst before I had touched a drop, so I do. The curse of drowning be upon drink, I say!

Sarsfield: (*To First Williamite.*) I am in better humour now. War and hunger make rough manners. Were you in the battle? If so, you are brave men.

First Williamite: We were not in that battle. We were at the Lagan.

Sarsfield: There were good fighters there, too. I am sorry they were not on our side. I am sorry all the men of Ireland are not on the one side.

First Williamite: It is best to be on the winning side.

Sarsfield: The winning side – which is it? We think we know, but heaven and hell know better. Ups and downs. Winning and losing are in the course of nature, and there's no use in crying.

First Williamite: Some one must be the winner.

Sarsfield: Ups and downs, ups and downs; and we know nothing till all is over. He is surely the winner who gets a great tombstone, a figured monument, cherubs blowing trumpets, angels' tears in marble -- or maybe he is the winner who has none of these, who but writes his name in the book of the people. I would like my name set in clean letters in the book of the people.

Mrs Kelleher: (*To James.*)   Take another bit of beef, sir; you
are using nothing at all. You might have hungry days yet.
Make hay while the sun shines. It isn't every day that Paddy
kills a deer!

James: (*In a muffled voice.*)   I have eaten enough.

Mrs Kelleher: It is well you came before these Northerners
had all swept. It's a rogue of a cat would find anything after
them.

James: (*Impatiently.*)   I have had quite enough.

Mrs Kelleher: Look now, don't be down hearted. Sure you
must be sorry for the King being in danger; but things might
change. It is they themselves might be dancing the back step
yet. There's more music than the pipes. The darkest hour
is before the dawn. Every spring morning has a black head.
It's a good horse that never stumbles. The help of God is
nearer than the door.

James: Let me be. That is enough.

Mrs Kelleher: (*Turning away.*)   I knew he hadn't enough ate.
It's the hungry man does be fierce.

Sarsfield: (*To the First Williamite.*)   I am sorry not to be
able to ask you, fellow-soldier, to sit down with us. But I
know you would sooner let the bones show through your coat
than lower that musket that is pointing at me.

First Williamite: I hope you won't take it unkindly, your
Majesty. But I am obeying orders.

Sarsfield: You are right; you are very right in not sitting
down. Suppose now you were sitting here, and the door
unguarded, and the King should make his escape—

First Williamite: Your Majesty would not get very far – we
have other men.

Sarsfield: Who knows? There are ups and downs. A King is
not as a common man – the moon has risen – there are horses
not far off – he might gallop through the night.

First Williamite: He would be overtaken.

Sarsfield: He might gallop – and gallop – and a few friends
would know the sound and would join him here and there.
He might go on very fast, away from the harbour, past the
wood, his own men gathering to him as he passed – to
Clonmel—

Second Williamite: Clonmel is full of King James's men, sure enough.

Sarsfield: And then, with all that gather to him there, he would go quietly, very quietly, very quickly to the Gap of the Oaks—

Second Williamite: Listen. That is where the convoy stops tonight.

Sarsfield: A little camp – four hundred horses well saddled, two hundred wagons with powder enough to blow up the Rock of Cashel – and in the middle of all, the yolk of the egg – the kernel of the nut – the pip of the orange.

Second Williamite: He knows that too. He knows that King William is making that secret march.

Sarsfield: A shout – the King!   Sarsfield – Ireland! – before there is time to pull a trigger, we have carried off the prize – we have him to treat with *inside* the walls of Limerick. We send the Dutchman back to his country. Will you go with him to the mud-banks, comrades, or will you stop in Ireland with your own King?

First Williamite: The King will win yet. I would never believe that he gave the word to run from Boyne.

Sarsfield: Now, if I were the King—

Matt: Sure you are King yet, for all I did to destroy you, God forgive me!

Sarsfield: That is true – yes, yes. I am a King tonight, even though I may not be one tomorrow.

Owen: (*Who has been listening eagerly.*)   It must be a wonderful thing to be a King!

Sarsfield: Wonderful, indeed – if he have the heart of a King – to be the son and grandson and great-grandson of Kings, the chosen and anointed of God. To have that royal blood coming from far off, from some source so high that, like the water of his palace fountain, it keeps breaking, ever breaking away from the common earth, starting up as if to reach the skies. How else would those who are not noble know when they meet it what is royal blood?

First Williamite: I would know in any place that this King has royal blood.

Second Williamite: It is easy to see among these three which of them is King.

Sarsfield: (*Looking at James.*)   A wonderful thing!   If he have the high power of a King, or if he take the counsel that should be taken by a King. To be a King is to be a lover – a good lover of a beautiful sweetheart.

First Williamite: I suppose he means the country, saying that.

Second Williamite: I am sure he must have a heart for Ireland.

Sarsfield: He goes out so joyous, so high of heart, because it is never possible for him to do any deed for himself alone, but for her as well that is his dear lady. She is in his hands; he keeps them clean for her; it is for her he holds his head high; it is for her he shows courtesy to all, because he would not have rude voices raised about her.

Second Williamite: The Dutchman would not have those thoughts for Ireland.

Mrs Kelleher: It's not from the wind he got it. Mouth of ivy and heart of holly. That is what you would look for in a King.

Sarsfield: If she is in trouble or under sorrow, this sweetheart who trusts him, that trouble, God forgive him, brings him a sort of joy! To go out, to call his men, to give out shouts because the time has come to show what her strong lover can do for her – to go hungry that she may be fed; to go tired that her dear feet may tread safely; to die, it may be, at the last for her with such glory that the name he leaves with her is better than any living love, because he has been faithful, faithful, faithful!

First Williamite: (*Putting down musket.*)   I give up the Dutchman's pay. This man is the best.

Second Williamite: He is the best. It is as good to join him.

Owen: I will follow him by every hard road and every rough road through the whole world.

Matt: I will never drink another drop till he has come to his rights! I would sooner shrivel up like a bunch of seaweed!

Mrs Kelleher: It is what I was often saying, the desire of every heart is the rightful King.

First Williamite: We will follow you! We will send our comrades away when they come, or we will turn them to you!

Second Williamite: We will fight for you five times better than we ever fought for the Dutchman. We will not let so much as a scratch on one belonging to you – even that lean-jawed little priest at the end of the table. (*Points at James.*)

Sarsfield: (*Rising.*) That is right. I knew you were good Irishmen. Now, we must set out for Clonmel.

James: No, no; we cannot go. We must wait for the men from the French ship.

Sarsfield: Write your orders to them. Tell them to come round, and bring us help at Limerick.

James: It would be best to see them.

Sarsfield: No time to lose! This good woman will give the letter safely.

(*Carter reluctantly gets out pen and paper. James begins to write. The door opens and the old Lady appears.*)

Owen: It is the poor Lady.

Matt: (*To Sarsfield.*) The poor Lady Dereen, your Majesty, that lost all for the Stuarts.

Owen: Come in, Lady, come; the King himself is here, King James.

Lady: The King! And safe! Then God has heard our prayers!

Owen: Come now, Lady; tell your story to the King.

Lady: I lost all for Charles. I will get all back from James. Charles was great; James will be greater! See here I have the King's own seal.

Sarsfield: That is the seal indeed. The King will honour it when he comes to his own.

Lady: No more beggary; no more wandering. My white halls again; my kinsmen and my friends!

Sarsfield: (*To James.*) Have we any token to give this poor distracted lady?

James: Give her a promise. We have nothing else to part with.

Sarsfield: (*Taking off his ring.*) Here, Lady; here is a ring. Take this in pledge that the King will pay you what he owes.

Lady: (*Taking it.*) Is it the sunrise? See how it shines! I knew the lucky sun would rise at last. I watched in the east for it every morning.

(*She childishly plays with the ring.*)

Matt: Wouldn't you thank the King now, Lady, for what he is after giving you?

Lady: I had forgotten. I forgot I was in the Court! I was dreaming, dreaming of hard, long roads and little houses – little dark houses. I forgot I was at Whitehall. I have not been to Whitehall for a long time to kiss the King's hand. (*She gives her stick to Owen, and stands very tall and straight.*) I know the Court well. I remember well what to do. A curtsy to the right to the Queen (*curtsies*); a curtsy to the left to the princesses (*curtsies*). Now I kneel to kiss the King's hand. (*She sweeps her dress back as if it were a train and kneels. Sarsfield gives her his hand; she puts her lips to it. She gets up uncertain and tottering, and cries out*) – You have befooled me! That is not the King's hand; that is no Stuart hand; that is a lucky hand – a strong, lucky hand!

Sarsfield: You have forgotten, Lady. It was a long time ago.

Lady: That is no Stuart voice! (*Peers at him.*) That is no Stuart face! Who was it said the King is here? (*She looks into Carter's face.*) That is no King's face. (*Takes his hand.*) That is no royal hand. (*Going to James.*) Let me look at your face. (*He turns away.*) Let me look at your hand.

James: Do not touch me! Am I to be pestered by every beggar that comes in?

Lady: (*In a shriek.*) That is the voice! That is the voice! (*Seizes his hand.*) That is the hand! I know it – the smooth, white, unlucky Stuart hand!

(*James starts up angrily. Williamites have gone to listen at the door. 'Lillibulero' is heard sung outside*) –

> Dey all in France have taken a swear,
>   Lillibulero bullen a la!
> Dat dey will have no Protestant heir:
>   Lillibulero bullen a la!
> Lero, lero, lero, lillibulero bullen a la!
>
> Though by my shoul de English do prate,
>   Lillibulero bullen a la!
> De Laws on dere side, and Christ knows what:
>   Lillibulero bullen a la!
> Lero, lero, lero, lillibulero bullen a la!

First Williamite: It is the Newry troop!

Owen: (*Bolting door and putting his back to it.*) They must not see the King!

Second Williamite: It is too late to escape. We will fight for you.

Matt: (*Going to door and putting his back to it.*) Believe me I won't let them in this time.

Sarsfield: (*Drawing sword and going before James.*) We will cut our way through them.

Mrs Kelleher: (*Pushing back dresser and opening door.*) It's a poor mouse that wouldn't have two doors to its hole! (*She pushes James and Carter in. Sarsfield stands at it.*) Go in now. When all is quiet, you can get through to the pier.

Voice of Williamite Captain outside: (*With a bang at door.*) Open! I say!

Matt: (*Rattling at door while he keeps it fast.*) Sure, I'm doing my best to open it – if I could but meet with the latch.

Voice: Open, open!

Matt: I have an unsteady hand. I am after taking a little drop of cordial— (*Another bang at door.*)

Owen: I'll quench the light!

(*Blows out candles. Sarsfield has followed James. Mrs Kelleher is pushing dresser back to its place. The door is burst open.*)

Captain: Who is here?

Matt: Not a one in the world, Captain, but myself and herself, and the son I have, and a few men of King William's army.

First Williamite: We are here, sir, according to orders.

Captain: Strike a light! (*Williamite strikes it and lights candle.*) What is going on here?

First Williamite: We are watching the pier, sir.

Captain: Why are the lights out?

Matt: It was I myself, sir – I will confess all. It was not purposely I did it. I have an unsteady hand; it was to snuff them I was striving.

Captain: Have you any news of King James?

First Williamite: Great news!

Captain: What is that?

First Williamite: He was seen to the east – up in the wood.

Captain: We must follow him at once.

First Williamite: It is said he is going north – on the road to –
Wexford!

CURTAIN

ACT III

Scene: The pier at Duncannon the same night. James and Carter talking together.

James: Upon my word, I am as glad to escape from that dark cellar as I was to get into it an hour ago.

Carter: I wonder how long Sarsfield will be away gathering his men.

James: It should take him a little time; but one never knows with him when he may appear. He makes me start up. He has no feeling for repose, for things at their proper time, for the delicate, leisurely life. He frets and goads me. He harries and hustles. I hear him now! (*Starts.*)

Carter: It is only the French sailors taking away another barrel of their meat from the cellar.
(*French sailors enter from left, singing as before. They roll a barrel away to the right.*)

James: The long and the short of it is, it will not be my fault if I spend another night in this abominable island.

Carter: That is good news indeed.

James: The only difficulty is how to get away.

Carter: Why, your Majesty has but to get into the ship.

James: Ah, if I could once get into it! But the question is how am I to escape – from Sarsfield? Of course, he is under my orders. I made him obey orders when we left the Boyne. But since then there is something about him – some danger in his eye, or in the toss of his head. Of course, I am in no way afraid of him.

Carter: Of course not, indeed.

James: But for all that, when he begins drawing maps with a flourish of his sword (*Mimics Sarsfield.*) or talking as if he were giving out the Holy Scriptures, there is something – a something – that takes away my strength, that leaves me bustled, marrowless, uncertain.

Carter: Not a doubt of it.

161

James: I am resolved I will strike a blow for myself. I will take my own way. I will be King again. I will be my own master! I am determined that here, this moment before he has time to come back, before I cool, before my blood goes down, I will make these sailors take me into their boat and row me out to the ship.

Carter: Well said, indeed.

James: When Sarsfield comes back to this pier, if he wants to preach to me again, he will have to swim for it!

Carter: Ha, ha, very good! (*Enter sailors from right.*)

James: (*To sailors.*)   Here, my men. I must go to the ship at once. You must take me in your boat.

First Sailor: Boat not ready yet, sir. More meat, more pork, more sau-sa-ges.

James: I must go at once. Here, I will give you money if you will take me at once.

Sailor: Give it now, sir, and I will take you   (*James gives it*) – after one more barrel.

James: At once!

Sailor: At once, sir. Only *one* more barrel. I will not be two or three minutes. You go, sir, wait in the boat. We will follow you very quick.   (*They go left.*)

James: Come to the boat at once, Carter. We shall be safe there. Oh, once at sea I shall be King again!

Carter: Not a doubt of it!

James: Come, come, no time to lose!

(*They turn right. Music is heard from right, 'Lillibulero' suddenly turning into 'White Cockade'. The two Williamites appear playing fife and drum, Owen with them.*)

First Williamite: That is right! We are changing the tune well now. We had to keep up the old one so long as our Newry comrades were within hearing. That they may have a quick journey to Wexford! Now for the white cockade!

(*Owen gives them each one, and they put them in their hats.*)

Owen: You did well, getting leave to come back and to watch the pier.

Second Williamite: So we will watch it well.

James: Let me pass, if you please.

First Williamite: Where are you going, my little priest?

James: I am going on my own business. Let me pass.

First Williamite: I don't know about that. I have orders to watch the pier. Double orders. Orders from King William to let no one leave it, and orders to let no one come near it, from King James.

James: I tell you I am going on King James's business.

First Williamite: He will be here in a minute. He is gathering men and horses below to the west of the town. Wait till he comes.

James: No, no, I cannot wait. (*Tries to get through.*)

First Williamite: You will have to wait. No hurry! The Mass can't begin without you!

James: I can make you let me go with one word.

Second Williamite: (*Catching hold of him.*) Faith, I can hold you without any word at all.

James: (*Wrenching himself free.*) Back, fool, back. I am the King!

Both the Williamites: Ha, ha, ha! Ho, ho, ho!

Second Williamite: O the liar!

Carter: You must believe his Majesty.

First Williamite: I do, as much as I believe you yourself to be *Patrick Sarsfield.*

Owen: *That* Patrick Sarsfield!

Carter: How dare you doubt that this is the King?

First Williamite: I don't. I have no doubt at all upon the matter. I wouldn't believe it from Moses on the mountain.

James: You common people cannot recognize high blood. I say I am the King. You would know it quickly enough if you could see me in my right place!

First Williamite: We might. Your reverence would look well upon the throne. Here, boys, make a throne for His Majesty. (*They cross hands and put him up as if on a throne.*) Hur-rah! This is the third King we have shouted for within the last six hours!

James: Let me down, I say!

First Williamite: Throw out gold and silver to the crowd! Every King throws out gold and silver when he comes to the throne!

Second Williamite: Give us your fee! Give us an estate! I would like mine in the County Meath.

First Williamite: Can you touch for the evil? Here is a boy that has the evil! We'll know you are King if you can cure the evil!

All: Ha, ha, ha! Ho, ho, ho!

James: Let me down, traitors!   (*A sound of keening heard.*)

Owen: Here is the poor Lady.

(*She comes in keening. They put down the King.*)

James: Here is a witness for me. She knew me last night.

Carter: She knew the true King's hand.

James: Lady Dereen, you knew me last night. Tell these fools what they will not believe from me, that I am the King?

(*He holds out his hand; she takes it, looks vacantly at it, drops it, and is silent for a minute.*)

Lady: (*Crying out.*)   The King! There is no King! The King is dead; he died in the night! Did you not hear me keening him? My lord is dead, and my kinsmen are dead, and my heart is dead; and now my King is dead! He gave his father a bad burying; we will give him a good burying – deep, deep, deep. Dig under the rivers, put the mountains over him; he will never rise again. He is dead, he is dead!   (*She sits down rocking herself and sings.*)

> Ochone, ochone, my pleasant Stuart;
> Ochone, heart-secret of the Gael!

(*Sarsfield comes in hurriedly, motions them all back. Speaks to James.*)

Sarsfield: All is well, sir. Our men are coming in fast. There are two hundred of them to the west of the harbour. We are late for the surprise – that chance is gone; but we can bring good help to hearten Limerick. The King's presence will bring out the white cockade like rush-cotton over the bogs.

James: Yes, yes; very good, very good.

Sarsfield: Are you ready, sir?

James: Oh, yes, ready, very ready – to leave this place.

Sarsfield: This way, sir, this way!

James: I know the way; but I have left my papers – papers of importance – in that cellar. I must go back and get them.

Sarsfield: Now William's troop has left, I will have the horses brought to the very edge of the pier – all is safe now.

James: Yes, yes, I am sure there is no danger. Yes, go for the horses; take care they are well saddled.

(*He goes out left; Sarsfield right. Matt and Mrs Kelleher come on from the left.*)

Mrs Kelleher: And is it true, Owen, my son, that you are going following after the King?

Owen: It is true, surely.

Mrs Kelleher: You that would never stir from the hearth to be taking to such hardship! Well, I wouldn't like to be begrudging you to the King's service. What goes out at the ebb comes in on the flood. It might be for profit.

Matt: Here is the belt your grandfather owned, and he fighting at Ross; pistols there are in it. Do your best now for the King. I'll drink – no, I swore I would never drink another drop till such time—

Mrs Kelleher: There is my own good cloak for you – there is something in the pocket you will find no load. (*Owen puts on cloak and belt.*) And here's cakes for the journey – faith, you'll be as proud now as a cat with a straddle!

Owen: You will hear no story of me but a story you would like to be listening to. Believe me, I will fight well for the King.

(*Sailors come from left, rolling a very large barrel; they are singing their song. Carter is walking after it.*)

Matt: Stop there! What is that barrel you are bringing away?

Sailor: It is one bacon-barrel.

Matt: It is not. It is one of my big wine barrels.

Sailor: Oh, ah! I assure you there is meat in it.

Matt: (*Putting his hand on it.*) Do you think I would not know the size of one of my own barrels if I met with it rolling through the stars? That is a barrel that came from France, and it is full of wine.

Carter: (*To sailors.*) Go on with the barrel.

Matt: I will not let it go! Why would I let my good wine go out of the country, even if I can have no more than the smell of it myself? Bring it back to the cellar, I say, and go get your meat.

Carter: It must be taken to the ship. It is the King's wish.

Matt: The King's wish? If that is so – where is the King, till I ask him? (*Looks around.*)

Carter: I tell you it must go. I will pay you for it – here is the money. What is it worth?

Matt: Well, if you pay fair, I have nothing to say. If it was to the King himself it was going, I would take nothing at all. He would be welcome.

Carter: (*Giving money.*) Here, here. (*To sailors.*)   Go on, now; hurry! Be careful!

First Williamite: It is a pity now, to see good wine leaving the country, and a great drouth on the King's good soldiers.

Second Williamite: He should not begrudge us a glass, indeed. It will strengthen us for all we will have to do at Limerick. (*Puts his hand on barrel.*)

Carter: This belongs to me! This is my property. If you commit robbery, you must account to the King!

Matt: Look here, I have still whisky in a jar. I brought it out to give you a drop to put courage into you before you would go. That is what will serve you as well.

First Williamite: We will let the barrel go, so.

Second Williamite: We could bring away the jar with us. I would sooner have wine now to drink the King's health.

Lady: (*Standing up, suddenly, and coming in front of the barrel.*)   Wine, wine, red wine! Do you grudge it for the King's wake? White candles shining in the skies, red wine for the King's pall-bearers!
(*She lifts up her hands.*)

First Williamite: She is right, she is right. (*To Matt.*)   Since you yourself turned sober, you are begrudging wine for the King!   Here!
(*Tilts up barrel. A muffled groan is heard from inside.*)

Second Williamite: That is a queer sort of a gurgling the French wine has – there is ferment in it yet. Give me an awl till I make a hole. (*Another stifled groan.*)

Carter: Oh, oh, oh, oh!
(*Puts his cloak over his ears, and retires to back.*)

First Williamite: (*Taking out bayonet.*)   Here, let me at it!
(*Knocks head off barrel; Carter giving short groans at every stroke.*)

Carter: Oh! be gentle.

First Williamite: Never fear. I have no mind to spill it.
(*Takes off top.*)
(*The King stands up pale and shaking. His cloak has fallen off and chain and order are displayed.*)

First Williamite: It is the little priest!

Second Williamite: Is he King yet? Or fairy?

Matt: (*Looking in.*) Would anyone, now, believe that he has drunk the barrel dry!

First Williamite: I wish I had been in his place.

Mrs Kelleher: It is trying to desert he was. That's as clear as a whistle.

Owen: The traitor! Wanting to desert the King!

Matt: But will anyone tell me now, what in the wide world did he do with all the wine?

Lady: Is not that a very strange coffin, a very strange coffin to have to put about a King?

Mrs Kelleher: Here is King James!
(*They all turn to right. Sarsfield comes in. He stands still.*)

Owen: Deserting your Majesty, he was!

Matt: Making away in my barrel!

First Williamite: Having drunk all the wine!

Mrs Kelleher: Let a goat cross the threshold, and he'll make for the altar!

Sarsfield: (*Taking off his hat,*) Your Majesty!

James: I wish, General Sarsfield, you would control this dangerous rabble.

All: Sarsfield!

Mrs Kelleher: Who are you at all?

Sarsfield: I am Patrick Sarsfield, a poor soldier of King James.

Mrs Kelleher: And where, in the name of mercy, is King James?

Sarsfield: You are in His Majesty's presence.
(*He goes to help James out of the barrel.*)

All together: *That* His Majesty!

Mrs Kelleher: It seems to me we have a wisp in place of a broom.

Owen: Misfortune on the fools that helped him!

First Williamite: Is it for him we gave up William?

Matt: And that I myself gave up drink!

Sarsfield: (*Who has helped the King out of the barrel, takes him by the hand.*)   Any roughness that was done to the King was done, I am sure, unknowingly. But now, if there are any little whisperings, and hidden twitterings, as to what his Majesty has thought fit to do, it is I myself who will give a large answer! (*He unsheaths sword.*)

James: I have business in France. You may stay here, General Sarsfield, if you will. But I will lead you no longer; I will fight no more for these cowardly Irish. You must shift for yourselves; I will shift for myself.

Carter: Not a doubt of it!

James: (*Going off, stops and turns.*)   When I come back as a conqueror, with my armies and my judges, there are some I may pardon – my servants who deserted me, my daughters who turned against me. But there are some I will never forgive, some I will remember now and ever, now and forever – those of you who stopped the barrel, those who tilted it up, and those who opened it!

(*He goes out right followed by Sarsfield and sailors. Owen, throwing off cloak and belt, and tearing cockade from his hat, throws himself down and begins to play jackstones as in First Act.*)

Lady: (*Turning to face the other way.*)   Where is the sun? I am tired of looking for it in the east. The sun is tired of rising in the east; it may be in the west it will rise tomorrow!

Mrs Kelleher: Gone is he? My joy be with him, and glass legs under him! Well, an empty house is better than a bad tenant. It might be for profit.

Matt: (*Taking up jar.*)   Well, I am free from my pledge, as the King says, now and ever, now and forever! (*Drinks from jar.*)   No more pledges! It's as well to be free. (*He sits down beside Owen.*)

First Williamite: Which King are we best with; the one we left or the one that left us?

Second Williamite: Little I care. Toss for it. (*Tosses a penny.*)   Heads, William; harps, James!

First Williamite: (*Picking it up.*)   Heads it is. (*Taking cockade from his hat.*) There's good-bye to the white cockade.

(*He and others throw cockades on the ground, and walk off.*)

Mrs Kelleher: (*To Owen.*) And what will you be doing, Owen? You will hardly go fighting now.

Owen: What business would I have fighting? I have done with kings and makings of kings. (*Throws up jackstones and catches all.*) Good, that's buttermilk!

Mrs Kelleher: You are right; you are right. It's bad changing horses in the middle of a ford. (*She takes back her cloak.*) Is all safe in the pocket? It's long before I'll part with it again – once bit, twice shy. It might all be for profit.

(*Sarsfield comes back. Stands still a minute, holding hat in his hand. Lets sword drop on the ground.*)

Sarsfield: Gone, gone; he is gone – he betrayed me – he called me from the battle – he lost me my great name – he betrayed Ireland. Who is he? What is he? A King or what? (*He pulls feathers one by one from cockade.*) King or knave – soldier – sailor – tinker – tailor – beggarman – thief. He has stolen away; he has stolen our good name; he has stolen our faith; he has stolen the pin that held loyalty to royalty! A thief, a fox – a fox of trickery! (*He sits down trembling.*)

Mrs Kelleher: (*Coming to him.*) So you have thrown away the white cockade, Sarsfield, the same as Owen.

Sarsfield: (*Bewildered.*) The same as Owen?

Mrs Kelleher: Owen threw away the King's cockade the same as yourself.

Sarsfield: Threw it away! What have I thrown away? Have I thrown away the white cockade?

Mrs Kelleher: You did, and scattered it.

(*Sarsfield lifts his hat and looks at it.*)

Mrs Kelleher: If you want another, they are here on the ground as plenty as blackberries in harvest.

(*Takes up a cockade.*)

Sarsfield: Give it here to me. (*He begins putting it in his hat, his hand still trembling.*)

Matt: You will go no more fighting for King James! You are free of your pledge! We are all free of our pledge!

Sarsfield: Where is my sword?

(*Mrs Kelleher gives it. He puts it in sheath.*)

Mrs Kelleher: Look, now, the skin is nearer than the shirt. One bit of a rabbit is worth two of a cat. It's no use to go looking for wool on a goat. It's best for you fight from this out for your own hand and for Ireland. Why would you go spending yourself for the like of *that* of a King?

Sarsfield: (*Buckling on his sword-belt.*)   Why, why? Who can say? What is holding me? Habit, custom. What is it the priests say? The cloud of witnesses. Maybe the call of some old angry father of mine, that fought two thousand years ago for a bad master! (*He stands up.*) Well, good-bye, good-bye. (*To Mrs Kelleher, who is holding out cakes.*)   Yes, I will take these cakes. (*Takes them.*)   It is likely I will find empty plates in Limerick. (*Goes off.*)

Lady: (*To Mrs Kelleher.*)   Is not that a very foolish man to go on fighting for a dead king?

Mrs Kelleher: (*Tapping her forehead.*)   Indeed, I think there's rats in the loft!

Lady: (*Tapping her forehead.*)   That is it, that is it – we wise ones know it. Fighting for a dead king! – ha! ha! ha! Poor Patrick Sarsfield is very, very mad!

CURTAIN

NOTES

SOME TIME ago I was looking through some poems taken down in Irish from the country people, and a line in one of them seemed strange to me 'Prebaim mo chroidhe le mo Stuart glegeal' – 'My heart leaps up with my bright Stuart'; for I had not heard any songs of this sort in Galway and I remembered that our Connacht Raftery, whose poems are still teaching history, dealt very shortly with the Royal Stuarts. 'James,' he says, 'he was the worst man for habits, he laid chains on our bogs and mountains. The father wasn't worse than the son Charles, that left sharp scourges on Ireland. When God and the people thought it time the story to be done, he lost his head. The next James – sharp blame to him – gave his daughter to William as woman and wife; made the Irish English and the English Irish, like wheat and oats in the month of harvest. And it was at Aughrim on a Monday many a son of Ireland found sorrow without speaking of all that died.'

So I went to ask some of the wise old neighbours who sit in wide chimney nooks by turf fires, and to whom I go to look for knowledge of many things, if they knew of any songs in praise of the Stuarts. But they were scornful. 'No indeed,' one said, 'there are no songs about them and no praises in the West, whatever there may be in the South. Why would there, and they running away and leaving the country the way they did? And what good did they ever do it? James the Second was a coward. Why didn't he go into the thick of the battle like the Prince of Orange? He stopped on a hill three miles away, and rode off to Dublin, bringing the best of his troops with him. There was a lady walking in the street at Dublin when he got there, and he told her the battle was lost and she said: "Faith you made good haste; you made no delay on the road." So he said no more after that. The people liked James well enough before he ran; they didn't like him after that.'

And another said: 'Seumas Salach, Dirty James, it is he brought all down. At the time of the battle there was one of his men said, "I have my eye cocked, and all the nations will be done away with," and he pointing his cannon. "Oh!" said James, "Don't make a widow of my daughter." If he didn't say that, the English would have been beat. It was a very poor thing for him to do.'

And one who lives on the border of Munster said: 'I used to hear them singing "The White Cockade" through the country; King James was beaten and all his well-wishers; my grief, my boy that went with them! But I don't think the people had ever much opinion of the Stuarts, but in those days they were all prone to versify.' And another old man said: 'When I was a young chap knocking about in Connemara, I often heard songs about the Stuarts, and talk of them and of the blackbird coming over the water. But they found it hard to get over James making off after the battle of the Boyne.' And when I looked through the lately gathered bundle of songs again, and through some old collections of favourite songs in Irish, I found they almost belonged to Munster. And if they are still sung there, it is not, as I think, for the sake of the Kings, but for the sake of the poets who wrote them. And in these songs of sorrow for Ireland and the indictment of England, the Stuart himself is often forgotten, or when he appears, he is but a faint and unreal image; a saint by whose name a heavy oath is sworn.

It is different with Patrick Sarsfield, Earl of Lucan, a 'great general that killed thousands of the English'; the brave, handsome, fighting man, the descendant of Conall Cearnach, the man who, after the Boyne, offered to 'change Kings and fight the battle again.' The songs about him are personal enough. Here is one I have put into English:

'O Patrick Sarsfield, health be to you, since you went to France and your camps were loosened; making your sighs along with the King, and you left poor Ireland and the Gael defeated – Och, Ochone!

'O Patrick Sarsfield, it is a man with God you are, and blessed is the earth you ever walked on. The blessing of the bright sun and the moon upon you since you took the day from the hands of King William – Och, Ochone!

'O Patrick Sarsfield, the prayer of every person with you; my own prayer and the prayer of the Son of Mary with you, since

you took the narrow ford going through Biorra, and since in
Cuilenn O'Cuanac you won Limerick – Och, Ochone!

'They put the first breaking on us at the Bridge of the Boyne;
the second breaking at the Bridge of Slaney; the third breaking
in Aughrim of O'Kelly; and O sweet Ireland, my five hundred
healths to you – Och, Ochone!

'O'Kelly has manuring for his land, that is not sand or dung,
but ready soldiers doing bravery with pikes, that were left in
Aughrim stretched in ridges – Och, Ochone!

'Who is that beyond on the hill Beinn Edar? I, a poor soldier
with King James. I was last year in arms and in dress, but this
year I am asking alms – Och, Ochone!'

As to the poor Lady, she was not the only one to wander
miserably, having spent all for the Stuarts.

The attempted escape of King James in the barrel has
already been used by Dr Hyde in a little play written in Irish.
In these days, when so much of the printed history we were
taught as children is being cast out by scholars, we must refill
the vessel by calling in tradition, or if need be our own imaginings. When my *White Cockade* was first produced I was pleased
to hear that J. M. Synge had said my method had made the
writing of historical drama again possible.

GRANIA

PERSONS

Grania
Finn
Diarmuid
Two Young Men

ACT I

*Scene: The scene is laid at Almhuin, in Ireland. Time, evening.
Inside a richly decorated tent; a fire in brazier centre, a high
candlestick at each side; a table with round loaves and wine. An
opening at each side of tent. Finn is leading in Grania; she is
wearing a golden dress and jewels. Music and joyous shouts are
heard outside.*

Finn: My five hundred welcomes to you, Grania, coming into
Almhuin.

Grania: I thank you, Finn.

Finn: Who would be welcome if it was not the King of
Ireland's daughter, that will be my wife tomorrow?

Grania: Your people that were outside and on the road lighted
all the district with fires as I came.

Finn: We would have been better prepared if your coming was
not so sudden at the last. You did not come too soon, that is
a thing that could not happen. But the big house of Almhuin will
not be set out fit for you till tomorrow, and it is in the tents of
our captains you and your company must be sheltered tonight.

Grania: It was my father, before going to Lochlann, said he
must leave me in a husband's care.

Finn: Who would protect you if I would not?

Grania: I am sure of that. Are you not the best of all the
world's big men?

Finn: They told me you could have made great marriages,
not coming to me?

Grania: My father was for the King of Foreign, but I said I
would take my own road.

Finn: He has great riches and a great name.

Grania: I would have been afraid going to him, hearing talk
of him as so dark and wild looking, and his shield tusked
with the tusks of a boar.

Finn: You were not in dread coming to me, and you so delicate
and so cherished?

Grania: I had an old veneration for you, hearing all my lifetime that you are so gentle to women and to dogs and to little
children, and you wrestling with the powers of the world
and being so hard in war.

Finn: It would be strange any person not to be gentle with
you.

Grania: And another thing. I had no wish to go travelling
forth and hither to strange countries and by strange seas. I
have no mind for going through crosses. I would sooner pass
my life at Almhuin, where I ever and always heard there are
wide white halls and long tables, and poets and fine company.

Finn: Your father has a good house.

Grania: There was little to listen to but my father planning
the wars in Lochlann. There was no pleasant stir in it, unless
what there might be in myself.

Finn: It may be you will tire of Almhuin itself after a while.

Grania: There will be good company. I have heard talk of the
men and the captains of the Fenians, of Oisin and Osgar and
Goll, that came to meet me a while ago.

Finn: The man you will think most of is not with them today,
that is my own kinsman, Diarmuid.

Grania: I heard of him often. They say him to be the best
lover of women in the whole world, and the most daring in
the war.

Finn: He has a good name from gentle and simple, from the
big man and from the poor. Those even that have no call to
him, cannot but love him.

Grania: It was he fought seven days and seven nights with
the terrible wild ox upon the mountains.

Finn: Any time I am tired or fretted, all he could do for me
he would not think it enough.

Grania: Where is he at this time, that he did not come to meet
me with the rest ?

Finn: I sent him to a far lonesome hill where I have a secret
store of treasures and of jewels. It is right there should be a
good man to guard them upon the road. It is for you he is
bringing them, he will be here within a short while.

Grania: It is likely it is a man of that sort a woman would
find it easy to love.

Finn: Did you ever give a thought to any man in the way of love?

Grania: I did – at least I think I did – but that was a long time ago.

Finn: Who was he? Did he belong to your own place?

Grania: I do not know. I never heard his name – but I saw him.

Finn: Did you speak to him?

Grania: No, he was but as if a shadow, that came for a moment and was gone.

Finn: Tell me all the story.

Grania: They had been hunting – there were a great many strangers. I was bade keep away from the hall. I was looking from a high window – then there was a great outcry in the yard – the hounds were fighting, the hounds the strange men had brought with them. One of them made as if to attack a little dog I owned at the time – I screamed out at the hounds. Then a young man ran out and beat them away, and he held up my little dog to me, laughing, and his cap fell off from his head.

Finn: Did they not tell you his name?

Grania: I was shy to ask them, and I never saw him again. But my thoughts went with him for a good while, and sometimes he came through my dreams. – Is that now what you would call love?

Finn: Indeed, I think it is little at all you know of it.

Grania: I heard often in the stories of people that were in pain and under locks through love. But I think they are but foolishness. There was one of a lover was made go through a fire for his sweetheart's sake, and came out shivering. And one that climbed to his darling's window by one golden thread of her hair.

Finn: There are many such tales and there are more in the making, for it is likely the tearing and vexing of love will be known so long as men are hot-blooded and women have a coaxing way.

Grania: I asked the old people what love was, and they gave me no good news of it at all. Three sharp blasts of the wind they said it was, a white blast of delight and a grey blast of discontent and a third blast of jealousy that is red.

Finn: That red blast is the wickedest of the three.

Grania: I would never think jealousy to be so bad a smart.

Finn: It is a bad thing for whoever knows it. If love is to lie down on a bed of stinging nettles, jealousy is to waken upon a wasp's nest.

Grania: But the old people say more again about love. They say there is no good thing to be gained without hardship and pain, such as a child to be born, or a long day's battle won. And I think it might be a pleasing thing to have a lover that would go through fire for your sake.

Finn: I knew enough of the heat of love in my time, and I am very glad to have done with it now, and to be safe from its torments and its whip and its scourge.

Grania: It being so bad a thing, why, I wonder, do so many go under its sway? That should be a good master that has so many servants and is so well obeyed.

Finn: We do not take it up of ourselves but it sweeps us away before it, and asks no leave. When that blast comes upon us, we are but feathers whirled before it with the dust.

Grania: It is a good thing surely, that I will never know an unhappy, unquiet love, but only love for you that will be by my side for ever. (*A loud peal of laughter is heard outside.*) What is that laughter? There is in it some mocking sound.

Finn: (*Going to the door.*) It is not laughter now – it is a merry outcry as if around some very welcome friend. It is Diarmuid that is come back.

(*Diarmuid comes in. Grania shrinks back from him.*)

Diarmuid: I am here, Finn, my master.

Finn: What way are you, Diarmuid? There is some wound upon your arm.

Diarmuid: It is a wound I was given on the road. But all you sent me for is safe.

Finn: I knew you would mind them well. But was that hurt cared and eased?

Diarmuid: It is nothing to signify. I drove the robbers off. All is safe. They are bringing the bags in here.

(*Two fair-haired young men come in two or three times laying bags on floor during the next sentences.*)

I will stop here and mind them through the night time. I

would sooner keep charge until you will open them for the
wedding on the morrow. I will sit there by the hearth. They
are jewels would be coveted by the witches of the lakes, or
the sea-women sporting among the golden ribs and the
wreckage of the ships of Greece.

Finn: It is to a woman worthy of them they are to be given.

Diarmuid: I am sure of that, indeed, and she being worthy
to wed with you.

Finn: Come here, Grania, until I make you acquainted with
the branch and the blossom of our young men.

Grania: (*Coming forward.*)   It is – who is it?
(*She gives a little cry and goes back a step as Diarmuid takes
off his cap.*)

Finn: What is it ails you, Grania, that you are turned to be so
wild and so shy?

Grania: It is that – that – he is wounded.

Finn: You have lost your talk on the road, Diarmuid, you,
that were always so ready to string words and praises for
comely young women.

Diarmuid: I had no time to wash away the dust and the sweat.
I did not know Grania was in the place. You should have
forewarned me.

Finn: He thinks you are vexed because he is not settled out
in handsome clothes.

Grania: It is strange – it is all strange to me – I will get used
to meeting strangers. Another time – in a very short while –
my voice will be more steady – my heart will leave starting.

Finn: You will get courage knowing you are a queen. Where,
Diarmuid, is the crown I bade you bring? It is not the high
crown of pearls from the far Indies I want, but the thin
golden crown shaped like the rising sun, that I thought of
late would be never used, and that I had been keeping till I
met with my own queen and my bride.

Diarmuid: It is wrapped about with tanned marten skins and
bound with purple thongs.

Finn: (*Unwrapping it.*)   Come to me, Grania.   (*He puts the
crown on her head.*)   Courage will come into your heart now,
with this sign and token of your estate.

Grania: I am tired. It is weighty on my head – it is time for

me to be with myself only. I have seen too much company
since morning.

Finn: That is so, and I am much to blame, not taking better
thought for you. Come to your women, they will bring you
to your tent that is close at hand. You have travelled a long
strange road, and tomorrow is your wedding day.

Grania: Tomorrow? Could it not be put off for a while?
This is but May, and no great luck in the moon. There is
more luck in the last moon of July – or the first new moon
after it. Put it off until that time.

Finn: That cannot be. Your father looked to me to put you
in your right place without delay. You must be my wife
tomorrow.

Grania: Must it be tomorrow?

Finn: All the armies are gathered together for that, and the
feasts are ready. You yourself will be ready when you have
taken your sleep through the night time.

Grania: Sleep – sleep – yes, I will go sleep if I can.

Finn: Diarmuid is tired as well as you.

Diarmuid: I have no desire to sleep. I will sit and watch here
till the dawn.

(*He sits down by the hearth, pulling cloak over his head.
Grania turns back to look at him from the door as Finn takes
her out. After a moment Finn comes back and sits near the fire.*)

Finn: Tell me, Diarmuid, is it right that a man past the
mering of age should give any thought to love?

Diarmuid: It is right for a man with a great burden of care
upon him to have a place of his own where he can let it fall
from him. And what is a home or a house without a wife
and a companion at the hearth?

Finn: That is so, and that is what I had in mind at the time
this marriage was settled and pressed on, for the good of
Ireland and my own good. But as to love, that is another
thing.

Diarmuid: It is another thing, sure enough.

Finn: I thought myself on the far side of it and of its trouble
and its joy. But now this young girl has come to me, so fearless, so mannerly, so plain and simple in her talk, it seems to
me I should wed with her, and she not a king's daughter but

a poor girl carrying the bag. (*Diarmuid nods, but is silent.*)
It is not the one way with you and me, Diarmuid, for many
women have offered you their beauty and themselves; but
as for myself there is no one I ever gave my heart to but was
swept from me in some hard way. And this is come like good
wine to the mouth that was filled for a long while with grey
mist and rain. And indeed, indeed my heart leaps up with
her. Is not that natural, Diarmuid, and she so well reared
and so young?

Diarmuid: It is natural, indeed.

Finn: Would you not say her to be well shaped and of good
blood and wise?

Diarmuid: She is all that, indeed.

Finn: It is not often I have known you to be so begrudging of
praise.

Diarmuid: What call have I to be praising her? I could tell
you no more than you knew before, through your own heart
and through your eyes.

Finn: But, tell me this, now. Is she that is so airy and beautiful
any sort of a fitting wife for me?

Diarmuid: You are brave and she will put her pride in you.
You are the best of all, and she is a woman would only join
with the best.

Finn: With all that, I would be well pleased if I could change
my years for yours, Diarmuid. I would give you in their
place all the riches I have ever won.

Diarmuid: Such a woman will be a right head for Almhuin.
She is used to a king's house, she will be open-handed, and
open-hearted along with that.

Finn: I think, indeed, she will be a right wife for me, and
loyal. And it is well that is so, for if ever any man should
come between her thoughts and mine I would not leave him
living, but would give him the sorrow of death.

Diarmuid: There is no good lover in Ireland but would do the
same, and his wife or his sweetheart failing him.

Finn: Yet, in the end there are but few do it; for the thought
of men that have passed their midday is mixed with caution
and with wisdom and the work they have in hand, or weakness is gaining on their limbs. And as for youngsters, they

do not know how to love, because there is always some tomorrow's love possible in the shadow of the love of today. It is only the old it goes through and through entirely, because they know all the last honey of the summer-time has come to its ferment in their cup, and that there is no new summer coming to meet them for ever. And so (*he gets up and stirs fire*) they think to carry that cup through life and death and even beyond the grave. But can I bring this young girl to be satisfied with that one love?

Diarmuid: There is no one among the men of Ireland can stand against your will. It should be easy for you to keep a woman faithful.

Finn: Yet the story-tellers make out that love is the disturber; that where it is on the road it is hard to be sure of any woman at all or any friend.

Diarmuid: It is I can give you out an answer to that. My master, you are sure of me.

Finn: I am sure of you indeed, and it is many a time you put your life in danger for my sake.

Diarmuid: (*Standing up.*)   I am your son and your servant always, and your friend. And now, at this marriage time, I will ask one asking.

Finn: Who would get his desire and you not to get it?

Diarmuid: I am tired of courts and of sports and of wars where we gain the day always. I want some hard service to put my hand to. There are the dark men of Foreign, their King has laid it down he will come and master Ireland. Let me go out now and put him down in his own country.

Finn: I will give you leave, but not till after the wedding moon.

Diarmuid: No, but let me go now, this very night at the brink of dawn.

Finn: No, but stop near me. You are more to me than any of my comrades or my friends.

Diarmuid: It is a strange thing, the first asking I have made, you have refused me.

Finn: Go then and take your own way, and my blessing go with you.

Diarmuid: I thank you for that leave.

Finn: But you will be tired out before morning. You have been on the road these three days, you got no sleep last night.

Diarmuid: I am drowsy enough and tired, but I will go.

Finn: Lie down over there upon the otter skins. I will sit here by the fire and keep a watch in your place.

Diarmuid: Make a promise then, to wake me at the first whitening of the dawn.

Finn: I will do that.

(*Diarmuid lies down on skins and sleeps. Finn looks at him a moment and covers him, then puts out candles and sits down where Diarmuid had been sitting, pulling his cloak over his head. Silence a moment, Grania comes in.*)

Grania: (*In a low voice.*) Diarmuid! (*No answer.*) Diarmuid! (*She comes nearer to Finn and speaks a little louder.*) Diarmuid, help me! (*Finn slightly moves.*) Give me your help now. I cannot wed with Finn. I cannot go to him as his wife. I do not know what has happened – half an hour ago I was content to go to him. You came in – I knew you – it was you I saw that day at Tara – my heart started like a deer a while ago. There is something gone astray – the thought of Finn is different. What way could I live beside him and my heart, as I am thinking, gone from him ? What name might I be calling out in my sleep ? (*She goes close to Finn and puts her hand on his shoulder.*) Have you no way to help me, Diarmuid ? It would be a terrible thing, a wedded woman not to be loyal – to call out another man's name in her sleep. (*Finn gets up and goes back into shadow.*) Oh, do not turn away from me! Do not leave me to the marriage I am in dread of. You will not help me ? Is it you, Diarmuid, are failing me, you that came to my help that other time? Is it to fail me you will now ? And is it my fault if this strange thing has come upon me, and that there is as if no one in all the world but you ? You are angry with me and vexed, and it is a bad day, the day I came into this place. But I am not ashamed. Was it my fault at all ? I will light now this candle, I will dare to show you my face. You will see in that I am not come to you as a light woman that turns this way and that way, but that I have given you the love I never gave to any man and never will give to any other! (*She lights candle and holds it up.*)

Finn: (*Sternly.*) Grania!

Grania: Oh! It is Finn! And where then is Diarmuid?

Finn: There he is before you. It is the boy lying down and rising with me has betrayed me.

Diarmuid: (*Moving and starting up.*) What is it? What has happened? Is that Grania?

Finn: You were looking for her to come. She was ready and willing. You are well fitted to rear traitors to one another.

Diarmuid: You are out of your wits. I had no thought she was coming here. What brought her?

Finn: Did she come giving you her love unasked? I thought she was a king's daughter.

Diarmuid: She is, and well worthy!

Finn: What was her mother then? Was she some woman of the camp? (*Pushes her from him.*)

Diarmuid: (*Putting his arm round her.*) I will not let any man say that. (*Half draws sword.*)

Finn: My life is a little thing beside what you have taken!

Diarmuid: You are talking folly. You never found a lie after me in any sort of way. But the time courage was put in your heart there was madness furrowed in your brain!

Finn: Was it every whole minute of your life you were false to me?

Diarmuid: You would not have said that, the day I freed you from the three Kings of the Island of the Floods.

Finn: It is quickly you have been changed by a false woman's flattering words!

Grania: It is not his fault! It is mine! It is on me the blame is entirely! It is best for me to go out a shamed woman. But I will not go knocking at my father's door! I will find some quick way to quiet my heart for ever. Forgive me, Finn, and I have more cause yet to ask you to forgive me, Diarmuid. And if there were hundreds brought together this day for my wedding, it is likely there will be at my burying but the plover and the hares of the bog! (*Goes towards door.*)

Diarmuid: (*Seizing her.*) I will not let you go out this way. I will not fail you!

Finn: There is all your talk of faith to me gone down the wind!

Diarmuid: I will not forsake her, but I will keep my faith with you. I give my word that if I bring her out of this, it is as your queen I will bring her and show respect to her, till such time as your anger will have cooled and that you will let her go her own road. It is not as a wife I will bring her, but I will keep my word to you, Finn.

Finn: Do you give me your oath to that?

Diarmuid: I do give it.

Finn: It is likely it will soon be broken. Grania is no withered pitiful hag with the hair matted wild to her knees.

Diarmuid: It will not be broken. Let my own heart break and be torn by wild dogs before that promise will be broken at all.

Finn: The moon is coming now to the full, and before its lessening you will have lied to me.

Diarmuid: (*Taking up a loaf.*) Look at this cake of bread. I will send you its like, white and round and unbroken at every moon of the year, full moon and harvest moon, while I am along with her, as a sign my own oath is in the same way clean and whole and unbroken.

Finn: It is the woman will make you break that swearing. There will be another telling bye and bye.

Diarmuid: (*Taking Grania's hands.*) There is this league between us, Grania. I will bring you with me and I will keep you safe from every danger. But understand well, it is not as a wife I will bring you, but I will keep my faith with Finn.

Grania: Do as is pleasing to you. I have made an end of askings.

Diarmuid: Come out with me now, till I put you in some place of safety.

Finn: You will find no safety in any place or in any Connacht corner north or west. And out in the big world itself, there is no one will give my enemy so much as shelter from the rain.

Diarmuid: I know well I have earned enemies in the big world because I fought with all its best men for your sake.

Grania: Oh, take me, take me away out of this! For it is hard treatment is falling upon me!

Diarmuid: And I tell you, Grania, but that I am bound to Finn by my word I have given him, and by kindnesses past counting and out of measure, it would be better to me than the riches of the whole world, you to have given me your love!

Grania: I have given it to you indeed.   (*She puts up her face to be kissed.*)

Diarmuid: (*Kissing her forehead.*)   That is the first kiss and it will be the last.

Finn: You will give up your life as the charge for that kiss!

Grania: Come out! Come out! The very blood of my heart is rising against him!

Finn: I will not let you go! Let our wedding be here and now, and I will call in as my witnesses to that word Goll and Oisin and Osgar and the captains of the armies of the Fenians!

(*Finn goes to door, blows horn, then turns towards Grania as if to seize her, sways and falls.*)

Grania: Oh, is it death!

Diarmuid: It is but a weakness that took hold of him, with the scorching of his jealousy and its flame.

Grania: Come away before he will rise up and follow us. My father's horses are in the field outside.

Diarmuid: Come out then to the hunting – for it is a long hunting it will be, and it is little comfort we will have from this out. For that is a man driven by anger, and that will not fail from our track so long as the three of us are in the living world!

(*The sound of many horns and shouts is heard at Right. Diarmuid opens door at Left. Grania goes out quickly. He follows with bowed head.*)

CURTAIN

ACT II

*Scene: Interior of a rough tent. The door opens on a wood out-
side. A bed strewn with rushes. Diarmuid lying on it asleep.
Grania is moving about and singing.*

Grania: Sleep a little, a little little;
                Green the wild rushes under my dear.
                Sleep here quiet, easy and quiet,
                Safe in the wild wood, nothing to fear.

(*She stirs fire and puts some round cakes she has been making,
to bake over it. Then comes to Diarmuid and puts her hand on
him as she sings*) –

                Waken darling, darling waken!
                Wild ducks are flying, daylight is kind;
                Whirr of wild wings high in the branches.
                Hazel the hound stands sniffing the wind!

Diarmuid: (*Awaking and taking her hand.*)   There is a new
light in your eyes – there is a new blush in your cheeks –
there is a new pride stirring in your thoughts. The white
sun of Heaven should be well pleased shining on you. Are
you well content, Grania, my wife?

Grania: I am well content indeed with my comrade and my man.

Diarmuid: And did you love me ever and always, Grania?

Grania: Did I not tell you long ago, my heart went down to
you the day I looked from the high window, and I in my
young youth at Tara.

Diarmuid: It was a long waiting we had for our marriage time.

Grania: It was a long waiting, surely.

Diarmuid: Let us put it out of mind and not be remembering
it at all. This last moon has made up for all those seven years.

Grania: It was a troublesome time indeed and a very troublesome life. In all that time we never stopped in any place so
long as in the shades and the shelters of this wood.

Diarmuid: It seems to me only one day we have been in it. I would not be sorry in this place, there to be the length of a year in the day.

Grania: The young leaves on the beech trees have unfolded since we came.

Diarmuid: I did not take notice of their growth. Oh, my dear, you are as beautiful as the blossoming of the wild furze on the hill.

Grania: It was not love that brought you to wed me in the end.

Diarmuid: It was, surely, and no other thing. What is there but love can twist a man's life, as sally rods are twisted for a gad?

Grania: No, it was jealousy, jealousy of the King of Foreign, that wild dark man, that broke the hedge between us and levelled the wall.

Diarmuid: (*Starting up.*) Do not bring him back to mind! It was rage that cracked me, when I saw him put his arms about you as if to bring you away.

Grania: Was it my fault? I was but gathering a sheaf of rushes for our two beds, and I saw him coming alongside of the stream to the pool. I knew him by the tusks on his shield and the bristled boar-skin cloak.

Diarmuid: What was it ailed you not to call to me?

Grania: You were far away – you would not have heard me – it is he himself would have heard my call. And I was no way afraid – I hid myself up in the branches of the big red sally by the pool.

Diarmuid: That was a foolish place to go hiding.

Grania: I thought myself safe and well hidden on the branch that goes out over the stream. What way could I know he would stop at that very place, to wash the otter blood from his spear, and the blood from his hands, and the sweat?

Diarmuid: If I had been near, it is his own blood would have splashed away in the pool.

Grania: He stopped then to throw the water on his face – it was my own face he saw in the pool. He looked up of a sudden – he gave a great delighted laugh.

Diarmuid: My lasting grief that I was not there, and my hand gripping his throat.

Grania: He bent the branch – he lifted me from it – he not to have caught me in his arms I would have fallen in the stream.

Diarmuid: That itself might have been better than his hand to have rested on you at all!

Grania: Then you were there – within one minute. You should likely have heard the great shout he gave out and the laugh?

Diarmuid: I lifted my hand to strike at him, and it was as if struck down. It is grief to my heart that he escaped me! I would have crushed him and destroyed him and broken his carcass against the rocks.

Grania: It was I myself struck your hand down. I was well pleased seeing you in that rage of anger.

Diarmuid: If I had known that, it is likely I would have killed you in his place.

Grania: But you did not kill me.

Diarmuid: What was it happened? I was as if blind – you were in my arms not his – my lips were on the lips he had nearly touched, that I myself had never touched in all those seven years.

Grania: It was a long, long kiss.

Diarmuid: That moment was like the whole of life in a single day, and yet it was but a second of time. And when I looked around he was gone, and there was no trace of him and he had made away and I could not kill him.

Grania: What matter? You should forgive him, seeing it was he brought us together at the last. You should help him to win another kingdom for that good deed. There is nothing will come between us now. You are entirely my own.

Diarmuid: I am belonging to you, indeed, now and for ever. I will bring you away from this rambling life, to a place will be all our own. We will do away with this trade of wandering, we will go on to that bare shore between Burren and the big sea. There will be no trace of our footsteps on the hard flagstone.

Grania: We were in that craggy place before and we were

forced to quit it. To live on the wind and on the air you cannot. The wind is not able to support anybody.

Diarmuid: We will get a currach this time. We will go out over the waves to an island. The sea and the strand are wholesome. We shall sleep well, and the tide beating its watch around us.

Grania: Even out in those far Aran Islands we would be threatened and driven as happened in the time past.

Diarmuid: But beyond Aran, far out in the west, there is another island that is seen but once in every seven years.

Grania: Is that a real place at all ? Or is it only in the nurses' tales ?

Diarmuid: Who knows ? There is no good lover but has seen it at some time through his sleep. It is hid under a light mist, away from the track of traders and kings and robbers. The harbour is well fenced to keep out loud creaking ships. Some fisherman to break through the mist at some time, he will bring back news of a place where there is better love and a better life than in any lovely corner of the world that is known. (*She turns away.*)   And will you come there with me, Grania ?

Grania: I am willing to go from this. We cannot stop always in the darkness of the woods – but I am thinking it should be very strange there and very lonesome.

Diarmuid: The sea-women will rise up giving out news of the Country-under-Wave, and the birds will have talk as in the old days. And maybe some that are beyond the world will come to keep us company, seeing we are fitted to be among them by our unchanging love.

Grania: We are going a long time without seeing any of the people of the world, unless it might be herds and fowlers, and robbers that are hiding in the wood.

Diarmuid: It is enough for us having one another. I would sooner be talking with you than with the world wide.

Grania: It is likely some day you will be craving to be back with the Fenians.

Diarmuid: I was fretting after them for a while. But now they are slipping out of mind. It would seem as if some soul-brothers of my own were calling to me from outside the

world. It may be they have need of my strength to help them
in their hurling and their wars.

Grania: I have not had the full of my life yet, for it is scared
and hiding I have spent the best of my years that are past.
And no one coming to give us news or knowledge, and no
friendly thing at all at hand, unless it might be Hazel the
hound, or that I might throw out a handful of meal to the
birds to bring me company. I would wish to bring you back
now to some busy peopled place.

Diarmuid: You never asked to be brought to such a place in
all our time upon the road. And are you not better pleased
now than when we dragged lonely-hearted and sore-footed
through the days?

Grania: I am better pleased, surely – and it is by reason of
that I would wish my happiness to be seen, and not to be
hidden under the branches and twigs of trees.

Diarmuid: If I am content here, why would not you be
content?

Grania: It is time for you to have attendance again, and
good company about you. We are the same here as if settled
in the clay, clogged with the body and providing for its
hunger and its needs, and the readying of the dinner of today
and the providing of the dinner for tomorrow. It is at the
head of long tables we should be, listening to the old men
with their jokes and flatteries, and the young men making
their plans that will change the entire world.

Diarmuid: That is all over for me now, and cast away like
the husk from the nut.

Grania: They will be forgetting us altogether.

Diarmuid: No, but they will put us into songs, till the world
will wonder at the luck of those two lovers that carried love
entire and unbroken out beyond the rim of sight.

Grania: That may be. And some night at the supper the men
will turn their heads hearing that song and will say, 'Is
Diarmuid living yet?' or 'Grania must be withered now and
a great trouble to those that are about her.' And they will
turn to the women that are smiling beside them, and that
have delicate hands, and little blushes in their cheeks, and
that are maybe but my own age all the same, but have kept

their young looks, being merry and well cared. And Grania
and Diarmuid will be no more than a memory and a name.

Diarmuid: (*Taking her hand.*) These white hands were
always willing hands, and where, I wonder, was this discontent born? A little while ago it was the woods you
wanted, and now it is the palaces you want.

Grania: It is not my mind that changes, it is life that changes
about me. If I was content to be in hiding a while ago, now
I am proud and have a right to be proud. And it is hard to
nourish pride in a house having two in it only.

Diarmuid: I take pride in you here, the same as I would in
any other place.

Grania: Listen to me. You are driving me to excuses and to
words that are not entirely true. But here, now is truth for
you. All the years we were with ourselves only, you kept
apart from me as if I was a shadow-shape or a hag of the
valley. And it was not till you saw another man craving my
love, that the like love was born in yourself. And I will go
no more wearing out my time in lonely places, where the
martens and hares and badgers run from my path, but it is to
thronged places I will go, where it is not through the eyes of
wild startled beasts you will be looking at me, but through
the eyes of kings' sons that will be saying: 'It is no wonder
Diarmuid to have gone through his crosses for such a wife!'
And I will overhear their sweethearts saying: 'I would give
the riches of the world, Diarmuid to be my own comrade.'
And our love will be kept kindled for ever, that would be
spent and consumed in desolate places, like the rushlight in
a cabin by the bog. For it is certain it is by the respect of
others we partly judge even those we know through and
through.

Diarmuid: (*Getting up and speaking gravely.*)   There is no
going back for us, Grania, and you know that well yourself.

Grania: We will go to my father's house – he is grown old,
he will not refuse me – we will call to your people and to my
people – we will bring together an army of our own.

Diarmuid: That is enough of arguing. There is no sense or
no reason in what you are saying.

Grania: It is a bad time you have chosen to give up your mannerly ways. You did not speak that way the day you found me in the hand of the King of Foreign. You would maybe be better pleased if I had gone with him at that time.

Diarmuid: You are but saying that to vex and to annoy me. You are talking like an innocent or a fool.

Grania: He made me great promises. A great place and power and great riches.

Diarmuid: I can win you riches in plenty if that is what you are coveting in your mind.

Grania: I cared little for his talk of riches – but – when he put his arms about me and kissed me—

Diarmuid: You let him leave a kiss upon your mouth?

Grania: It as if frightened me – it seemed strange to me – there came as if a trembling in my limbs. I said: 'I am this long time going with the third best man of the Fenians, and he never came as near as that to me.'

Diarmuid: (*Flinging her from him.*) Go then your own way, and I would be well pleased never to have met you, and I was no better than a fool, thinking any woman at all could give love would last longer than the froth upon the stream!

(*The sound of a rattle is heard outside.*)

Grania: What is that? Who is it?

(*Finn disguised as a beggar is seen at door.*)

Diarmuid: It is but a beggar or a leper.

Finn: Is this a house is sheltering a handsome young woman and a lathy, tall young man, that are not belonging to this district, and having no follower but a hound?

Diarmuid: Who are you? Keep back from the door!

Finn: I am no leper if I am a beggar. And my name is well earned that is Half-Man – for there is left to me but one arm by the wolves, and one side of my face by the crows that came picking at me on the ridge where I was left for dead. And beyond that again, one of the feet rotted from me, where I got it hurted one time through a wound was given me by treachery in the heel.

Diarmuid: Take off that mask till I see your face.

Finn: I will and welcome, if you have a mind to see it, but it is not right a lovely young lady to get a view of a bare gnawed skull, and that is what this caul covers. It is by reason of that I go sounding the rattle, to scare children from the path before me, and women carrying child.

Diarmuid: If it is alms you are seeking it is a bare place to come, for we carry neither gold nor silver, there being no market in the woods.

Finn: Not at all, not at all – I am asking nothing at all. Believe me, the man that sent me is a good payer of wages.

Diarmuid: What call had he to send you here? We own nothing for any man to covet.

Finn: With a message he sent me, a message. You to be the man and the young woman I am searching after, I have to give a message and get a message. That is all the business I have to do. I will get fair play, never fear, from the man that sent me.

Diarmuid: Tell me who is that man, till I know is he enemy or friend.

Finn: You to see him you would not forget him. A man he is, giving out gold from his hand the same as withered leaves, and having on his shield the likeness of the rising sun.

Grania: That can surely be no other than Finn. What did he want sending you?

Finn: I will tell you that, and it is little I know why would he want it. You would not say him to be a man would be in need of bread.

Grania: Tell out now what you have to tell.

Finn: Wouldn't you say it to be a strange thing, a man having that much gold in his hand, and the sun in gold on his shield, to be as hungry after bread as a strayed cur dog would have nothing to eat or to fall back on, and would be yelping after his meal.

Diarmuid: Give out the message.

Finn: It is what he bade me say: 'Tell that young woman,' he said, 'and that youngster with her,' he said, 'that on every first night of the round moon these seven years, there used to be a round cake of bread laid upon my road. And the moon was at her strength yesterday,' he said, 'and it has failed me to find on any path that cake of bread.'

Diarmuid: It is Finn that sent him! It is Finn is calling me to account because I have forgotten my promise to him, and my faith.

Grania: He has come upon our track. We must go our road again. It is often we escaped him before this. I am no way afraid.

Diarmuid: It is not fear that is on me, it is shame. Shame because Finn thought me a man would hold to my word, and I have not held to it. I am as if torn and broken with the thought and the memory of Finn.

Grania: It is time to put away that memory. It is long enough you gave in to his orders.

Diarmuid: I did that with my own consent. Nothing he put upon me was hard. He trusted me and he could trust me, and now he will never put trust in me again.

Grania: It may not be Finn will be getting his commands done, and our friends gathering to our help. Let him learn that time, not to thrust his hand between the wedges and the splint.

Finn: (*Who has been sitting crouched over fire.*) Have you the message ready and the bread I was bade bring back to the champion that met me on the path?

Grania: (*Taking up one of the cakes.*) It is best send it to him and gain the time to make our escape.

Diarmuid: No, no more lying. I will tell no more lies to my master and my friend!

(*Diarmuid takes cake from Grania and flings it down, then throws himself on the bed and covers his face with his hands. Grania takes up cake, breaks it again and again, and gives it to Finn.*)

Grania: That is the answer to his message. Say to him that as that bread is broken and torn, so is the promise given by the man that did right in breaking it. Tell Finn, the time you meet him, it was the woman herself gave that to you, and bade you leave it in his hand as a message and as a sign.

Finn: Take care now. Is that a right message you are sending, and one that you will not repent?

Grania: It is a right message for that man to get. And give heed to what I say now. If you have one eye is blind, let it be turned to the place where we are, and that he might ask news of. And if you have one seeing eye, cast it upon me, and tell Finn you saw a woman no way sad or afraid, but as airy and high-minded as a mountain filly would be challenging the winds of March!

Finn: I can tell him that, surely, and you not giving it out to me at all.

Grania: And another thing. Tell him there is no woman but would be proud, and that oath being broken for her sake. And tell him she is better pleased than if she was a queen of the queens of the world, that she, a travelling woman going out under the weather, can turn her back on him this day as she did in the time that is past. Go now, and give that message if you dare to give it, and keep those words red scorched in your mind.

Finn: I will bring that message, sure enough, and there will be no fear on me giving it out. For all the world knows Finn never took revenge on a fool, or a messenger, or a hound. But it would be well for them that send it to bear in mind that he is a hard man – a hard man – a hard man, surely. As hard as a barren stepmother's slap, or a highway gander's gob.

Grania: Go, go on your road. Or will you take food and drink before you go?

Finn: Not at all, I will eat in no man's house or in any place at all, unless in the bats' feeding time and the owls', the way the terror of my face will not be seen. I will be going now, going my road. But, let you mind yourself. Finn does be very wicked the time he does be mad vexed. And he is a man well used to get the mastery, and any that think to go daring him, or to go against him, he will make split marrow of their bones.

Diarmuid: (*Looking up.*) There might kindness grow in him yet. It is not big men, the like of him, keep up enmity and a grudge for ever.

Finn: Who can know, who can know? Finn has a long memory. There is Grania he doted down on, and that was robbed from him, and he never threw an eye on any woman since and never will, but going as if crazed and ransacking the whole country after her. As restless as the moon of Heaven he is, and at some times as wasted and as pale.

Grania: It is time for him to leave thinking about her.

Finn: A great memory he has and great patience, and a strong fit of the jealous, that is the worst thing ever came from the skies. How well he never forgave and never will forgive Diarmuid O'Duibhne, that he reared on his knee and nourished with every marrow-bone, and that stole away his wife from him, and is dead.

Grania: That is no true story. Diarmuid is not dead, but living!

Finn: That's my hearing of the thing. And if he is on the earth yet, what is he doing? Would you call that living? Screening himself behind bushes, running before the rustling of a wren on the nest. In dread to face his master or the old companions that he had.

Grania: There is no man but must go through trouble at some time; and many a good man has been a stranger and an exile through a great share of his lifetime.

Finn: I am no friend to Diarmuid O'Duibhne. But he to be my friend, I would think it a great slur upon him it being said a man that had so great a name was satisfied and content, killing hares and conies for the supper, casting at cranes for sport, or for feathers to stuff a pillow for his sweetheart's head, the time there is an army of the men of Foreign in Ireland.

Grania: I can tell you it will not be long till he will be seen going out against them, and going against some that are not foreign, and he having an army of his own.

Finn: It is best for him make no delay so, where they are doing every whole thing to drag the country down.

Diarmuid: (*Standing* up.) I will go out and fight. I will delay no minute.

Grania: No, but do as I tell you. Gather your friends till you can make your own stand. Where is the use of one man only, however good he may be?

Finn: A queer thing indeed, no queerer. Diarmuid, that was the third best man of the whole of the armies of the Fenians, to be plucking and sorting pigeon's feathers to settle out a pillow and a bed.

Diarmuid: I will go as I am, by myself. There is no man

living would let his name lie under reproach as my name is under it.

Grania: (*To Finn.*) Go quick—you have brought messages – bring another message for me, now, to the High King's house at Tara.

Diarmuid: I will wait for no man's help. I will go.

Grania: Is it that you will leave me? It is certain Finn has tracked us – we have stopped too long in the one place. If Finn is there his strength will be there. Do not leave me here alone to the power and the treachery of Finn! It is in at this door he may be coming before the fall of night.

Diarmuid: I will stop here. I will not leave you under Finn's power for any satisfaction to myself. (*To Finn.*) Go, as you are bidden, and bring help from the King at Tara.

Finn: Very good, very good. That now is the message of a wise housekeeping husband.

Diarmuid: I give my word it needs more courage at some times to be careful than to be forward and daring, and that is the way with me now.

Finn: Maybe so, maybe so. And there is no wonder at all a common man to be tame and timid, when Diarmuid, grandson of Duibhne has a faint miserable heart.

Diarmuid: That is the wicked lie of some old enemy.

Finn: (*Going to door.*) Very likely, very likely; but maybe it would be better for Grania I was speaking of, to have stopped with the old man that made much of her, in place of going with the young man that belittles her.

Grania: That is a slander and no true word.

Finn: (*At door.*) Ha! Ha! Ha! It is a story makes great sport among gentle and simple in every place. It is great laughing is given out when the story is heard that the King of Foreign put his arms about Grania's neck that is as white as a hound's tooth, and that Diarmuid saw him do it – and that the King of Foreign is living yet, and goes boasting on his road! (*Goes out.*)

Diarmuid: (*Fastening on sword.*) Give that to me. (*Points at spear.*)

Grania: (*Throwing it from her.*) Oh, stop with me, my darling, and my love, do not go from me now or forsake me!

And to stay in the lonely woods for ever or in any far desolate place, you will never hear a cross word or an angry word from me again. And it is for you I will wear my jewels and my golden dress. For you are my share of life, and you are the east and the west to me, and all the long ago and all that is before me! And there is nothing will come between us or part us, and there will be no name but yours upon my lips, and no name but my own spoken by your lips, and the two of us well contented for ever!

Finn: (*Comes back and looks in at door.*)   It is what they were saying a while ago, the King of Foreign is grunting and sighing, grunting and sighing, around and about the big red sally tree beside the stream! (*He disappears. Diarmuid rushes out.*)

CURTAIN

ACT III

Scene: In the same tent. Grania has put on her golden dress and jewels, and is plaiting gold into her hair. Horns and music suddenly heard, not very near. She goes, startled, to door, and falls back as Finn comes in. He is dressed as if for war and has his banner in his hand. He looks older and more worn than in the First Act.

Finn: I have overtaken you at last, Grania.

Grania: Finn! It is Finn!   (*She goes a step back and takes up a spear.*)

Finn: It would be no great load upon you to bid me welcome.

Grania: What is it has brought you here?

Finn: Foolishness brought me here, and nature.

Grania: It is foolishness for a man not to stop and mind his own estate.

Finn: A wild bird of a hawk I had, that went out of my hand. I am entitled to it by honest law.

Grania: I know your meaning well. But hearken now and put yourself in a better mind. It is a heavy punishment you put upon us these many years, and it is short till we'll all be in the grave, and it is as good for you leave us to go our own road.

Finn: A queer long way I would have walked for no profit. Diarmuid is gone out from you. There is nothing to hinder me from bringing you away.

Grania: There is such a thing.

Finn: Is it your own weak hand on that spear?

Grania: (*Throwing it down.*)   No, but your own pride, if it has not gone from you and left you snapping and angry, like any moon-crazed dog.

Finn: If there is madness within me, it is you yourself have a right to answer for it. But for all that, it is truth you are speaking, and I will not bring you away, without you will come with me of your own will.

Grania: That will be when the rivers run backward.

Finn: No, but when the tide is at the turn. I tell you, my love that was allotted and foreshadowed before the making of the world will drag you in spite of yourself, as the moon above drags the waves, and they grumbling through the pebbles as they come, and making their own little moaning of discontent.

Grania: You have failed up to this to drag or to lead me to you.

Finn: There is great space for rememberings and regrettings in the days and the nights of seven years.

Grania: I and Diarmuid stopped close to one another all that time, and being as we were without hearth or frolic, or welcome or the faces of friends.

Finn: Many a day goes by, and nothing has happened in it worth while. And then there comes a day that is as if the ring of life, and that holds all the joy and the pain of life between its two darknesses. And I am thinking that day has come, and that it will put you on the road to myself and Almhuin.

Grania: You think I will give in to you because I am poor in the world. But there is grief in my heart I not to have strength to drive that spear through you, and be quit of your talk forever.

Finn: Would you think better of me if I had been satisfied to put this crown on some other woman's head, and it having rested upon your own for one moment of time? (*Takes crown from under his cloak and holds it up.*)

Grania: It would have been best. I would be well pleased to see you do it yet.

Finn: But I would not do that to gain the whole world entirely. And I to have my youth seven times over, it is after you I would come searching those seven times. And I have my life spent and wasted following you, and I have kissed the sign of your foot in every place all through Ireland.

Grania: I have no forgiveness for you that have been a red enemy to my darling and my man. I have too long a memory of all the unkindness you have done.

Finn: It is your fault if I did them. Every time the thought of kindness came to me, the thought of you came with it, and put like a ring of iron around my heart.

Grania: It is turned to iron indeed. And listen to me now, Finn, and believe what I say. You to have hunted us through crags and bushes, and sent us out in the height of hailstones and of rain, I might overlook it and give you pardon. But it is the malice you showed, putting a hedge between myself and Diarmuid that I never will forgive, but will keep it against you for ever. For it is you left my life barren, and it was you came between us two through all the years.

Finn: I did right doing that. There is no man but would keep the woman he is to wed for himself only.

Grania: It was your shadow was between us through all that time, and if I carry hatred towards you, I leave it on your own head. And it is little I would have thought of hardships, and we two being lovers and alone. But that is not the way it was. For the time he would come in, sweaty and sorefooted from the hunting, or would be dull and drowsy from the nights of watching at the door, I would be down-hearted and crabbed maybe; or if I was kind itself, it would be like a woman would be humouring a youngster, and her mind on some other track. But we to have a settled home and children to be fondling, that would not have been the way with us, and the day would have been short, and we showing them off to one another, and laying down there was no one worthy to have called them into the world but only our two selves.

Finn: You are saying what is not true, and what you have no right to say. For you know well and you cannot deny it, you are man and wife to one another this day.

Grania: And if we are, it is not the same as a marriage on that day we left Almhuin would have been. It was you put him under a promise and a bond that was against nature, and he was a fool to make it, and a worse fool to keep it. And what are any words at all put against the love of a young woman and a young man? It was you turned my life to weariness, and my heart to bitterness, and put me under the laughter and the scorn of all. For there was not a poor man's house where we lodged, but I could see wonder and mockery and pity in the eyes of the woman of the house, where she saw that poor as she was, and ugly maybe and ragged, a king's daughter was thought less of than herself. Because if Diarmuid never left his watch upon my threshold, he never came across it, or never gave me the joy and pride of a wife! And it was you did that on me, and I leave it on your own head; and if there is any hatred to be found in the world, and it to be squeezed into one cup only, it would not be so black and so bitter as my own hatred for you!

Finn: That hatred is as if crushed out of the great bulk of my love for you, that is heaped from the earth to the skies.

Grania: I am not asking it or in need of it. Why would I listen to a story I have heard often and too often?

Finn: But you will listen, and you will give heed to it. You came of your own free will to Almhuin to be my wife. And my heart went out to you there and then, and I thought there would be the one house between us, and that it was my child I would see reared on your knee. And that was known to every one of my people and of my armies, and you were willing it should be known. And after that, was it a little thing that all Ireland could laugh at the story that I, Finn, was so spent, and withered, and loathsome in a woman's eyes, that she would not stop with me in a life that was full and easy, but ran out from me to travel the roads, the same as any beggar having seven bags. And I am not like a man of the mean people, that can hide his grief and his heart-break, bringing it to some district where he is not known, but I must live under that wrong and that insult in full sight of all, and among mockery and malicious whisperings in the mouth of those maybe that are shouting me!

Grania: I have a great wrong done to you, surely, but it brings me no nearer to you now. And our life is settled, and let us each go our own course.

Finn: Is it not a great wonder the candle you lighted not to have been quenched in all that time? But the light in your grey eyes is my desire for ever, and I am pulled here and there over hills and through hollows. For my life was as if cut in two halves on that night that put me to and fro; and the half that was full and flowing was put behind me, and it

has been all on the ebb since then. But you and I together
could have changed the world entirely, and put a curb upon
the spring-tide, and bound the seven elements with our
strength. And now, that is not the way I am, but dragging
there and hither, my feet wounded with thorns, the tracks
of tears down my cheeks; not taking rest on the brink of any
thick wood, because you yourself might be in it, and not
stopping on the near side of any lake or inver because you
might be on the far side; as wakeful as a herd in lambing
time, my companions stealing away from me, being tired
with the one corn-crake cry upon my lips always, that is,
Grania. And it is no wonder the people to hate you, and but
for dread of me they would many a time have killed you.

Grania: If I did you wrong, did I do no wrong against
Diarmuid? And all the time we were together he never cast
it up against me that it was I brought him away from his
comrades, or, as he could have done, that I asked him without waiting for his asking. He never put reproaches on me,
as you are reproaching me, now that I am alone and without
any friend at hand.

Finn: Diarmuid has no harm in his heart, and he would find
it hard to do anything was not mannerly, and befitting a man
reared in kings' houses, if he is no good lover itself.

Grania: Diarmuid that gave all up for love is the best lover of
the whole world.

Finn: No, for his love is not worth a reed of straw beside
mine.

Grania: His love knows no weakening at all. He would
begrudge me to walk the road! Listen to this now. The King
of Foreign had put his arms about me – he had left but one
kiss on my mouth – and for that much Diarmuid is gone out
at this time to take his life!

Finn: Diarmuid to be a good lover, it is my own life he would
have shortened. If he had any great love for you, it is I myself
he would not have left living.

Grania: You are belittling Diarmuid, and I will judge you
by your own words. You boast that you are a better lover.
Then why are you wasting talk here, and you having let him
go out of your hand today?

Finn: He is not gone out of reach of my hand.

Grania: He is! He is safe and gone from you. Would I have been so daring in talk, and I not certain of that?

Finn: It is hard for any man to escape the thing was laid down for him, and that he has earned.

Grania: It is no friend of yours he went out fighting. It is that foreign king. He will be well able to put him down.

Finn: It is not a man weakened with love that goes out to win in a fight. It is a foreign hand will do judgment upon him, but it was I myself sent him out to that judgment.

Grania: That is not true! It is a boast and a bragging you are making to threaten me. You would never dare to do it. He is of your own blood.

Finn: You are beautiful and I am old and scarred. But if it was different, and I to be what I was, straight as a flag-flower, and yellow-haired, and you what the common people call out that hate you, wide and low-born, a hedgehog, an ugly thing, I would kill any man at all that would come between us, because you are my share of the world and because I love you.

Grania: You are speaking lies – I know it is a lie and that it was not you sent him out to that fight. It was not you, it was that sharp-tongued beggar, that spiteful crippled man.

Finn: There is no man only a lover, can be a beggar and not ashamed.

Grania: It was not you – you were not that cripple.

Finn: This is the hand where you put the broken bread.

Grania: It was you sent Diarmuid out! It was you came between us! It was you parted us! It was your voice he obeyed and listened to, the time he had no ears for me! Are you between us always? – I will go out after him, I will call him back – I will tell him your treachery – he will make an end of it and of you. He will know you through and through this time. It will fail you to come between us again.

(*A heavy shout is heard.*)

Finn: Hush, and listen!   (*Goes to the door.*)

Grania: What is it? Let me find Diarmuid—

Finn: (*Holding her back.*)   It is Diarmuid is coming in.

(*Diarmuid's body is carried in by two fair-haired young men.*

They lay it on the bed and take off their caps. Finn looks at him, takes his hand, then lays it down and turns away.)

Death and the judgment of death have overtaken him.

Grania: (*Bending over him.*) Oh, Diarmuid, you are not dead! You cannot be dead! It is not in this hour you could die, and all well between us, and all done away with that had parted us!

Finn: He is dead indeed. Look at that wound in his neck. He is bleeding and destroyed with blood.

Grania: Come back to me, come back, my heart's darling, my one love of the men of the world! Come back, if but for one moment of time. Come back, and listen to all I have to tell. And it is well we have the world earned, and is it not a hard thing, a young man to die because of any woman at all casting an eye on him, and making him her choice, and bringing her own bad luck upon him, that was marked down for her maybe in the time before the world. And it is hunger I gave you through my love, and it is a pity it is around you it was cast, and it is a pity now, you to be loosed out of it. And it would have been better for you, some girl of the ducks and ashes, hard reared and rough, to have settled out your pillow, and not myself that brought ill will upon you, and the readying of your grave!

Finn: Where is the use of calling to him and making an outcry? He can hear no word at all, or understand anything you say. And he has brought with him a good memory of happiness and of love; and some of the world's great men bringing with them but empty thoughts of a life that was blasted and barren.

Grania: Ochone, my grief! For all is at an end, and you are clean wheat ground and bruised and broken between two hard stones, the luckless love of a woman, and the love turned to anger of a friend.

Finn: (*Putting his hand on her arm.*) That is enough. A red death is a clean death, and the thing that is done cannot be undone, and the story is ended, and there is no other word to say.

Grania: (*Pushing him away.*) You stood between us long enough and he living, but you cannot come between us and he dead! And I own him from this time anyway, and I am glad and could nearly laugh, knowing your power is spent and run out, and that it will fail you to come meddling any more between us that are lovers now to the end!

Finn: Your bitter words are no matter. There is no one to give heed to them.

Grania: It is well I will keen him, and I never will quit his grave till such time as the one flagstone will cover the two of us from the envious eyes of the women of Ireland and from your own. And a woman to lose her comrade, she loses with him her crown! And let you go to some other place, Finn, for you have nothing to say to him at all, and no other hand will be laid on him from this out but my own!

Finn: (*Bending over him.*) He is not dead – his lips are stirring – there is a little blush in his face—

Grania: (*Stooping.*) Oh, Diarmuid, are you come back to me? (*He moves.*) Speak to me now. Lift now your lips to my own – hush! He is going to speak. Oh, Diarmuid, my darling, give me one word!

Diarmuid: (*Turns his head slightly and looks at Finn.*) Is that you, my master, Finn? I did not know you were dead along with me.

Grania: You are not dead, you are living – my arms are about you. This is my kiss upon your cheek. (*Kisses him.*)

Diarmuid: (*Not noticing her.*) The King of Foreign is dead. I struck him down by the sally tree – as he was falling he struck at me, and the life went out of me. But what way did you meet with your death, my master Finn?

Grania: You are living I say – turn towards me. I am Grania, your wife.

Diarmuid: (*Still speaking to Finn.*) It is a very friendly thing you to have met me here, and it is Ireland and the world should be lonesome after you this day!

Grania: Speak to him, Finn. Tell him he is astray. Tell him he is living. Bring the wits back to him.

Finn: Diarmuid, you are not dead, you are in the living world.

Grania: Come back, now, come back to life! Finn thought he had sent you to your death, but it failed him – he is

treacherous – he is no friend to you. You will know that now.
Come back, and leave thinking of him!

Diarmuid: (*Still speaking to Finn.*) There was some word
I had to say meeting you – it is gone – I had it in my mind a
while ago.

Grania: Do you not see me ? It is I myself am here – Grania!

Diarmuid: Some wrong I did you, something past forgiving.
Is it to forgive me you are waiting here for me, and to tell me
you are keeping on anger against me after all ?

Finn: Come back now, and put out your strength, and take a
good grip of life, and I will give you full forgiveness for all
you have done against me. And I will have done with anger,
and with jealousy that has been my bedfellow this long time,
and I will meddle with you no more, unless in the way of
kindness.

Diarmuid: Kindness – you were always kind surely, and I a
little lad at your knee. Who at all would be kind to me and
you not being kind ?

Finn: I will turn back altogether, I will leave you Grania
your wife, and all that might come between us from this
time.

Diarmuid: What could there be would come between us two ?
That would be a strange thing indeed.

Finn: I will go, for the madness is as if gone from me; and
you are my son and my darling, and it is beyond the power
of any woman to put us asunder, or to turn you against me
any more.

Diarmuid: That would be a very foolish man would give up
his dear master and his friend for any woman at all.   (*He
laughs.*)

Grania: He is laughing – the sense is maybe coming back to
him.

Diarmuid: It would be a very foolish thing, any woman at all
to have leave to come between yourself and myself. I cannot
but laugh at that.

Finn: Rouse yourself up now, and show kindness to the wife
that is there at your side.

Diarmuid: There is some noise of the stream where I died.
It is in my ears yet – but I remember – I am remembering

now – there was something I begrudged you, the time our bodies were heavy about us. Something I brought away from you, and kept from you. What wildness came upon me to make me begrudge it? What was it I brought away from you? Was not Hazel my own hound? (*He dies.*)

Finn: Lift up your head, open your eyes, do not die from me! Come back to me, Diarmuid, now!

Grania: He will say no word to either one of us again for ever. (*She goes to wall, leaning her head against it, her hands working.*)

Finn: Are you gone indeed, Diarmuid, that I myself sent to your death? And I would be well pleased it was I, Finn, was this day making clay, and you yourself holding up your head among the armies. It is a bad story for me you to be dead, and it is in your place I would be well satisfied to be this day; and you had not lived out your time. But as to me, I am tired of all around me, and all the weight of the years is come upon me, and there will be no more joy in anything happens from this day out forever. And it is as if all the friends ever I had went to nothing, losing you. (*After a moment's silence he turns to the young men.*) Bring him out now, slaves of Britain, to his comrades and his friends, and the armies that are gathering outside, till they will wake him and mourn him and give him burial, for it is a king is lost from them this day. And if you have no mind to keen him, let you raise a keen for the men of your own country he left dumb in the dust, and a foolish smile on their face. For he was a good man to put down his enemies and the enemies of Ireland, and it is living he would be this day if it was not for his great comeliness and the way he had, that sent every woman stammering after him and coveting him; and it was love of a woman brought him down in the end, and sent him astray in the world. And what at all is love, but lies on the lips and drunkenness, and a bad companion on the road?

(*The body is carried out. The bearers begin to keen. The keen is taken up by the armies outside. Finn sits down, his head bowed in his hand. Grania begins fastening up her hair and as if preparing for a journey.*)

Finn: You are doing well going out to keen after him.

Grania: It is not with him I am going. It is not with Diarmuid
I am going out. It is an empty thing to be crying the loss of a
comrade that banished me from his thoughts, for the sake of
any friend at all. It is with you I will go to Almhuin. Diarmuid is no more to me than a sod that has been quenched
with the rain.

Finn: I will meddle no more with what belongs to him. You
are the dead man's wife.

Grania: All the wide earth to come between Diarmuid and
myself, it would put us no farther away from one another
than what we are. And as for the love I had for him, it is dead
now, and turned to be as cold as the snow is out beyond the
path of the sun.

Finn: It is the trouble of the day that is preying on you.

Grania: He had no love for me at any time. It is easy know
it now. I knew it all the while, but I would not give in to
believe it. His desire was all the time with you yourself and
Almhuin. He let on to be taken up with me, and it was but
letting on. Why would I fret after him that so soon forgot his
wife, and left her in a wretched way ?

Finn: You are not judging him right. You are distracted with
the weight of your loss.

Grania: Does any man at all speak lies at the very brink of
death, or hold any secret in his heart ? It was at that time he
had done with deceit, and he showed where his thought was,
and had no word at all for me that had left the whole world
for his sake, and that went wearing out my youth, pushing
here and there as far as the course of the stars of Heaven.
And my thousand curses upon death not to have taken him
at daybreak, and I believing his words! It is then I would
have waked him well, and would have cried my seven
generations after him! And I have lost all on this side of
the world, losing that trust and faith I had, and finding him
to think of me no more than of a flock of stairs would cast
their shadow on his path. And I to die with this scald upon
my heart, it is hard thistles would spring up out of my grave.

Finn: Quiet yourself, for this is grief gone wild and that is
beyond all measure.

Grania: I to have known that much yesterday I would have

left him and would have gone with that King that clutched
at me. And I would have said words to Diarmuid would have
left a burn and a sting.

Finn: I will call in women to cry with you and to be comfort-
ing you.

Grania: You are craving to get rid of me now, and to put me
away out of your thoughts, the same as Diarmuid did. But I
will not go! I will hold you to your word, I will take my
revenge on him! He will think to keep your mind filled with
himself and to keep me from you – he will be coming back
showing himself as a ghost about Almhuin. He will think to
come whispering to you, and you alone in the night time.
But he will find me there before him! He will shrink away
lonesome and baffled! I will have my turn that time. It is I
will be between him and yourself, and will keep him outside
of that lodging for ever!

Finn: I gave him my promise I would leave you to him from
this out, and I will keep it to him dead, the same as if he was
still living.

Grania: How well he kept his own promise to you! I will go
to Almhuin in spite of you; you will be ashamed to turn me
back in the sight of the people, and they having seen your
feet grown hard in following and chasing me through the
years. It is women are said to change, and they do not, but
it is men that change and turn as often as the wheel of the
moon. You filled all Ireland with your outcry wanting me,
and now, when I am come into your hand, your love is
rusted and worn out. It is a pity I that had two men, and
three men, killing one another for me an hour ago, to be left
as I am, and no one having any use for me at all!

Finn: It is the hardness of trouble is about my heart, and is
bringing me down with its weight. And it seems to me to be
left alone with December and the bareness of the boughs;
and the fret will be on me to the end.

Grania: Is it not a strange thing, you, that saw the scores and
the hundreds stretched dead, that at the sight of one young
man only, you give in to the drowning of age? It is little I
will give heed from this out to words or to coaxings, and I
have no love to give to any man for ever. But Diarmuid that

belittled me will not see me beating my hands beside his grave, showing off to the cranes in the willows, and twisting a mournful cry. It is the thing I will give him to take notice of, a woman that cared nothing at all for his treachery.

Finn: Wait till the months of mourning are at an end, and till your big passion is cold, and do then what you may think fit, and settle out your life, as it is likely there will be another thought in your mind that time. But I am putting no reproach on you, for it is on myself the great blame should be, and from this out I have no more to say to love or friendship or anything but the hard business of the day.

Grania: I will not wait. I will give my thoughts no leave to repent. I will give no time to those two slaves to tell out the way I was scorned!

Finn: The men of the armies will laugh and mock at you, seeing you settle out a new wedding in the shadow of your comrade's wake.

Grania: There is many a woman lost her lord, and took another, and won great praise in the latter end, and great honour. And why should I be always a widow that went so long a maid? Give me now the crown, till I go out before them, as you offered it often enough. (*She puts it on her head.*) I am going, I am going out now, to show myself before them all, and my hand linked in your own. It is well I brought my golden dress.

Finn: Wait till the darkness of the night, or the dusk of the evening itself.

Grania: No, no. Diarmuid might not see me at that time. He might be gone to some other place. He is surely here now, in this room where he parted from the body – he is lingering there by the hearth. Let him see now what I am doing, and that there is no fear on me, or no wavering of the mind. Open the door now for me!

(*Finn opens door and they go to the opening, she taking his hand. There is a mocking laugh heard. She falls back and crouches down. Finn tries to raise her.*)

Finn: I thought to leave you and to go from you, and I cannot do it. For we three have been these seven years as if alone in the world; and it was the cruelty and the malice of love made its sport with us, when we thought it was our own way we were taking, driving us here and there, knocking you in between us, like the ball between two goals, and the hurlers being out of sight and beyond the boundaries of the world. And all the three of us have been as if worsted in that play. And now there are but the two of us left, and whether we love or hate one another, it is certain I can never feel love or hatred for any other woman from this out, or you yourself for any other man. And so as to yourself and myself, Grania, we must battle it out to the end.

(*Finn raises her up. A louder peal of laughter is heard.*)

Grania: (*Going towards the door.*)   It is but the armies that are laughing! I thought I heard Diarmuid's laugh.

Finn: It is his friends in the armies gave out that mocking laugh.

Grania: And is it not a poor thing, strong men of the sort to be mocking at a woman has gone through sharp anguish, and the breaking of love, on this day? Open the door again for me. I am no way daunted or afraid. Let them laugh their fill and welcome, and laugh you, Finn, along with them if you have a mind. And what way would it serve me, their praise and their affection to be mine? For there is not since an hour ago any sound would matter at all, or be more to me than the squeaking of bats in the rafters, or the screaming of wild geese overhead!

(*She opens the door herself. Finn puts his arm about her. There is another great peal of laughter, but it stops suddenly as she goes out.*)

CURTAIN

NOTES

I THINK I turned to Grania because so many have written about sad, lovely Deirdre, who, when overtaken by sorrow, made no good battle at the last. Grania had more power of will, and for good or evil twice took the shaping of her life into her own hands. The riddle she asks us through the ages is, 'Why did I, having left great, grey-haired Finn for comely Diarmuid, turn back to Finn in the end, when he had consented to Diarmuid's death?' And a question tempts one more than the beaten path of authorized history. If I have held but lightly to the legend, it is not because I do not know it, for in *Gods and Fighting Men* I have put together and rejected many versions. For the present play I have taken but enough of the fable on which to set, as on a sod of grass, the three lovers, one of whom had to die. I suppose it is that 'fascination of things difficult' that has tempted me to write a three-act play with only three characters. Yet where Love itself, with its shadow Jealousy, is the true protagonist I could not feel that more were needed. When I told Mr Yeats I had but these three persons in the play, he said incredulously, 'They must have a great deal to talk about.' And so they have, for the talk of lovers is inexhaustible, being of themselves and one another.

DAVE

PERSONS

Nicholas O'Cahan
(*Elderly, very neatly dressed in old-fashioned clothes, with knee breeches.*)

Kate O'Cahan . . . . . . HIS WIFE
(*A good deal younger. She is winding a ball of wool from skeins on the back of a chair. She walks back and forward to this.*)

Timothy Loughlin . . . . A SERVING MAN

Josephine Loughlin . . . . . A YOUNG GIRL
(*His niece.*)

Dave . . . . A YOUTH
(*In poor working clothes. Looks sullen and slouches. His hair hangs over his forehead.*)

Time: A hundred years ago.

DAVE

Scene: A room well furnished with old-fashioned things, a settle, a chest, an armchair, a turf basket. The door L. opens into a little entry; door R. leads to the kitchen. Timothy is on his knees arranging the fire.

Timothy: (*Shouts.*) Bring in, Dave, the turf! (*No answer.*) Come on, you lazy cur! Hurry now.
(*Dave comes in with an armful.*)
Couldn't you come when I called you?

Dave: (*Sullenly.*) I could if I brought the turf wet.

Timothy: Don't be giving impudence. You know well you were scheming or slouching around some hole or corner.

Dave: Have it your own way so. (*He is putting the turf in the basket.*)

Timothy: If I had my own way it's walking the road you would be – put out of this house.

Dave: I wouldn't please you to go out, or it's out of the reach of your tongue I'd be gone before now.

Timothy: I'll get quit of you in spite of yourself. Hurry on, now, go get another load of the turf. What, now, is keeping that little girl of mine so long in the village?

Dave: There she is at the door. (*Josephine enters as he goes out.*)

Josephine: I left the message for the driver of the long car, that Nicholas O'Cahan and the Missis would be wanting a seat to the town when he'll be passing.

Timothy: You took your time doing that. Idling in the shop I'll engage you were, and the dark of the evening coming on. Fingering ribbons and fooleries.

Josephine: You're out there. I was not in the shop at all.

Timothy: What kept you so? Fooling and gabbing with idlers, the same as yourself. Here now is the Missis.
(*Kate comes in from the other door.*)

Timothy: (*Getting up.*) Josephine that is after bidding the car to wait for you and the Master, ma'am, to bring you to the town for the night.

Kate: I thought you were talking as if vexed with someone.

Timothy: So I am vexed with that lad that's slow bringing in the turf. Come on, now – come, fill up the basket. (*Dave comes in and begins putting in more sods.*) And I was telling this niece of mine she had too much time lost with chattering down in the village.

Josephine: Well, I was not chattering or saying any word at all – but listening.

Timothy: That's it. To some person with as little sense as yourself.

Josephine: You're out again. It was to a holy man was preaching in the street.

Kate: (*Interested.*) Was it a priest that was preaching – or a friar?

Josephine: I don't rightly know. He was a stranger – a sort of a missioner. Asking help he was for the people of Iar Connacht that are down under the fever and the famine.

Timothy: What brought him questing here? All the help we have to give, it is for ourselves we should keep it as is right.

Kate: Tell me, now, Josephine, what account did he give?

Josephine: The fever is running through the country, he was saying. It is a terrible scourge. It is what he said, the people are dying in empty walls with no roof over them, or in a shed in the haggards, or out by the side of the road.

Kate: God help them, they are surely under great trouble.

(*Dave has stopped filling basket, and is listening.*)

Timothy: The right place for them is the poorhouse, that was built for the like of that class.

Josephine: It is what he was saying, the poorhouses are filled till there is no more room in them. The people are dying, he said, without help of priest or friar or anything at all.

Kate: That is a terrible story, if it is true.

Josephine: And worse again—

Kate: There could hardly be worse than that.

Josephine: The breath would hardly be gone out of them, he said, before they'd be put into the earth. No one to give them

burial, but a bag made and the body put in it and thrown in a
hole in the wild bog, and the shaking sod closing over their
head. And he said 'in Connemara over it is the dogs bring
the bodies out of the houses, and ask no leave!'

Kate: (*Puts her hand over her eyes.*) The poor creatures!
What are we doing that we cannot come to their help! The
Lord have mercy on them, and bring them to the comfort of
Heaven!

Timothy: I wouldn't believe a word of it. It's certain the half
of them should be in gaol, as it's likely the gaol fever is
rotting the most of them.

Josephine: I tell you the Missioner said it, and he rising up
his hand.

Timothy: Talk is easy. It's hard trust any of Adam's race.

Dave: (*Comes a step forward, lets fall the sods of turf from his
arm. To Josephine.*) Where is that man was preaching? Is
he in the street yet?

Timothy: (*Taking hold of his arm.*) Mind your own business.
Have you the gap in the wall settled yet? Come on, now.
There are things to make ready before the master will make
his start.

(*Pushes Dave before him out of door. Kate takes her skein of
wool that is on the back of a chair, and begins winding it into
a ball.*)

Josephine: I'm in dread, Ma'am, you'll get a wetting going to
the town. There is rain overhead yet, and all that came down
through the night and through the morning is lying in pools
and in splashes on the road.

Kate: What is weather and a wetting beside what we are after
hearing? That is as pitiful a story as any ever I heard.

Josephine: Ah, the weather might cheer up before you will
make your start. It's myself would like to be going with you,
and to see all the grandeur and the people of the town.

(*She goes into kitchen as Nicholas comes in.*)

Nicholas: (*Closes a book he has been reading as he comes in,
keeping his finger in the place.*) This is a great book I got
from the pedlar. I nearly begrudge going to the town, and
not to be reading it through from start to finish.

Kate: Indeed, I myself have not much heart to go there after all I have been hearing of the fever and the famine, but to stop and say a prayer for all that are under trouble.

Nicholas: Pup, pup, woman. You know your witness is required at the court-house along with my own in that case that concerns Thomas O'Cahan's right of way, and he my third cousin by the two great-grandfathers. Stop now interrupting me till you'll hear what this old poet says (*Sits down in his armchair, and reads.*)

The Kingdom started up altogether,
To put out the Danes who put trouble on Ireland;
The Kennedys and the strength of the Lorcans,
Morans and Brogans armed and dressed (*looks up*)
– the whole of them were in the battle of Clontarf.

Kate: The poor men!

Nicholas: Don't be interrupting me!
They travelled from Munster as may be read,
O'Sullivan out from the west of Ireland –   (*Excited.*)
Ha! Here it is put down clear and plain!

Kate: What is it?

Nicholas: The name I was in search of! And that I made sure should be in the poem. And that is my own name.

Kate: Is it Nicholas O'Cahan?

Nicholas: What about Nicholas? That is a name is well enough, but that likely may not have been in the world in those early times. Listen, now:
O'Donovan of the deer, O'Maher and O'Cahan.
The Battle of Clontarf was not fought without them being in it!

Kate: That should be a long time ago.

Nicholas: Near to a thousand years!

Kate: And was he killed in it?

Nicholas: Killed or not killed what signifies? How do I know did he ever strike a blow, or get a blow? Battle or no battle he would be dead now anyway.

Kate: It is for the people dying of the hunger at this time I am fretting. You might have heard the Missioner down in the village?

Nicholas: Wait now till I'll see is it put down were there any more of my old fathers in the world at that time. O'Malley,

O'Mara – O'Shaughnessy. It is a great book. You would know, reading it, what people are worth nothing, and which of them are worth while.

Kate: We'd mostly know that living anear them.

Nicholas: Believe me, high blood and ancient blood is the best property at all to run in a family. – Do you know what I'm thinking?

Kate: I do not, without you'd tell me.

Nicholas: It is going through my mind that if the Lord had sent us a son we would find it hard to make our mind up what name to bestow on him, among all the big names in my family.

Kate: (*Coming back with her ball of wool, interested.*) I used often to be thinking I would call him Patrick.

Nicholas: Not at all. It is well enough for people with no genealogy to go seeking a name among the saints. But where there is family, it is right to show respect to the family. I should have a good deal of quality belonging to me.

Kate: I was only saying—

Nicholas: Go easy, now! It is natural for you to be running down race. I am finding no fault with yourself. But it is the first time an O'Cahan ever joined with a Heniff! You'll be saying, I suppose, that lad Dave, that is a foundling is not far from being equal to myself!

Kate: (*Turning back to her chair.*) You need not be running down my people. I never saw poverty out of my father or my mother. Everyone belonging to me came from the old stock of the parish, and my grandmother coming to Mass every Sunday on a pillion and a black mare!

Nicholas: Don't be talking. Where is Timothy? (*Calls.*) Timothy! I must tell him about the antiquity of the O'Cahans.

Timothy: (*Coming in.*) I sent the message, sir, to the driver of the long car—

Nicholas: Stop a minute and listen. (*Takes up book.*) Did you ever hear news of the families that drove out the Danes, the Lochlanach, from Ireland?

Timothy: What way would I hear it, sir? I have not learning like yourself.

Nicholas: Long ago as it was, Timothy, near to a thousand

years, they were not without one of my own race and
name.

Timothy: Why wouldn't there be one of them? It's easy
know that out of yourself – or twenty-one of them! The
O'Cahans are a great breed, surely. It's the finest thing in the
known world to have high generations behind you.

Nicholas: It is proud my third cousin Thomas O'Cahan will
be tomorrow, hearing he had a far-off father living close on a
thousand years ago. Hurry on, now, Kate, and make ready
for the road.

Kate: I will, so soon as I'll have this ball of wool wound. I
have but to put on my bonnet and my shawl. I hope no bad
thing will happen the house, and we away from it through
the whole of the night-time.

Nicholas: Timothy Loughlin will be in charge, and the little
girl Josephine, his niece, till such time as we'll come back
tomorrow.

Timothy: Believe me, sir, I'll take good care of all – only that
lad—

Nicholas: Give me here my Sunday boots. (*Begins taking
off the boots he is wearing.*)

Timothy: (*Bringing boots.*) It is what I was saying, that lad
Dave – I'd sooner you'd bring him along with you. It is hard
for me to keep control of him. He is a bad class of a scamp.

Nicholas: I have it in my mind you were making some report
of him a while ago.

Timothy: I give you my word, sir, in the twelve-month I
lived with you, I had but the half of it peaceable, before that
lad was brought in here. (*He kneels to lace Nicholas's boots.*)

Nicholas: I have some memory it was yourself brought him
in from where he was standing, a *spailpin* with his spade in
his hand, seeking work at the Easter fair. Saying, you were,
he would be easy brought on his back, having no kindred to
be running to.

Timothy: There is not a day but I'll hear some troublesome
thing of him. Rambling and idling, card-playing up in the
mountains – that's where he was through last night.

Kate: Ah, there's boys will do that sort of thing to the end
of time.

Timothy: He's tricky, and has too much tricks in him. He is a holy terror.

Kate: Well, he should be as God made him.

Nicholas: Do not be taking his side now. It was against my own judgment I brought him into the house. A lad whose race and kindred no one knows, and whose father and mother no one knows.

Kate: He is but a youth of a boy. It's a pity to put on him the sins of the generations before him.

Nicholas: He has no generations before him, bad or good to give him that excuse.

Timothy: That's it. A by-child reared in the workhouse. It's likely a tinker's brat.

Nicholas: That's a class I don't like, and I wouldn't like it, and I'm a man that couldn't like it.

Kate: He was maybe born into his troubles. It's easy be good having good means and a good way and plenty of riches.

Nicholas: Hurry on, now, Kate, and make ready. Give me here the key till I'll lock this book in the chest. (*Takes keys and puts one in the lock.*)

Timothy: The vagabone! It's a skelping he should get to bridle him that would take the skin off him. He is bad out and out. He brought badness into the world with him, the same as you might bring a birthmark.

Kate: (*Going over to take last threads of the skein off the chair.*) Maybe so, maybe so. I never got learning out of books. But it's often I heard said there is no child comes into the world but brings with him some grain of the wisdom of Heaven. It's the mother can know that, watching his little ways. The Spirit of God given in the beginning wasn't given to one or to two. I myself can tell you that much if I never had a child of my own. (*Goes.*)

Timothy: (*As Nicholas is about to lock the chest.*) There is Dave coming. Have a care, sir, where you would conceal your choice things—

(*Dave comes in.*)

Timothy: Where were you?

Dave: Where you bade me go. Putting up the gap in the wall—

Timothy: I'll believe that when I'll see myself is it done. It's likely you would make a poor job of it with the drowsiness is on you after being out rambling through the night-time.

Dave: I hear what you're saying.

Nicholas: (*Who is turning over the pages of his book, and putting a mark in.*)   Tut, tut, try and behave now.

Timothy: You see the way he is, sir, a sullen miserable hound.

Nicholas: It is right you should learn behaviour. But I would not be hard on you, as I would on one who had a good rearing and a good name.

Dave: What fault have you to find with my name ? Anyway I got no other name. Dave, short and sharp like you would shout for a dog.

Timothy: Have some shame on you! I tell you, you not to have come into the world would be no loss at all.

Nicholas: That's enough, Timothy. I don't know where are my glasses ? (*He puts down the book and looks for them.*)

Timothy: Hearken now. Your master is going away for one night – or two nights. I myself will be in charge of all here. I lay it on you that you will not be drinking or stealing, or be going to night sports or dance-houses with scamps and schemers, gambling or smoking or snuffing – fighting and quarrelling – bringing bad lads into the house on top of me.

Dave: (*With a bitter laugh.*)   Go on with your A.B.C. Put on me all the sins you can find to put on me, and I'll not deny them! Swearing big oaths and blasphemy! To laugh at my neighbour's downfall! To make nothing of breaking the Ten Commandments! I've a right to be put running with a price on my head, the same as a wild dog of the hills.

Timothy: Oh, to listen to him! It is to the assizes he should be dragged by the hair of his head!

Dave: Have a care now. I could put curses out of myself as quick as you!

Nicholas: (*Putting on his hat.*)   Leave off that uproar and go in there to the Missis. (*He goes. Calls out.*) Hurry now, Kate, or we'll miss the car. Dave will bring out all your little packages and wearables.

(*Kate comes out, followed by Dave, with packages. She is dressed for the journey.*)

Timothy: God speed you, sir, and come back to us safe and sain. I'll mind the house well. (*They go out.*) It's a pity you're not bringing that lad before the judge that might put the terror of the law on him!

(*He turns back as Josephine comes in bringing a kettle in her hand.*)

Josephine: Oh, are they gone! (*Calls from door.*) Oh, Ma'am, won't you stop a minute, and I'll have the tea wet for you! (*She turns round.*) She beckons she could not come back. (*She puts kettle down on hearth.*)

Timothy: (*Looking from window.*) They are going down the road in a hard trot. I was in dread the wet would come down again, and turn them back from making their start.

Josephine: (*Flinging herself into Nicholas's armchair.*) My joy go with them in a bottle of moss. If they never come back they'll be no great loss! Here's his old book on the floor! (*Kicks it.*)

Timothy: (*Giving it a kick, and then picking it up.*) Himself and his ancient generations! And looking at myself over the top of it as if I was dirt! If I didn't make up my mind to humour him I'd like well to face him on the head of that.

Josephine: He hasn't a great deal of sense. Will you look what they left after them? Their whole bunch of keys. Stuck in the lockhole of the chest one of them is.

Timothy: Do you say so! I never knew Nicholas O'Cahan leave that chest open till now.

Josephine: (*Opening it.*) Well, we'll take a view of it. Here is a grand shawl I never saw. It would suit myself well. (*Puts it on, gets up on a chair to look at herself in the mirror.*) A great pity it to be lying there idle. (*Looks in chest again.*) And the silk skirt she put on at the time of the wedding at the Keanes. (*Slips it on.*) I would be well pleased to wear silk clothes, and to have a lady's life.

Timothy: (*Who has taken the keys and opened the cupboard.*) Here is where he keeps his cellar. (*Takes out a jar, pours some of its contents into a glass, and drinks it off. Pours some more into the glass and leaves it on the table.*) That's good stuff, and no mistake.

Josephine: (*Kneeling at the chest.*)   Linen sheets as white as if they were for her burying – and towels of the finest flax, fit for any bishop, or any big lord.

Timothy: (*Stooping over chest.*) Here is some weighty thing—

Josephine: A teapot – and a milk jug. Is it silver they are?

Timothy: (*Examining.*)   White pewter they might be – no it's silver sure enough.

Josephine: (*Putting her hand deeper in the chest:*)   There is some weighty thing here below – a stocking—

Timothy: Give it here to me. (*Unrolls it.*)   Why wouldn't it be weighty, and the foot of it being full of golden guineas! (*Shakes it.*)

Josephine: Gold! That is better again than silver.

Timothy: What use is it to him where he has full and plenty? He cannot bring it with him to the tomb. (*Starts, and drops stocking.*)   There is some noise.

Josephine: (*Getting up, goes to window.*)   It is but thunder. I was thinking it would be coming with the weight of blackness gathering overhead. There now is the rain pouring down.

Timothy: (*Taking stocking again, and weighing it in his hand.*) By cripes! if I got this I'd knock a good turn out of it.

Dave: (*Comes in unheard, shakes the rain from his hat, claps his hands, and calls ironically.*)   God bless the work!

Timothy: (*Hastily stuffing stocking into his pocket while Josephine shuts lid of chest.*)   What brings you snaking in here, idling and spying around?

Dave: It's well for yourselves it is not Nicholas O'Cahan that came in and his Missis.   (*He takes up the glass of whisky, and drinks it off.*)

Timothy: If they did itself what signifies? I'm not like yourself that no one would trust with a fourpenny bit without he'd keep his two eyes fixed on you through the hours of the day and night.

Dave: You can save your chat. I know you well to be a class of a man that is gathering up for himself. You not to have crookedness in you, how would you go picturing it in every other one ? I know well what happened the three lambs you told Nicholas O'Cahan were torn and ate with the fox!

Timothy: You'll go bringing every lie and every bad story to him, I suppose ?

Dave: Why would I ? It is not for him I ever said a prayer, or to please him I'll ever turn informer.

Timothy: You'd best not. There's many a thing I can say about yourself.

Dave: Do your best! There is no wrong thing ever I did since I came to the place but you have it told out ere this, and ten times as much told, and the most made of it, and the worst, the way I never got a penny in my hand for wages, but all stopped for fines or for punishment. I don't know at all what is it holds me back from doing every crime and every robbery, when there could not be put upon me a worse name for badness than what is put upon me now.

Timothy: What could there be in you but badness, you that were left at the side of a ditch by vagabones of tinkers that were travelling the roads of the world since the day of the Crucifixion!

Dave: Didn't I hear enough of that story the seventeen years I am in the world ? In the poorhouse, in the street, in this house, nothing but the one bad word. I got no chance in any corner but what my two hands gave me and God! I don't know in the world wide what kept me back that I didn't kill and destroy the whole of ye, and bring down the roof over your head. I declare to my God it's often I'd have choked the breath out of yourself and your master if it wasn't there is a look of pity in the old woman's face, if she hasn't the courage to stretch a hand to me itself.

Timothy: Why would any Christian stretch a hand to you or the like of you ?

Dave: What now is the worst thing and the most thing I could do to punish the world and the whole of ye ?

Josephine: Ah, let you quieten down, and not be shouting to call in the country entirely.

Dave: To put a wisp of lighted straw in among the lumber in the chest, and to put another in the thatch of the roof ? To burn the house and all that's in it, and to leave the whole of ye without a roof over your head! That is what I owe to the world that gave me nothing only insult since ever I made my start upon its plains! (*He begins flinging things into the chest.*)

Josephine: (*Seizing his arm.*) Stop, now – can't you only let on to have burned them, and we ourselves will share with you whatever is worth while.

(*Timothy hastily collects what things are best in the chest and puts them in the basket, from which he throws out the turf.*)

Dave: Bring here and throw on them the vessel of sheep's fat was rendered for to dip the candles! That will make a bone-fire will sparkle up to the rafters of the roof. I'll put fire to the house, and all that's in it – only that jar I'll bring out on the road till I'll call to some of the wild class – thieves and sheep-stealers, and the worst of the world's rogues! (*To Timothy.*) It's yourself should come drink with me then! (*He seizes a handful of paper thrown out from the chest, and lights a twist of it at the fire.*)

Josephine: There is someone opening the door. Who could be coming in on this night of thunder and of rain?

Dave: (*Going to door with the lighted wisp in his hand.*) Come in, come in fellow law-breakers! There's a fire lighting will make you a ladder to the stars! There is whisky before you in the jar!

(*Nicholas and Kate O'Cahan come in, she shaking the rain from the umbrella she holds before her. Dave falls back.*)

Nicholas: Dave! Leave down that wisp of fire in the hearth! Are you gone clean mad! (*Snatches wisp from him, and puts it out.*)

(*Timothy rushes at Dave from behind, gives him a violent blow, and strikes him down. He falls heavily with a cry, striking his head against a chair, and lies senseless.*)

Kate: Oh, is it killed he is!

Timothy: Lift him up on the settle till I bind him to it. (*He and Nicholas lift and bind him with the cord that has bound the parcels.*)

Nicholas: You did well to down a lad of that sort. He is a terrible type of a ruffian.

Timothy: He's one of the old boy's comrades. If you had seen him ten minutes ago, he was all one with a wild beast. (*He binds Dave's feet.*)

Kate: I give him up now. He is a holy terror to the whole world.

Timothy: It would be well to put a gag in his mouth.

Josephine: He can say nothing. He has his senses lost with the dint of the fall.

Timothy: With the dint of drunkenness. But I now have something to say. Look now the way the room is. He that got hold of the keys – it's likely picked them from your pocket, and he attending you along the road—

Kate: Oh, no! I couldn't hardly believe that!

Timothy: Myself and the little girl being in the kitchen – attending to the work we had to do – and when we came in – there as you see— (*Points to chest.*)

Kate: Ah, to look at the way all is tossed and turned. No, but the choice things put within in the basket.

Timothy: He was to bring them away through the darkness—

Nicholas: He should be a thief out and out.

Timothy: He'd take the sheet from your side, with respects to you. And when he got at the drink—

Kate: Ah, it should be the drink that did it—

Timothy: He drank the devil into him. He rose the shovel at me to let my blood, and maybe knock out my brains. Only for I have a good coat on my shoulders he'd split me.

Nicholas: The Lord be praised he has no family to bring under disgrace!

Timothy: And worse again. He was to put a light in the clothes that's within the chest – and in the rafters, and to burn the house entirely, the way you would not see all he had robbed. He was on the brink of doing it!

Kate: (*Covering her face with her hands.*) Oh, tell me no more. The fire is the last of all!

Timothy: (*To Josephine.*) Here's my little girl can bear witness did he call for the pan of sheep's tallow for to give a heart to the flame.

Josephine: (*Sullenly.*) You can tell your own story without me.

Nicholas: I will commit him to justice in the morning. Let the Sheriff come bring him away with his men.

Timothy: It is this very minute he should be brought away. He is that crafty you couldn't trust him not to make his escape. He might rise up in his senses and break his cords and make an attack on us all.

Nicholas: It is likely the car-driver went no farther than the post-house at the cross. Out on the car, and the rain down, we got more wet than all the men of the world. You should go around the whole of the province before you would come to the town.

Kate: The flood had us made fools of. The water on the public road had leave to cover the bridge.

Josephine: Oh, let me loosen your cloak, ma'am. You are wet-drowned and perished.

(*She takes Kate's cloak and bonnet and shakes them before the fire.*)

Timothy: To follow the car-driver to the post-house, and to catch him, he could bring word to the barracks to send a sergeant to our aid. Let you go tell him that sir, and I'll stop and mind this lad.

Nicholas: Not at all, but you will come holding the lantern. The night is come on, and the road is as slippery as a road of ice. (*To Kate.*) We'll be back in a while's time.

Kate: Oh, what way can I stop here in the room after all has happened. The fright's gone into my heart!

(*She takes cloak and bonnet from Josephine and goes through door to kitchen.*)

Nicholas: (*Sarcastically.*) The girl Josephine will maybe have the courage to stop for ten minutes, or twelve minutes, of time to guard you against a lad that has lost his senses and is tied with knots and with a rope.

(*They go out, Timothy carrying lantern.*)

Josephine: (*Stands looking out after them.*) I'll go back to my mother's friends in the village. I'm not willing to stop longer in this place, and my uncle beckoning me to tell lies. (*She slips out, knocking over the umbrella that is in her way. Bangs the door after her. The room is almost dark. Dave stirs and moans. Kate, coming back, goes over and looks at him. She lights a candle, then goes to him again.*)

Kate: They were surely too hasty and too hard, treating him

the way they did. I would hardly believe looking at him he
could be so bad as what they say. And if he was itself, is it his
fault, being as he was a child without a home? (*She touches
his hair.*)   There is blood on it, and a sharp wound upon his
head.

Dave: (*Cries out.*)   Where am I? Loosen my hands. I cannot
move!

Kate: Lie quiet, now, and I will do what I can for you.
(*She takes one of the fine towels from the chest, takes the silver
bowl and pours water into it from the kettle.*)

Dave: Let me up out of this! Are they gone out, the cowards!
My thousand curses on them! Loosen my hands till I will
light a wisp in earnest! I'll get my revenge on them! That
death may perish them! That I may see them kicked roaring
through the provinces! Oh! there is a sting of pain – I cannot
move – I cannot see – the blood is coming into my eyes.
(*His voice fails as his head sinks back, and he lies still.*)

Kate: Close your eyes now till I'll wash the blood from them.
(*She rolls up a sheet, and puts it as a pillow under his head, and
washes the blood from his face.*)   Here now is a knife. I will
cut the cords from your hands (*does so*) and from your
feet. (*He moves his limbs, and then lies quite still.*)   He is in a
doze of weakness. The poor child, all of them telling him he
was bad, what way could he believe there was the breath of
God in him? (*He moans as she washes the blood from his
hair.*)   Astray in the lonesome world, he never met with
kindness or the love of kindred, to make his heart limber.
(*She stoops and listens to his breathing.*)   That he may get
comfort in his sleep, where he is used to little comfort in his
waking! That is all I can do for him now, but to bless him
with the sign of Christ's cross.   (*She makes the sign over him,
and sits down on a chair near the fire and bows her head.*)   Oh,
King of Mercy come to his help! He is as lonesome as a
weaned lamb gone astray among the stones. It is as if he had
lost his way in the world, and been bruised on the world's
roads. The dust has darkened his eyes, it is hard for him lift
his head into the light. He is under clouds of trouble. Bring
him to the dawn of the white day. Send a blessing on him
from the Court of the Angels!   (*She sings*) –

There lust and lucre cannot dwell,
There envy bears no sway,
There is no hunger, heat nor cold,
But pleasure every day.

Thy gardens and thy gallant walks
Continually are green,
There grow such sweet and pleasant flowers
As nowhere else are seen.

Quite through the trees with silver sound
The flood of life doth flow
Upon whose banks on every side
The wood of life doth grow.

There trees for evermore bear fruit,
And evermore do spring;
There evermore the angels sit
And evermore do sing!

(*Music is heard outside as she ceases.*)
There is music outside – sweet quieting music. It might be
some poor wandering fiddler going the road through the
provinces. (*She stands up and looks at Dave, then sits down
again facing him.*) He is sleeping very easy. There is surely
someone having a wish for him, in or out of the world.

Dave: (*Moves and mutters, then raises himself on his elbow as if
listening. He laughs.*) I am coming – I could not see the
path, but I heard the music and the laughing – merry laughter
not mocking. Is it me you're calling brother? It is long since
I was called by that name. Am I your brother, and you with
your head held so high? I see the door open – but there is a
dyke between us. Reach me out your hand – it is hard to
get over the dyke. There is the music again. (*He closes his
eyes.*)

Kate: He is maybe listening to the birds of Heaven. It is
sometimes a vision is sent through the passion sleep of the
night.

Dave: (*He has moved a little, but is still listening.*) I had a
bad dream. I dreamed I was on a rough road – with ugly
words – with mean company – the mud was splashed on me

and the dirt. (*Listens.*) I will, I will do your bidding as it is your will. I will go back till I have leave to come to you – till such time as you will beckon me to come. (*He lays down his head and sleeps again.*)

Kate: He surely got comfort in his sleep. There is a bright appearance on his face.

Dave: (*Starting up.*) Where am I ? What is this place ?

Kate: (*Standing up, and coming nearer.*) Where were you, agra ?

Dave: Some good place it was – a very green lawn. It had no bounds to its beauty. (*Puts his hand over his eyes.*)

Kate: It was surely a good dream.

Dave: There were some that held the hand to me. Who were they ? I was to find something. Oh! it is going astray on me! I cannot keep it in my mind!

Kate: It will likely come back to you again.

Dave: It was as if all the herbs of summer were in blossom – I think no one could be sick or sorry there. I would nearly say it had what should be the sound and the feeling of home.

Kate: It was maybe not in this world you saw that good harbour.

Dave: And a very laughable thing. It was nearly like as if I was a king's son or a great gentleman. I could not but laugh thinking that. (*He lays down his head.*)

Kate: (*Moving away.*) It is nearly a pity he had not the power to awake at the time that door was open. It is likely he will walk with his head up from this out, for it may be it was himself he saw in that dream.

Dave: (*Sitting up on the side of the settle.*) Tell me, now, will it ever chance me to get there again ?

Kate: It will surely at the last, with the help of God.

Dave: I will never be content or satisfied till I will come again to that dream.

Kate: You will come to it again, surely, and it will be no dream.

Dave: I want to be in it now.

Kate: Any place that has the love of God in it is a part of that garden. You have maybe brothers under trouble to reach a hand to, and to beckon them to it, as there was a hand reached out to you.

Dave: What way could I do that, being as I am all badness, without goodness or grace?

Kate: Poor child, it is because they were always putting a bad name on you that you don't know you are good.

Dave: Good – You are the first ever said that to me.

Kate: It is certain the Man Above never sent you here without some little flame of His own nature being within you.

Dave: That is a great thought if it is true.

Kate: It is true, surely. Mind you never let that flame be quenched in you.

(*Dave buries his face in his hands.*)

Kate: You might maybe sleep again. The Lord be with you by noon and by night from this out, in the day and in the darkness!   (*Goes taking candle.*)

Voice of Nicholas: (*At the door.*)   I hear no sound. It is likely his senses are astray from him yet.

Voice of Timothy: A great pity it failed us to get word to the sergeant. With all the run I put on myself, the car was gone before me.

(*They come inside.*)

Nicholas: It will be time enough to get help in the morning. He is well tied and bound.

Timothy: He to start defaming or blaspheming, it's what we'll put a gag over his mouth. Or to redden the tongs, and threaten him with cruelty. It's little myself or the world would care he never to rise up again. He is a danger to the whole of the universe.

Nicholas: Bring in here the lantern before we'll fall over some chair.

(*Timothy brings it in at the same moment as Kate comes back with the candle. Dave stands up.*)

Timothy: (*Going behind Nicholas.*)   His hands are free! He'll do murder on us!

Nicholas: (*Seizing a chair, and holding it up.*)   Have a care now!

Dave: (*As if surprised.*)   I have no wish to do hurt or harm.

Timothy: Do not trust him!

Nicholas: It is best for you quit this house before any worse thing might come about!

Dave: I will go. I think I did some foolish thing a while ago. (*Puts his hand over his eyes as if trying to remember.*) There was anger on me – I must have done with foolishness.

Nicholas: Whether or no, you will go do it in some other place than this.

Timothy: That's right – let him go beg his bread.

(*Dave goes towards the door.*)

Kate: Ah, Dave, stop awhile! I would be sorry to see you go begging your bread.

Dave: It would not be for honour, I to go quest or beg. I am going out as I came in, with my spade and the strength of my two hands that are all my estate. I am going in search of – to give help to – (*passes his hand over his eyes*) my people.

Timothy: It is in the gaols you will likely find them, or among those paupers that are rotting with the fever, and are thrown out by the side of the road.

Dave: (*Turning back, his eyes shining.*) That is it! Those are the ones I will go to! The miserable people the preacher was seeking aid for. I will go look for them in Connacht over, and through the whole wilderness of Connemara!

Timothy: Much good you'll do coming to them, unless drinking and scheming!

Dave: (*Taking up his spade and hat.*) If it should fail me to earn a handful of meal to keep the life in them, I can show service to the dead. Those that die on the roadside I will not leave to be dragged by a dog, or swallowed down in a bog-hole. If I cannot make out a couple of boards to put around them, I will weave a straw mat with my hands. If the dead-bells do not ring for them, I will waste a white candle for their wake!

Kate: Oh! You aren't hardly fit for that work, and your cheeks so pale, and the drops of blood on your brow.

Dave: I give you my word I never felt so merry or so strong. I am like one that has found his treasure and must go share it with his kin. Why wouldn't I be airy doing that? (*Goes out.*)

Timothy: A good riddance. I hate the living sight of him. Strutting out like a lord on the mall!

Kate: Stop your bad talk, Timothy. He is a good boy, and a decent boy, and a boy that doesn't deserve it from God or man.

Timothy: He is a thief and a robber. I will swear it before any judge. Dave is a lad that belongs to the gallows.

Josephine: (*Who has come in and heard his last words.*)   I hear what you are saying, and it is not truth. I saw Dave going down the road, and I have it in my mind it was your lies turned him out. (*Comes forward.*)

Timothy: Take care what you are saying!

Josephine:·   I know well what I am saying. Give up now to Nicholas O'Cahan what you have your hand on at this minute, and are keeping for your own profit. Hold him, sir!—

(*Timothy goes towards door, but Nicholas seizes his arms from behind, and while he struggles she tears his pocket open, and bag falls on to floor. Nicholas picks it up.*)

Nicholas: The girl is speaking truth. It is best for you to quit this. It is often it came across me that you, having the bad word so ready on your tongue, should have some bad drop in yourself. But I made allowance for you, because of you being of a poor class, and of no ancient family or good blood.

Timothy: Ancient, is it ? Let me tell you that if your family is ancient my own is more ancient again! Yourself and your generations and your Battle of Clontarf, that was for driving out the Danes! My own family was of the Danes, and came in with the Danes, and it's likely were long in the country before those families were born that drove them out! The seed and breed of the Loughlins is more ancient, and is seventeen times better than any O'Cahan at all!

Nicholas: Of all the impudence! Quit this house before I'll give you up to the Sheriff that will put you in the dock! (*He takes up his book and hurls it at him. Timothy escapes by the door. He sinks into an armchair.*)

Kate: (*Tearfully.*)   That is best. He had a bad thought of everyone, and that breeds badness in a house.

Josephine: Will you put me out, Ma'am, along with him, or will you let me stop and care you ?

Kate: (*Tearfully.*)   I'll put no one out. But the world is turned to be very queer. Too many hard knocks, and I do be tired in my legs. I've near a mind to go follow that poor lad that went out, not having a red halfpenny to handle, and wear out what is left of my life poor and banished like himself. And maybe get more respect that ever I got here, with my name not showing out in any old book!

Nicholas: (*Agitated.*) What is on you, Kate? Don't be talking about leaving me, and the way the wheel is going around I take my oath I will never bring down my pedigree upon you again the longest day I'll live! (*Gets up and flings the book on the hearth.*) Let it turn to ashes and my joy go with it, for nothing in the mighty world will ever make me open it again!

Kate: I'm in dread you will be fretting after it yet, and make that a new reproach against my name.

Nicholas: Well, will this content you, that I'll give up my own name, and call myself Heniff from this out?

Kate: You cannot do that, and Nicholas O'Cahan being cut in clean letters on the slab you have ordered for your burying.

Nicholas: Ah, my poor Kate, what can I do to satisfy you? Listen now, you have leave to call that lad Dave back here from his poverty, if it is your will.

Kate: (*Goes to the window and looks into the darkness, and then turns back.*) I wouldn't ask it. God has surely some great hand in him. He had the look of being very glad in the mind. His head held high, and a light on his brow as bright as the bow of heaven. May friends and angels be around him and steer him to a good harbour in the Paradise of the King!

CURTAIN

NOTES

A thought long dwelling in my mind and that I had heard put by a poor woman in a workhouse into such simple words as, 'There is no child comes into the world but brings with him some grain of the wisdom of Heaven,' was brought nearer to dramatic expression when I saw in the *Irish Statesman* a poem by its Editor, A. E., who has allowed me to print it here and to dedicate the little play to him:

> 'The gods have taken alien shapes upon them
> Wild peasants driving swine
> In a strange country. Through the swarthy faces
> The starry faces shine.
>
> Under grey tattered skies they strain and reel there;
> But cannot all disguise
> The majesty of fallen gods, the beauty,
> The fire beneath their eyes.
>
> They huddle at night within low, clay-built cabins,
> And, to themselves unknown,
> They carry with them diadem and sceptre
> And move from throne to throne.'

EXTRACTS FROM 'OUR IRISH THEATRE'

THE PLAYBOY in Dublin

It was another story when, in 1907, *The Playboy of the Western World* was put on. There was a very large audience on the first night, a Saturday, January 26th. Synge was there, but Mr Yeats was giving a lecture in Scotland. The first act got its applause, and the second, though one felt the audience were a little puzzled, a little shocked at the wild language. Near the end of the third act there was some hissing. We had sent a telegram to Mr Yeats after the first act – 'Play great success'; but at the end we sent another – 'Audience broke up in disorder at the word shift.' For that plain English word was one of those objected to, and even the papers, in commenting, followed the example of some lady from the country, who wrote saying 'the word omitted but understood was one she would blush to use even when she was alone.'

On the Monday night *Riders to the Sea*, which was the first piece, went very well indeed. But in the interval after it, I noticed on one side of the pit a large group of men sitting together, not a woman among them. I told Synge I thought it a sign of some organized disturbance and he telephoned to have the police at hand. The first part of the first act went undisturbed. Then suddenly an uproar began. The group of men I had noticed booed, hooted, blew tin trumpets. The editor of one of the Dublin weekly papers was sitting next to me, and I asked him to count them. He did so, and said there were forty making the disturbance. It was impossible to hear a word of the play. The curtain came down for a minute, but I went round and told the actors to go on playing to the end, even if not a word could be heard. The police, hearing the uproar, began to file in, but I thought the disturbers might tire themselves out if left alone, or be satisfied with having made their protest, and I asked them to go outside but stay within call in case of any attempt being made to injure the players or the stage. There were very few people in the stalls, but among them was Lord Walter Fitzgerald, grand-nephew of the patriot, the adored

Lord Edward. He stood up and asked that he and others in the audience might be allowed to hear the play, but this leave was refused. The disturbance lasted to the end of the evening, not one word had been heard after the first ten minutes.

Next day Mr Yeats arrived and took over the management of affairs. Meanwhile I had asked a nephew at Trinity College to come and bring a few fellow athletes, that we might be sure of some able-bodied helpers in case of an attack on the stage. But, alas! the very sight of them was as a match to the resin of the pit, and a roar of defiance was flung back – townsman against gownsman, hereditary enemies challenging each other as they are used to do when party or political processions march before the railings on College Green. But no iron railings divided pit and stalls, some scuffles added to the excitement, and it was one of our defenders at the last who was carried out bodily by the big actor who was playing Christy Mahon's slain father, and by Synge himself.

I had better help from another nephew. A caricature of the time shows him in evening dress with unruffled shirt cuffs, leading out disturbers of the peace. For Hugh Lane would never have worked the miracle of creating that wonderful gallery at sight of which Dublin is still rubbing its eyes, if he had known that in matters of art the many count less than the few. I am not sure that in the building of our nation he may not have laid the most lasting stone; no fear of a charge of nepotism will scare me from 'the noble pleasure of praising', and so I claim a place for his name above the thirty, among the chief, of our own mighty men.

There was a battle of a week. Every night protestors with their trumpets came and raised a din. Every night the police carried some of them off to the police courts. Every afternoon the papers gave reports of the trial before a magistrate who had not heard or read the play and who insisted on being given details of its incidents by the accused and by the police.

We held on, as we had determined, for the week during which we had announced the play would be acted. It was a definite fight for freedom from mob censorship. A part of the new National movement had been, and rightly, an attack on the stage Irishman, the vulgar and unnatural butt given on the

English stage. We had the destroying of that scarecrow in mind among other things in setting up our Theatre. But the societies were impatient. They began to dictate here and there what should or should not be played. Mr Colum's plays and Mr Boyle's were found too harsh in their presentment of life. I see in a letter about a tour we were arranging: 'Limerick has not yet come to terms. They have asked for copies of proposed plays that they may "place same before the branch of the Gaelic League there." '

At Liverpool a priest had arranged an entertainment. The audience did not like one of the plays and hooted. The priest thereupon appeared and apologized, saying he would take the play off. In Dublin, Mr Martin Harvey, an old favourite, had been forced to take off after the first night a little play because its subject was Irish belief in witchcraft. The widow of a writer of Irish plays that had been fairly popular was picketed through Ireland with her company and was nearly ruined, no one being allowed to enter the doors. Finally, at, I think, Athlone, she was only allowed to produce a play after it had been cut and rearranged by a local committee, made up of the shopkeepers of the town. We would not submit Mr Synge's work or any of the work we put on to such a test, nor would we allow any part of our audience to make itself final judge through preventing others from hearing and judging for themselves. We have been justified, for Synge's name has gone round the world, and we should have been ashamed for ever if we had not insisted on a hearing for his most important work. But, had it been a far inferior play and written by some young writer who had never been heard of, we should have had to do the same thing. If we had been obliged to give in to such organized dictation, we should of necessity have closed the Theatre. I respected the opinion of those among that group who were sincere. They, not used to works of imagination and wild fantasy, thought the play a libel on the Irish countryman, who has not put parricide upon his list of virtues; they thought the language too violent or it might be profane. The methods were another thing; when the tin trumpets were blown and brandished, we had to use the same loud methods and call in the police. We lost some of our audience by the fight; the pit was weak for a while, but one after another said, 'There is no other theatre to go to,' and came back. The stalls, curiously, who appeared to approve of our stand, were shy of us for a long time. They got an idea we were fond of noise and quarrels. That was our second battle, and even at the end of the week, we had won it.

SYNGE

I first saw Synge in the north island of Aran. I was staying there, gathering folklore, talking to the people, and felt quite angry when I passed another outsider walking here and there, talking also to the people. I was jealous of not being alone on the island among the fishers and sea-weed gatherers. I did not speak to the stranger, nor was he inclined to speak to me. He also looked on me as an intruder. I heard only his name. But a little later in the summer Mr Yeats, who was staying with us at Coole, had a note from Synge, saying he was in Aran. They had met in Paris. Yeats wrote of him from there: 'He is really a most excellent man. He lives in a little room which he has furnished himself; he is his own servant. He works very hard and is learning Breton; he will be a very useful scholar.'

I asked him here and we became friends at once. I said of him in a letter: 'One never has to rearrange one's mind to talk to him.' He was quite direct, sincere, and simple, not only a good listener but too good a one, not speaking much in general society. His fellows guests at Coole always liked him, and he was pleasant and genial with them, though once, when he had come straight from life on a wild coast, he confessed that a somewhat warlike English lady in the house was 'civilization in its most violent form.' There could be a sharp edge to his wit, as when he said that a certain actress (not Mrs Campbell), whose modern methods he disliked, had turned Yeats' *Deirdre* into *The Second Mrs Conchubar*. And once, when awakened from the anaesthetic after one of those hopeless operations, the first words that could be understood were, 'Those damned English can't even swear without vulgarity.'

While with us, he hardly looked at a newspaper. He seemed to look on politics and reforms with a sort of tolerant indifference, though he spoke once of something that had happened as 'the greatest tragedy since Parnell's death.' He told me that the people of the play he was writing often seemed the real people among whom he lived, and I think his dreamy look came

247

from this. He spent a good deal of time wandering in our woods where many shy creatures still find their homes – marten cats and squirrels and otters and badgers – and by the lake where wild swans come and go. He told Mr Yeats he had given up wearing the black clothes he had worn for a while, when they were a fashion with writers, thinking they were not in harmony with nature, which is so sparing in the use of the harsh colour of the raven.

Simple things always pleased him. In his long illness in a Dublin hospital, where I went to see him every day, he would ask for every detail of a search I was making for a couple of Irish terrier puppies to bring home, and laugh at my adventures again and again. And when I described to him the place where I had found the puppies at last, a little house in a suburb, with a long garden stretching into wide fields, with a view of the hills beyond, he was excited and said that it was just such a Dublin home as he wanted, and as he had been sure was somewhere to be found. He asked me at this time about a village on the Atlantic coast, where I had stayed for a while, over a post-office, and where he hoped he might go for his convalescence instead of to Germany, as had been arranged for him. I said, in talking, that I felt more and more the time wasted that was not spent in Ireland, and he said: 'That is just my feeling.'

The rich, abundant speech of the people was a delight to him. When my *Cuchulain of Muirthemme* came out, he said to Mr Yeats he had been amazed to find in it the dialect he had been trying to master. He wrote to me: 'Your *Cuchulain* is a part of my daily bread.' I say this with a little pride, for I was the first to use the Irish idiom as it is spoken, with intention and with belief in it.

THE PLAYBOY in New York

Tuesday, November 28th. The papers give a fairly accurate account of what happened last night. There was a large audience, *The Gaol Gate* was put on first, which, of course, has never offended anyone in Ireland, but there was a good deal of coughing going on and there was unrest in the gallery. But one man was heard saying to another, 'This is all right. You needn't interrupt this. Irishmen do die for their neighbours.' Another said, 'This is a part of *The Playboy* that is going on now, but they are giving it under another name.' Very soon after the curtain went up on *The Playboy* the interruptions began. The managers had been taking much too confident a view, saying, 'These things don't happen in New York.' When this did happen, there were plenty of police, but they wouldn't arrest anyone because no one gave the order, and the disturbance was let go on nearly all through the first act. I went round, when the disturbance began, and knelt in the opening of the hearth, calling to every actor who came within earshot that they must not stop for a moment but must spare their voices, as they could not be heard, and we should do the whole act over again. At the end Tyler came round and I was delighted when he shouted that it should be played again. O'Donovan announced this and there were great cheers from the audience. And the whole play was given then in perfect peace and quiet. The editor of the *Gaelic American* and his bodyguard were in the stalls, two rows of them. They were pointed out to me when I came in. The disturbers were very well arranged; little groups here and there. In the box office this morning they have a collection of spoils left by the enemy (chiefly stink-pots and rosaries). A good many potatoes were thrown on the stage, and an old watch, and a tin box with a cigar in it, and a cigarette box. Our victory was complete in the end.

Ten men were arrested. Two of them were bar-tenders; one a liquor dealer; two clerks; one a harness-maker; one an instructor; one a mason; one a compositor, and one an electrician.

Some of the police who protected us were Irish. One of them said to our manager, Mr Robinson: 'There's a Kerryman says he has you pictured, and says he'll have your life.' Mr Robinson had had some words with this Kerryman and had said: 'We'll give you a supper when you come to Dublin,' and the Kerryman had answered, 'We'll give you a wake.'

The disturbers were fined sums from three to ten dollars each.

28th. I was talking to Roosevelt about the opposition on Sunday and he said he could not get into the plays: Mrs Roosevelt not being well, he did not like to leave home. But when I said it would be a help to us, he said, 'Then I will certainly come,' and settled that tonight he will dine with me and come on.

Wednesday, 29th. I was in such a rush last night I sent off my letters very untidily. I hadn't time even to change my dress for dinner. It went off very well. John Quinn, Col. Emmet, grand-nephew of the Patriot, Mr Flynn. I had asked Peter Dunne (Mr Dooley) but he was engaged to dinner at eight at the Guinnesses. He came, however, at seven and sat through ours. He was very amusing, and he and Roosevelt chaffed each other. . . . When we got to the theatre and into the box, people saw Roosevelt and began to clap and at last he had to get up, and he took my hand and dragged me on my feet, too, and there was renewed clapping. . . . Towards the end of *Gaol Gate* there was a great outbreak of coughing and sneezing, and then there was a scuffle in the gallery and a man throwing pepper was put out. There was a scuffle now and then during *The Playboy*, but nothing violent, and always great clapping when the offender was thrown out. We played with the lights up. After the first act I took my party on to the stage and introduced the players, and Roosevelt spoke separately to them and then made a little speech saying how much he admired them and that he felt they were doing a great deal to increase the dignity of Ireland (he has adopted my phrase) and that he 'envied them and Lady Gregory for America.' They were quite delighted and Kerrigan had tears in his eyes. Roosevelt's daughter, who was with another party, then appeared and he introduced her to them, remembering all the names, 'This is Mr Morgan, this is Miss

Magee. . . .' I brought him a cup of tea and it was hard to tear him away when the curtain went up.

I stayed in my room writing letters through the second act, and when I came back, a swarm of reporters was surrounding Roosevelt and he was declaring from the box, 'I would as soon discuss the question as discuss a pipe dream with an out-patient of Bedlam.' This was about an accusation they had just shown him in some paper, saying he had had a secret under-standing with some trusts. He was shaking his fist, and saying, 'I am giving you that straight; mind you, take it down as I say it.' When the play was over, he stayed in the box a few minutes discussing it; he said he would contribute a note on an article he wants John Quinn to write about us. When we left the box, we found the whole route to the door packed, just a narrow lane we could walk through, and everyone taking off hats and looking at him with real reverence and affection, so unlike those royal crowds in London. It was an extraordinary kindness that he did us.

EXTRACTS FROM
'LADY GREGORY'S JOURNALS'

ery bitterly, he was a Labour man, I a Labour
had helped him and worked in the movement,
em all, and that is how I was treated.
d at one time a workers' union, we were to carry
selves without employers, we were to earn big
ge Russell gave £50 towards it. We did well for
o, there was one of us worked from 8 o'clock in
until 7 o'clock at night. But, after a little, work
would read the papers and not work more than a
urs. I saw it was a hopeless business. I had done
lp. I have helped strikers and revolution according
then my lights. I was a Socialist then.'
esire and hope is rather to lead the workers into a
n interest in reading, in drama especially. The
re has done so much. He has a great belief in drama.
ht has always been weak, a sort of film over the
or advised him not to read, but he said, 'Then I
norant,' and he refused an operation because there
andth chance he might go blind and so remain
had been sent to a National School as a child for
s but learned little more than his letters. Then one
e was fourteen, he listened to his brother and a
y talked of William of Orange, trying to make out
the Battle of the Boyne, 'and I thought to myself
ot I tell them that?" and I determined to learn to
were a lot of old primers lying about and I learned
and then I went through a grammar and learned
he first book I ever read was Merle D'Aubigny's
he Reformation.' (I said here I had never heard that
since I was a child; there was a copy then at
'It was hard to understand, at least the long notes
many of them were in German. I thought of learning
read them. But the second book I read was harder
on the Human Understanding. But when I got a
s together I would buy a book here and there from
Dickens, because he was cheap, and some of the
ovels. But one day for a shilling I bought the Globe
hakespeare, and that began a new life. I read it over
d learned a great deal of it by heart.'

DISCOVERING SEAN O'CASEY

April 15, 1923. The Shadow of a Gunman (*Sean O'Casey's first play*) was an immense success, beautifully acted, all the political points taken up with delight by a big audience. Sean O'Casey, the author, only saw it from the side wings the first night but had to appear to make his bow. I brought him into the stalls the other two nights and have had some talk with him.

Last night there was an immense audience, the largest, I think, since the first night of *Blanco Posnet*. Many, to my grief, had to be turned away from the door. Two seats had been kept for Yeats and me, but I put Casey in one of them and sat in the orchestra for the first act, and put Yeats in the orchestra for the second. I had brought Casey round to the door before the play to share my joy in seeing the crowd surging in (Dermod O'Brien caught in the queue), and he introduced me to two officers, one a Colonel. (Yeats had wanted me to go with them to a *ball* given by the army, 'good names being wanted'!)

Casey told me he is a labourer, and, as we talked of masons, said he had 'carried the hod.' He said, 'I was among books as a child, but I was sixteen before I learned to read or write. My father loved books, he had a big library. I remember the look of the books high up on shelves.'

I asked why his father had not taught him and he said, 'He died when I was three years old through those same books. There was a little ladder in the room to get to the shelves, and one day when he was standing on it, it broke and he fell and was killed.'

I said, 'I often go up the ladder in our library at home,' and he begged me to be careful.

He is learning what he can about art, has bought books on Whistler and Raphael, and takes *The Studio*. All this was as we watched the crowd.

I forget how I came to mention the Bible, and he asked 'Do you like it?' I said, 'Yes. I read it constantly, even for the beauty of the language.' He said he admires that beauty, he was brought up as a Protestant but has lost belief in religious forms. Then, in talking of our war here, we came to Plato's *Republic*, his dream city, whether on earth or in heaven not far away from the city of God. And then we went in to the play. He says he sent us a play four years ago, *The Frost in the Flower*, and it was returned, but marked, 'not far from being a good play.' He has sent others, and says how grateful he was to me because when we had to refuse the Labour one, *The Crimson in the Tri-colour*, I had said, 'I believe there is something in you and your strong point is characterization.' And I had wanted to pull that play together and put it on to give him experience, but Yeats was down on it. Perrin says he offered him a pass sometimes when he happened to come in, but he refused and said, 'No one ought to come into the Abbey Theatre without paying for it.' He said, 'All the thought in Ireland for years past has come through the Abbey. You have no idea what an education it has been to the country.' That, and the fine audience on this our last week, put me in great spirits.

March 8, 1924. In the evening to the Abbey with W. B. Yeats, *Juno and the Paycock* (*Sean O'Casey's*) – a long queue at the door, the theatre crowded, many turned away, so it will be run on next week. A wonderful and terrible play of futility, of irony, humour, tragedy. When I went round to the Green-room I saw Casey and had a little talk with him. He is very happy.

I asked him to come to tea after the next day, the matinée, as I had brought up a barmbrack for the players, but he said, 'No. I can't come. I'll be at work till the afternoon and I'm working with cement, and that takes such a long time to get off.'

'But after that ?'

'Then I have to cook my dinner. I have but one room and I cook for myself since my mother died.'

He is, of course, happy at the great success of his play, and I said, 'You must feel now that we were right in not putting on that first one you sent in – *The Crimson in the Tri-colour*. I was inclined to put it on because some of it was so good and I thought you might learn by seeing it on the stage, though some was very poor, but Mr Yeats was firm.'

Casey likes Larkin, tells how he knows all the workmen personally and tries to improve life for them. He had bought an open place for them to use, to come to on Sundays and have games and see the flowers, saying to one man, 'Where is your wife, So-and-so. Cooking the dinner? Well now, can't you do without a hot dinner for once in a way on a Sunday and bring her here and push the pram yourself?' In some religious procession the priests were saying, 'Hail to thee, St Patrick,' and the workers drowned it with, 'Hail to thee, Jim Larkin!'

He is very happy walking in the woods and dipping into the books in the library.

February 14, 1926, Sunday. On Friday I left for Dublin to see *The Plough and the Stars.* I got the post and papers in Gort, and when the train had started opened the *Independent* and saw a heading right across the page, 'Riotous Scenes at the Abbey. Attempt to stop O'Casey's play,' and an account of wild women, especially, having raised a disturbance, blown whistles, etc., prevented second act from being heard and had then clambered on to the stage – a young man had struck Miss Delany on the face, etc., etc. Then the police had been sent for, and quiet apparently restored, for the rest of the play to be given. It is so lucky I had set out and not seen this, at Coole, when too late to take the train.

At Athenry I got the *Irish Times*, which gave a fuller account. Yeats had spoken from the stage but the clamour had drowned his speech, but the reporters had got some of it. The train was very crowded, groups of men getting in at each station. I thought at first there must be a fair going on, but they were going up for the football, England *v.* Ireland, next day.

Yeats met me at the station and gave his account of the row; thought of inviting the disturbers to a debate as we had done in the *Playboy* riots, but I was against that. In *Playboy* time our opponents were men. They had a definite objective, they thought the country people were being injured by Synge's representation of them. These disturbers were almost all women who have made demonstrations on Poppy Day and at elections and meetings; have made a habit of it, of the excitement.

We found the Abbey crowded, many being turned away. Yeats said that last night he had been there by accident, for he does not often go to more than one performance. Robinson had not come that evening, and when the disturbance began and he wanted to call for police he found it was Perrin's night off and the telephone had been closed up. But at last the Civic Guards came and carried the women off the stage and the play went on without interruption to the end. At the end of the second act, a good many people had thought it was not to be resumed and had gone, and the disturbers had seized their places and kept up the noise from there, while some climbed on to the stage breaking two lamps and tearing a piece out of the curtain and attacked the actresses.

The papers said Miss Delany had been struck on the face by a young man. But the actors said he came next morning, very indignant at the accusation, said he had thrown something at Seaghan Barlow and it had accidentally hit Miss Craig. Miss Richards says she herself threw a shoe at one of the intruders and it missed its aim and one of them took it up and threw it at Yeats, but it then also missed its aim. I went round to see them in the Green-room and they were very cheerful. There was no attempt at disturbance, though one man said from the gallery, in the public-house scene, 'This is an insult to the memory of Pearse,' and walked out. Someone else cried out, when two men of the Citizen Army came into the pub holding one the flag of the Republic, the other of the Citizen Army – the Plough and Stars Flag – it was designed by 'A.E.' – 'Those flags were never in a public-house!' And it is natural they might object to that, though they don't know that scenes can't be re-arranged for every episode – the flags had to be shown and that scene was the most convenient.

And their bearers did but take a modest glass at the bar, and carried the flags out again with decency and order.

I thought the play very fine indeed. And the next day at the matinée, when, though the house was full and overflowing, there was no danger of riot, and I could listen without distraction, it seemed to me a very wonderful play – 'the forgiveness of sins,' as real literature is supposed to be. These quarrelling, drinking women have tenderness and courage, showing all through, as have the men. At intervals in the public-house scene one hears from the meeting being held outside fragments of a speech of Pearse (spoken in Stephenson's fine voice with extraordinary effect). One feels those who heard it were forced to obey its call, not to be afraid to fight even in the face of defeat. One honours and understands their emotion. Lionel Johnson's lines to Ireland came into my mind:

> 'For thy dead is grief on thee?
> Can it be thou dost repent
> That they went, thy chivalry
> Those sad ways magnificent?'

And then comes what all nations have seen, the suffering that falls through war, and especially civil war, on the women, the poor, the wretched homes and families of the slums. An overpowering play. I felt at the end of it as if I should never care to look at another; all others would seem so shadowy to the mind after this.

EXTRACTS FROM 'COOLE'

WOODS, VISIONS AND THE LAKE

ALTHOUGH this house of Coole that has been my home for half a hundred years lies but seven miles from the home of my childhood, Roxborough, the estate being separated indeed at one point but by a field or two from the high demesne walls within which my childhood was passed, there had ever seemed to be a strangeness and romance about Coole. Its owner during his earlier years was in Parliament, abroad, on the Turf; then later governing tropical Ceylon; the house for long periods closed. The demesne even was but seldom visited by the County Hunt, because it did not possess, as do most of the Galway estates, small coverts from which a fox hearing sounds of danger would make for the open country; but the long stretch of wooded acres, counted by hundreds, where he could twist and turn and never break to give opportunity for that scamper through open fields and over loose stone walls that is the joy of huntsmen and hounds. Nor did hunt breakfasts magically appear in the closed rooms to lift the foiled horseman's heart.

But the woods did not always keep a winter silence, and the frost that hardening the slippery ground gives foxes their safe season in their earths, brings in the woodcocks from the icy bogs and streams, or the frigid terraced limestone of the hills, to snug shelter under hazel boughs and roots and the soft moss that harbours juicy grubs. They even breed here, and disturbed will, like the lapwing, try to tempt the supposed enemy (my grandchildren it may be) from their brood. . . .

Four-footed creatures also make themselves at home in the woods. Even at no great distance from the garden gate I have seen a fox pacing slowly, silently, in the centre of one of the green walks; turning his head right and left, listening also, no doubt, with those pricked ears for the rustling of a rabbit moving in the grass, or more mischievously nibbling bark from the young tree stems. In Pairc-na-Carraig, the rocky wood, a badger once crossed Yeats's path so close, so absorbed in its quest, that he touched with his hand its thick covering before it vanished in alarm. . . .

Weasels have a bad name with our gamekeepers although a kindly neighbour says: 'The poor creatures, they will touch nothing at all on you if you behave well to them and let them alone. But if you do not, they will not leave a chicken in the yard.' And 'to see a weasel passing the road before you, there's nothing in the world like that to bring you all sorts of good luck. . . .'

And the river, passing under a natural bridge formed of great limestone flags, again sinks, again rises, then joining with another stream flows on till we see it shining through the spreading beech trees of Kyle Dortha, a wood destroyed, tradition says, by some calamity of burning that is not kept so clearly in the mind of the people as 'the Big Wind' of 1847. And a later storm, of 1903, was troublesome enough to me, and comes sadly to mind as I pass by those acres of Pairc-na-Carraig where thousands of tall conifers were overthrown by the fierce wind that cut its wide path through our demesne. The news had come to me one evening in London, the very evening as I well remember when friends, Yeats and Arthur Symons and Florence Farr – I forget if there were two or three others – had come to dine with me. I was about to read them Synge's new play, but seeing a home letter and taking it in to read in another room with no ill presentiment, line after line told of some new disaster – nine great elms felled between house and stable yard; our demesne walls broken by falling trees, the public roads blocked; the great ilex on the lawn under which men and boys used to gather to watch our cricket matches (in which we had never been beaten until after its fall). I said nothing to my guests, and the play being *Riders to the Sea*, its tragedy suited my mood.

And I think it was these Coole woods and not those of Alban that were in Synge's mind later when he wrote 'Who'll pity Deirdre has lost the twilight in the woods with Naisi, when beech trees were silver and copper and ash trees were fine gold.' For when staying here he never went out upon the roads, those sylvan walks were his delight. . . .

For if the sharp report of guns is still heard in winter-time, a sudden volley as I listened telling that the woodcock have been disturbed, another poet than Synge has wandered here these many summers and enriched their tradition with his imaginings. The lake also he has loved, taking rod and line in the boat and bringing in many a pike or perch. . . .

And yesterday evening, August 16, 1928, some days after I had written so far, Yeats having come to stay for a while, we walked down to the river in the evening, some afternoon visitors having left. And there, close to the bank, having as it seemed come from the clump of blackthorn on the other side, two swans were sailing along towards the lake, one leading, one to the rear, very white and stately; and between them in single file three cygnets, grey, And Yeats said, 'I have known your lake for thirty years, and that is the first time a swan has built here. That is a good omen. . . .' They passed on, dignified, not breaking their line until they were out of sight in the wider water, beyond a ridge of rocks.

And the wild ducks, even more mysterious in their nesting places, might have been given a stanza in Yeats's poems had he been with me one evening as I sat in an opening between the woods and counted in twos, in threes, once or twice in fives, over three score of these altogether, flying towards the source of the river. So still the air, I remember, that as I watched them I could hear the ringing of the Angelus bell two miles away in Gort.

These woods have been well loved, well tended by some who came before me, and my affection has been no less than theirs. The generations of trees have been my care, my comforter. Their companionship has often brought me peace.

THE BUST OF MACAENAS

THE sun, nearing its evening disappearance behind the grey garden wall, the great row of sheltering beech, the distant Burren hills, shines with a special warmth as it seems on the colossal marble bust of Macaenas at the end of the flower-bordered gravel walk. Kiltartan tradition says this image was carried across Europe on wagons drawn by oxen; but it is likely the width of land between its birthplace and an Italian seaport is a truer measure of its journey; and I know not from what harbour in Ireland it was carried to its resting place here.

Yeats planned many a play or poem pacing up and down this gravelled walk before facing the blank paper on the writing table in his room; I stealing a pleasant half-hour with him between the ordering of the day's meals and the endless answering of letters that falls to a woman's share; turning just once again towards the great ilex, its silver grey calling to mind that of the olive against the Italian blue. John Morley spending a day here said he would like to spend his whole life pacing up and down in the same way. Sir Alfred Lyall, loving the calm grey walls after the brilliant hues of his Italian garden, would reproach me for planting even roses and would quote:

> Here there was laughing of old, there was weeping
> Haply of lovers none ever will know
> Whose eyes went seaward a hundred sleeping
> Years ago.

And on the great stem, smooth as parchment, of a copper beech whose branches sweep the ground as we come near the gate into the woods, many a friend who stayed here has carved the letters of his name. W.B.Y., of course, and Jack B.Y. with a graving of the little donkey he loves; and J. M. Synge and A.E. and An Craoibhin (Douglas Hyde) and John Masefield and Sean O'Casey and as it should be, a very large G.B.S. And this A.J. was cut by Augustus John after his descent from the very topmost boughs where he had left those letters also to astonish the birds of the air.

But alas! Once or twice country lads doing some work in the orchard, seeing those signatures, thought it natural to add their own, and these, unknown to literature, may puzzle some future antiquarian. And once I was just in time to catch hold of the penknives of some schoolboys from the United States, who with their friends were spending an afternoon with us. It may be that I was too rash, that some day in that wonder-country there may be signed by a President in the White House the letters of a name that I had disallowed. Have not even angels been entertained unawares ? . . .

A yet more sunny resting place is that under the bust of Macaenas that is itself sheltered overhead by a great mass of green ivy boughs, for in the afternoon the sun before vanishing westward sends its heat into the heavy iron bench and into the very bones of whoever rests there.

So that oldest of my father's sons, stepson of my mother, would in his later days come from his home some seven miles to the east, the home of my childhood, to bask for an afternoon hour; would be content there even alone, it may be his mind going back on autumn days to that Crimean September when he was one of those Royal Fusiliers who, as Kinglake tells, driving back a Russian column from the heights of the Alma, 'bought their triumph with blood'. In my childhood we were told he had shot seven Russians and I remember a coloured print which seemed to confirm this. I never heard him talk of those days, but one evening is clear in the eyes of memory; when a young brother, learning the piano, played with his little fingers 'Partant pour la Syrie', the air composed by Hortense, Napoleon's mother, and used by the French army of those days as its battle anthem.

And he, usually so reserved, crossed the room and giving the astonished child a sovereign, went back to his chair silently and, as we noticed, deeply moved. . . .

I have gone far out in the world, east and west in my time, and so the peace within these enclosing walls is fitting for the evening of my days.